Reinventing Government for the Twenty-First Century

State Capacity in a Globalizing Society

Edited by Dennis A. Rondinelli
and G. Shabbir Cheema

With a Foreword by
President Vicente Fox of Mexico

Kumarian
Press, Inc.

Reinventing Government for the Twenty-First Century:
State Capacity in a Globalizing Society
Published 2003 in the United States of America by Kumarian Press, Inc.,
1294 Blue Hills Avenue, Bloomfield, CT 06002 USA

Production and design by Rosanne Pignone, Pro Production
Copyedited by Beth Richards
Proofread by Phil Trahan, The Sarov Press
Index by Barbara J. DeGennaro

The text for *Reinventing Government for the Twenty-First Century*
is set in Times Roman 10.5/12.5.
Printed in Canada on acid free paper by Transcontinental Printing. Text printed with
vegetable oil-based ink.

∞ The paper used in this publication meets the minimum requirements of the American
National Standard for Information Sciences—Permanence of Paper for Printed Library
Materials, ANSI Z39.48–1948.

Library of Congress Cataloging-in-Publication Data

Reinventing government for the twenty-first century : state capacity in a globalizing
    society / edited by Dennis A. Rondinelli and G. Shabbir Cheema.
        p. cm.
    Includes bibliographical references and index.
    1-56549-179-3 (cloth : alk. paper) — ISBN 1-56549-178-5 (paper : alk. paper)
1. Public administration. 2. Organizational change. 3. Economic development.
4. Decentralization in government. 5. Public-private sector cooperation.
6. Globalization. I. Rondinelli, Dennis A. II. Cheema, G. Shabbir.
JF1525.O73R45 2003
    320'.6—dc21
                                                                2003013323

---

11 10 09 08 07 06 05 04 03 02   10 9 8 7 6 5 4 3 2 1   First Printing
2002

Reinventing Government
for the Twenty-First Century

Contents

Figures and Tables   vii
Foreword   ix
Preface   xiii
Acronyms   xvi

1 Reinventing Government for the Twenty-First Century:
   An Introduction   1
   Dennis A. Rondinelli and G. Shabbir Cheema

PART I GLOBALIZATION AND GOVERNMENT

2 Globalization and the Role of the State:
   Challenges and Perspectives   17
   Guido Bertucci and Adriana Alberti
3 Promoting National Competitiveness in a Globalizing Economy:
   The State's Changing Roles   33
   Dennis A. Rondinelli
4 Making Globalization and Liberalization Work for People:
   Analytical Perspectives   61
   Manuel R. Agosín and David E. Bloom
5 Pro-Poor Policies for Development   83
   Hafiz A. Pasha

PART II ENHANCING STATE CAPACITY

6 Strengthening the Integrity of Government:
   Combating Corruption Through Accountability and
   Transparency   99
   G. Shabbir Cheema
7 Mobilizing the State's Financial Resources for Development   121
   Suresh Narayan Shende

8   Building Social Capital Through Civic Engagement   143
    Khalid Malik and Swarnim Waglé
9   Creating and Applying Knowledge, Innovation,
    and Technology   163
    Jennifer Sisk

PART III GOVERNMENTS AS PARTNERS

10 Strengthening Local Governance Capacity for Participation   181
    John-Mary Kauzya
11 Decentralizing Governance: Participation and Partnership
    in Service Delivery to the Poor   195
    Robertson Work
12 Partnering for Development: Government–Private Sector
    Cooperation in Service Provision   219
    Dennis A. Rondinelli

PART IV CONCLUSION

13 The Competent State: Governance and Administration
    in an Era of Globalization   243
    Dennis A. Rondinelli and G. Shabbir Cheema

About the Contributors   261
Index   265

Figures and Tables

FIGURES

4.1 Three Spheres of Development Policy   63
4.2 The Conventional Approach   73
4.3 The Vision from Sustainable Human Development   73
10.1 Model for Analyzing Local Governance Stakeholders   184
10.2 Local Governance Stakeholders and Actors
Analysis Framework   185
10.3 Framework for Holistic Capacity Building   187
13.1 Roles of the Competent State   249

TABLES

11.1 Objectives of Case Studies as They Relate to Sustainable
Human Development Objectives   200
11.2 Relation of Case Studies to Good Governance Principles   201

Foreword

Vicente Fox
President, Republic of Mexico

IN RECENT DECADES major changes have taken place in our world. The progress made in science and technology, together with widespread democratization, have shaped a new reality. As a result, new and unique development opportunities—as well as new challenges—are now opening up for us.

The world is within our reach. We have easy access to services and products from all parts of the world; scientific advances are being applied rapidly, and, in some cases, are taking laws and traditional ethics by surprise. Knowledge is closer at hand, but lasts a shorter time. The world has been reshaped, and new actors have appeared on the international scene.

This situation demands new, rapid, and continuous responses by those of us who have a responsibility to govern. Facing this new reality calls for rethinking the concept of the state. We must redefine functions and capacities, being careful never to intrude into areas that are not our concern.

These are the demands of globalization. States cannot continue operating as they did when borders were practically closed and response and adaptation capacities were less rapid. In the past our highest priorities were our internal interests and administrative agendas. If we wish to take full advantage of the opportunities that the new global reality offers us and make them available to all citizens, states must now have a firm structure with the capacity to change and respond; a structure that will promote new forms of production, participation, education, and peaceful coexistence. It is time for innovation, for building new and better decision-making capabilities, and for consolidating and ensuring stability and the effective operation of our democracies. In brief, the state should be able to generate and ensure the conditions that allow us to join in and remain part of world development in the most effective manner possible.

In countries such as Mexico, where full development has not yet been achieved, these changes should not be limited to administrative management. We should develop an attitude of continuously addressing people's needs. To attain greater balance in human development, government decisions should unfailingly include all of society in economic processes. The solutions are not to be found in simple formulas that rule out all humanism. Societies are made by and for citizens. The redefinition of the state's roles demands that all the capacities of governments be enhanced through innovation and creativity to strengthen the resources of all people.

In a democracy, we should design and improve the strategies that will enable us to advance toward a government that will respond to citizens' needs and ensure better communication with them. We should rid ourselves of old paradigms—closed ideologies and false dilemmas that ask us to choose between the market and the state. Experience clearly tells us that we need broader internal and external markets and a better state. We need a global development strategy that will join competence and efficiency with equality.

In a democracy, governing also calls for honesty and accountability, the efficient use of resources, ongoing professionalization and training, intelligent and responsible deregulation, the use of new technologies that benefit citizens, and total commitment to quality in public sector activities. A democratic government should foster the decentralization of power and advocate the participation of both the private sector and civil society in government projects and processes.

Mexico is making efforts in that direction. The Mexican people are experiencing intense times of transformation. We have established and applied general guidelines through six points compiled into an "agenda for good government." This agenda is intended to direct efforts toward "doing more with less"; making government tasks more efficient through new technologies; combating corruption through education, prevention and penalties; building a government of quality under internationally accepted regulations; developing professional public servants through a professional career service; and encouraging a deregulated government that will work responsibly not to hinder its citizens from becoming a part of world development, but rather to contribute to expanding their horizons.

This book, *Reinventing Government for the Twenty-First Century: State Capacity in a Globalizing Society,* edited by Dennis A. Rondinelli and G. Shabbir Cheema, and published in the framework of the Fifth Global Forum on Government Innovation, promoted by the United Nations and held in Mexico, deals with these themes of such current importance in a clear and timely manner. It establishes and suggests innovative and creative guidelines and, at the same time, expands the frameworks and spaces for reflection on the topic.

The challenges remain. Facing them will require a genuine desire for innovation and modifying age-old patterns of behavior. This is the only way to generate the necessary confidence of citizens in their governments and in the changes in the state's role. We must take these actions so that all of us may share in our common development.

Preface

IN TIMES OF CHANGE AND UNCERTAINTY organizations must continually innovate and reinvent themselves in order to survive, adjust, and improve the quality of their performance. For leaders of most organizations, change and reinvention are among the most difficult tasks to plan and implement effectively. The larger and more complex the organization, the more difficult the process of change. Yet leaders in government, private enterprises, and organizations of civil society must be visionary and innovative in an era of rapid globalization and international interdependence. Leaders of all institutions and especially of the state—the sovereign political entity of national governance that emerged more than three hundred years ago—must rethink institutional goals and purposes, redefine missions, reformulate plans and policies for achieving objectives, reassess the most effective ways of implementing those policies and plans, and reevaluate performance continuously in order to improve standards of living for, and the human potential of, their citizens. During the twenty-first century, reinvention will become an essential process for political and administrative leaders in governments that seek to adjust to the rapid changes in their economies and societies brought about by globalization and technological innovation.

The thinking reflected in this book emerged from a series of global forums on reinventing government supported by the United Nations since 1999 and was used to stimulate debate and discussion in the Fifth Global Forum on Re-Inventing Government held in Mexico City in 2003. The government of the United States organized the first Global Forum in 1999 and since then it has emerged as one of the most significant international events dealing with reinventing government. The governments of Brazil, Italy, and Morocco organized subsequent forums, each focusing on a different theme: democratic institutions in Brazil, e-government in Italy, and partnerships for democracy and development in Morocco. For the Fifth Global Forum, Mexico's President Vicente Fox invited representatives from states around the world to focus on innovation and quality in government. In his speech to the World Economic Forum in Davos in 2003, President Fox emphasized the need for government reinvention. "Citizens and organizations from different parts of the world are demanding us to change—to change our way of thinking on how to promote a greater economy and social development in our countries, to change our policies, our strategies, and our way of relating to the world," he noted. "We must change in order to build a new era of democratic cooperation and shared responsibility in which the developing countries commit themselves to responsible economic policies, the developed countries accept to commit themselves in solidarity with the countries with lower incomes, and both show it in deeds."

The themes chosen for the Fifth Global Forum, based on the Government of Mexico's Presidential Agenda for Good Government, focus on quality government that costs less, and is professional, digital, deregulated, honest, and transparent. All of these themes and others related to redefining the state's role in achieving the United Nations Millennium Development Goals are explored in this book.

A heads of state meeting at the United Nations in 2000 agreed upon a declaration and road map for sustainable development embodied in the United Nations Millennium Declaration. Those leaders recognized explicitly the need to make globalization a positive force of opportunity for all of the world's people, to combat poverty, and to strengthen the institutional capacities of governments to serve their citizens more effectively.

The contributors to this volume assess how globalization affects the roles of states in attaining the goals set forth by their leaders in the United Nations Millennium Declaration, and how the state must reinvent itself in the wake of momentous changes that are taking place in international economic, political, social, and technological relationships. The implicit theme running through all of the chapters is the need for a "competent state"—one that guides, facilitates, and supports public and private sector activities aimed at achieving equitable and sustainable economic and social progress. In the final chapter we pull together the recurring themes in defining the roles of a competent state in the twenty-first century.

Because reinventing government is likely to be a continuing process for all states, the ideas explored in this book cannot be the final word. We seek instead to stimulate thinking and provide guidance and direction, based on experience, for the ongoing discussion of how governments can strengthen their institutional capacity to pursue sustainable development and make globalization the positive force envisioned by the heads of state in adopting the Millennium Declaration. We appreciate the assistance of the United Nations for providing support for the Fourth Global Forum to which authors of chapters in this volume contributed in an individual capacity. The views expressed in this book are those of the authors and not necessarily of the United Nations or Member States.

—Dennis A. Rondinelli
Chapel Hill, North Carolina

—G. Shabbir Cheema
New York, New York

Acronyms

DCEC	Directorate on Corruption and Economic Crime (Botswana)
ESCAP	Economic and Social Commission for Asia and the Pacific
FAO	Food and Agriculture Organization (UN)
FDI	Foreign direct investment
GATT	General Agreement on Tariffs and Trade
GDP	Gross domestic product
HIPC	Heavily indebted poor countries
ICAC	Independent Commission Against Corruption (Hong Kong)
ICTs	Information and communication technologies
IIADP	Irosin Integrated Area Development Program (Philippines)
IMF	International Monetary Fund
IP	Integrity Pact (Seoul, South Korea)
IT	Information technology
KITS	Knowledge, Information, and Technology Systems
MDGs	Millennium Development Goals
OECD	Organization for Economic Cooperation and Development
NGOs	Nongovernmental organizations
PPPs	Public-private partnerships
PRSPs	Poverty Reduction Strategy Papers
SKAA	Sindh Katchi Abadis Authority (Pakistan)
SOEs	State-owned enterprises
TNCs	Transnational corporations
UNCTAD	United Nations Conference on Trade and Development
UNDP	United Nations Development Programme
VAT	Value-added tax
WHO	World Health Organization
WIPO	World Intellectual Property Organization
WTO	World Trade Organization

1

Reinventing Government for the Twenty-First Century: An Introduction

Dennis A. Rondinelli and G. Shabbir Cheema

GLOBALIZATION IS THE DOMINANT FORCE shaping a new era of interaction and interdependence among nations and people in the twenty-first century. Globalization provides new opportunities for economic and social development to countries around the world through trade liberalization, foreign investment, capital flows, information exchange, and technological change. Yet rapid globalization has not led to equitable benefits for millions of people who live in countries where governments have not adjusted their functions and services to this global society's demands.

For more than two decades globalization has been changing the "rules of the game" for nation-states and international organizations. The roles of the state—as central planner and controller of the national economy, as the primary provider of goods and services, and as the engine of economic growth—have largely been discredited as effective functions for governments seeking to promote economic and social development. Indeed, some observers argue that the ability of states to exercise sovereign control over internal economic activities and transactions across their borders has weakened in the face of relentless globalization.[1]

Predictions of the demise of the state, however, as Mark Twain commented on reports of his death, are greatly exaggerated. Governments in countries seeking to participate in, and benefit from, globalization must increasingly assume new roles—as catalysts for economic and social development, enablers of productivity and efficiency, regulators ensuring that economies remain open and equitable, promoters of private sector expansion, and stimulators of financial and human resource development. At the same time they must use their resources to provide services and infrastructure that make productive activities competitive

1

nationally and internationally and to meet the needs of their citizens, especially the poorest. In a globalizing society, governments must work cooperatively with the private sector, civil society organizations, international financial institutions, and public interest groups to develop institutions that support and sustain economic and social development. Although governments in many countries with developing and transitional economies are transforming their roles, not all states have successfully abandoned traditional functions and embraced those needed to spread the benefits of globalization.

Globalization is the movement toward greater interaction, integration, and interdependence among people and organizations across national borders. The strongest manifestation of globalization has been the increasing economic interactions among countries in trade and investment and in the international flows of capital, people, technology, and information.[2] But globalization is also evident in the increasing levels of international political interaction and widespread social and cultural interchange that have occurred over the past quarter of a century.[3]

Globalization has brought both benefits and challenges to countries around the world.[4] Globalization brings not only new economic opportunities but also new political, social, technological, and institutional complexities, especially to poorer countries, which governments must address in order to stimulate economic and social development that is equitable, sustainable, and poverty-alleviating. To benefit from more open and widespread economic interaction, states must support an economic system that promotes and facilitates the ability of business enterprises to compete effectively in international markets and people at all economic levels to earn a decent livelihood.

This book explores the changing roles of the state in promoting and supporting sustainable economic and social development in an era of globalization. It examines the concepts of globalization that government policies should reflect in order to redefine the state's role in promoting participation in and spreading the benefits of global interaction. It describes the forces driving globalization, the factors that contribute to the state's capacity to promote development, and the policies and institutions essential for a competent state to carry out its responsibilities in a new era of international interaction.

THE EMERGENCE OF A GLOBALIZING SOCIETY

Since the early 1980s the economy has been globalizing rapidly—markets for goods and services have been expanding internationally, countries have been forming regional and global partnerships, and corporations have been expanding regionally and doing business worldwide. Few governments seeking economic and social development ignore the benefits and challenges of a globalizing society.

Globalization and Economic Growth

In a global market individuals, households, and businesses trade with each other within and across national borders. Although a globalizing economy is subject to cyclical spurts of growth and periodic downturns (much like the cycles of domestic economies) the world economy has grown rapidly since the 1960s. Regional recessions in Latin America in the early 1980s, in Africa in the 1980s and 1990s, and in Asia in the late 1990s—and the worldwide recession beginning in 2000—temporarily dampened the pace of economic globalization, but they did not reverse it. Despite cyclical downturns, globalization drove world economic growth by 140 percent (in real US dollars) between 1970 and 1998, to nearly $40 trillion in annual output of goods and services.[5]

The most recent surge of economic globalization, beginning at the end of World War II and accelerating in the early 1980s, was driven first by trade (exporting and importing), then by foreign direct investment (inward and outward purchases of productive assets), and now is driven by both pervasive trade and investment which are in turn accelerated by technological advances in communications and transportation. International trade grew substantially during the last half of the twentieth century. The value of world merchandise exports doubled from a little more than $2 trillion in 1980, to a little more than $4 trillion in 1994, and then increased to $6 trillion in 2001.[6] The ratios of merchandise exports to gross domestic product (GDP) grew from about 8 percent in 1960, to 13 percent in 1990, and to nearly 18 percent in 1998. In addition, the value of world exports of commercial services increased from $402 billion in 1980 to more than $1.4 trillion in 2001.

These trends generally held for both developing countries and advanced market economies. Between 1990 and 2000, trade in goods as a percentage of world GDP increased from 32 percent to 40 percent. Countries at all levels of income, on average, increased their participation in international trade and foreign direct investment (FDI). Gross FDI also increased as a percentage of GDP worldwide from 2.7 percent to 8.8 percent.[7] The economic growth of many developing countries has been closely associated with the shift from inward-looking protectionist development strategies to outward export-oriented liberal trade strategies. Those countries that have diversified their exports and opened their economies to imports and investment have grown faster than countries that maintained protectionist policies or that continued to export only basic commodities and raw materials.[8]

Although developing countries engaged in a smaller volume of trade than did richer countries, the value of their exports more than doubled from 1980 to 1994. The manufacturing export shares of developing countries increased from about 5 percent in 1913, to nearly 25 percent in 1994. By 2000, developing countries accounted for 30 percent of merchandise exports.[9] And all regions of the world saw growth in manufactured exports, although countries within regions differed drastically in their rates of growth.

By the 1990s, economic globalization was being driven more by FDI than by trade. Total world inward and outward FDI grew from 10 percent of world GDP in 1980 to 31 percent in 1999. The accumulated stocks of inward FDI increased from about $14 billion in 1914, to about $2.5 trillion in 1995, and to more than $6.8 trillion in 2001.[10] Both trade and investment were driven by the expansion of transnational corporations (TNCs). Between 1996 and 2001 the number of parent TNCs grew from 44,000 to more than 65,000, and their number of foreign affiliates (enterprises in which they had a 10 percent or more investment) increased from 280,000 to 850,000. The sales of foreign affiliates doubled during the same period from $6.4 trillion to $18.5 trillion, growing to twice the size of world exports. The total assets of TNCs' foreign affiliates grew from $8.3 trillion in 1996, to nearly $25 trillion in 2000. The gross product (value of output) of TNC parents and affiliates grew to $8 trillion in 1999, accounting for about 25 percent of world GDP. Foreign affiliates of TNCs now employ more than 53 million people.

The Benefits of Globalization

Most international economic studies conclude that the shift toward a more competitive global economy that accelerated in the early 1990s, and the opening of more countries' markets to world trade and investment over the past fifty years, benefit not only richer nations but also developing countries that liberalize their economies and those in transition from government-controlled economies to market-based systems. The Organization for Economic Cooperation and Development (OECD) concludes that countries that opened their markets to international trade and investment have achieved double the average economic growth of those that did not.[11] A broad range of studies concludes that the economies of countries that opened markets and participated in international trade and investment have grown faster than those that constrained their domestic markets and limited their participation in international trade.[12] Growth in GDP is positively associated with export growth. Growth rates are generally higher for all subgroups—small and large primary goods exporters and small and large manufacturing exporters—in outward-oriented countries. Open market economies have higher investment ratios, better macroeconomic balance, and stronger private sector roles in economic development than do nonmarket countries.

Criticisms that globalization rewards economic competitiveness at the cost of social progress often overlook the substantial improvements in social conditions around the world during the period of rapid population growth and economic integration. Overall, social conditions and quality of life indicators improved in much of the developing world during the last half of the twentieth century. The United Nations Food and Agriculture Organization (FAO) reports that by 2000, global agricultural production increased 1.6 times greater than the total production level achieved in 1950, which in that year was the highest in 10,000 years of agricultural history.[13] Between 1970 and 2000, infant mortality (per 1,000 live births) dropped in Sub-Saharan Africa from 132 to 92, in East Asia and the Pacific from 77 to 35, in South Asia from 138 to 75, and in Latin America and the Caribbean from 82 to 31.[14]

The United Nations Development Programme's (UNDP) *Human Development Report* indicates that since 1990, 800 million people obtained improved water supplies and 750 million gained access to improved sanitation. Primary school enrollments worldwide increased from 80 percent in 1990 to 84 percent in 1998. Countries in which half the world's population live have reduced hunger by 50 percent or are on track to do so.[15] About eighty-one countries moved significantly toward democracy, and more countries than ever before—140 of the world's nearly 200 nations—held multiparty elections. Analyses of the relationship between economic progress and "economic freedom" based on rankings of market characteristics—openness of trade policy, fiscal burden of government, government intervention in the economy, property rights, and others—have found a strong positive correlation between the two sets of indicators. Countries with high levels of economic freedom had higher per capita incomes, while those characterized as "mostly unfree" and "repressed" had lower per capita incomes.[16]

The OECD's studies also indicate that freer and more open market economies can bring both economic and social benefits to countries at all levels of development. Among the potential benefits are:

- greater freedom of choice for individuals about what to buy and sell and at what price, where to obtain inputs, where and how to invest, and what skills to acquire;
- comparative advantages in world trade that allow individuals and businesses to prosper by using their resources to do well compared to others;
- higher incomes to those employed in jobs producing goods and services for international markets;
- greater freedom for individuals to engage in specialization and exchange;
- lower prices and a greater availability of goods and services;
- opportunities to diversify risks and invest resources where returns are highest;
- access to capital at the lowest costs;
- more efficient and productive allocation of resources;
- greater opportunities for firms to gain access to competitive sources of materials and inputs; and
- inward transfer of technology and know-how.[17]

The Problems of Globalization

Globalization, however, does not confer benefits on all countries automatically, nor does it generate benefits at no cost. All of the market failures that can occur in domestic economies also appear in the global economy. In reality, markets do not always operate as they are supposed to in theory. When they deviate from fundamental principles, market failures can produce economically and socially undesirable consequences. Market failures appear when consumers and producers do not bear the full costs of their actions, when prices do not reflect social costs and benefits, when consumers are manipulated or misled by advertising or do not have access to appropriate or sufficient information to make good economic decisions, and when unfair trading practices prevent prices from being set by market signals. Moreover, adjustments in market economies can produce cycles of economic decline, financial crises, and recessions or depressions, casting some people into poverty. Strong inequalities in income distribution can put some people at economic disadvantage, preventing them from participating in or benefiting from market processes. Some segments of the population—the unskilled, the physically or mentally disabled, the aged, and those suffering from serious health problems, for example—may not be able to earn sufficient income to participate at all. Firms acting in their own self-interest may exploit natural or common resources or dispose of their environmentally harmful wastes without regard for human health or welfare and without paying the costs of the damage to the physical environment, thereby shifting costly burdens to society.

But what are often called "market failures" are really "policy failures"; the problems result either from the unwillingness or inability of governments to enact and implement policies that foster and support effective economic systems and prevent countries from participating in world trade and investment. One example of policy failure often attributed to worldwide economic competition is widespread inequality in the distribution of wealth and income, resulting in high levels of poverty. The UNDP *Human Development Report* notes that nearly 3 billion people live in relative poverty on incomes of less than $2 a day and that more than 1.1 billion people live in absolute poverty on less than $1 a day.[18] The social impacts of absolute poverty are devastating. In the poorest countries about 20 percent of children die before their first birthday, nearly half of those who survive are malnourished, a significant percentage of the population in poor countries do not have access to clean water, sanitation facilities, basic health services, or adequate education. Most of those living in poverty do not have the opportunity to participate effectively in a market economy or to benefit from it.

Is globalization the cause of abject poverty? World Bank economists argue that, to the contrary, "the current wave of globalization which started around 1980, has actually promoted economic equality and reduced poverty."[19] The World Bank contends that poverty results not from globalization but, instead, from the inability or unwillingness of governments to create the policy and institutional framework required to participate effectively in global economic interaction. From 1990 to 2000, during rapid globalization and a worldwide shift from centrally planned to competitive market economies, the number of people living in absolute poverty on less than $1 a day actually fell from 1.3 billion to 1.1 billion—or from 29 percent to 23 percent of the population in developing countries—during the same period when the world's population was growing rapidly. The share of the population living in deep poverty declined the most in countries and regions with the greatest participation in the global economy and the strongest economic growth rates in East Asia and the Pacific, South Asia, and Latin America and the Caribbean. Absolute poverty declined the least, or worsened, in countries (in the Middle East and North Africa, Sub-Saharan Africa, and Eastern Europe) with the weakest economic growth.[20]

Studies have consistently found a strong relationship between participation in the global economy and national economic growth.[21] During the 1990s the more globalized developing countries' economies grew faster than high-income countries, and both grew faster than less globalized developing countries.[22] As the Asian Development Bank points out, "the Asian experience shows that growth is the most powerful weapon in the fight against poverty. Growth creates jobs that use labor, the main asset of the poor. As growth proceeds, private sector employment becomes the major source of economic support for the majority of workers and their families."[23]

Government policies facilitating participation in the global economy and stimulating national economic growth made markets work for the poor by strengthening the assets of the poor so that they could participate more effectively in economic activities. The policies provided social and economic services—education, health services, and water and sanitation facilities—that reduce poverty and services and infrastructure that help expand small- and medium-sized enterprises. Encouraging effective private investment increased the number of jobs and raised labor incomes. By expanding into international markets many East and Southeast Asian and Latin American countries reduced poverty by opening new opportunities for trade of agricultural and industrial goods and services. By getting infrastructure and knowledge to the poor in cities and rural regions, and creating efficient systems of public administration, governments in these regions have fostered both growth and equity and have addressed asset inequalities across genders, races, ethnic groups, and social classes to reduce both relative and absolute poverty.

RETHINKING GOVERNANCE AND THE ROLE OF THE STATE

The reasons for inequitable distribution of the benefits of globalization vary from region to region and from one country to another, but one factor is constant: State capacity is a necessary condition to use the opportunities provided by globalization and to protect and promote the interests of vulnerable groups in society. The state plays a critical role in alleviating poverty, protecting the environment, promoting human rights and human security, and ensuring gender equity—all necessary conditions for spreading the benefits of global economic and social interaction more widely.

The need to improve governance and public administration and to enhance the state's capacity to carry out new functions and roles is now widely recognized. The United Nations Millennium Declaration calls for respect for human rights, the promotion of democracy, and good governance (including efficient and effective public administration). Good governance is a necessary condition to achieve each of the Millennium Development Goals (MDGs): eradicating extreme poverty and hunger, achieving universal primary education, promoting gender equality, reducing child mortality, improving maternal health, combating HIV/AIDS and other diseases, ensuring environmental sustainability, and promoting global partnership for development. Governments in developing countries and their international development partners have significantly increased their financial support to strengthen governance and enhance the efficiency and effectiveness of public administration.

This book explores the issues involved in reinventing government for a twenty-first century globalizing society. To compete effectively in the global economy and benefit socially from stronger international interaction, governments must provide their citizens and businesses with quality services that cost less and that reach more people. Governments that seek to participate in and benefit from a world becoming more integrated and interdependent must reinvent their structures and processes to become more professional, digital, technologically proficient, deregulated, honest, and transparent.

In Part I, contributors identify globalization forces that are reshaping economic interaction and the political and social conditions that lead to wider participation and sharing of benefits of international trade, investment, and technological progress. Guido Bertucci and Adriana Alberti make a vigorous argument in Chapter 2 that globalization and the forces driving it do not forecast the demise of the state. They point out that individual states make important decisions both nationally and internationally about almost all of the forces driving globalization. They argue that globalization requires the state to perform new roles not only in integrating countries into the global economy but also in reducing poverty and creating the conditions that spread the benefits of globalization more widely.

In Chapter 3, Dennis Rondinelli explores the concept of national competitiveness in a system of global trade and investment. He points out that although, in a narrow sense, only firms and organizations compete in global economic transactions, governments have an important role in creating economic, social, and political conditions that make their countries attractive as locations for domestic and foreign investment and enhance their private sectors' ability to participate in international trade. He outlines the types of policies and institutions that governments should strengthen in order to create a favorable business climate and enhance the competitiveness of enterprises that create jobs and expand employment.

Manuel Agosín and David Bloom, in Chapter 3, emphasize the potential negative impacts of globalization for countries that cannot integrate themselves into the world economy in ways that develop human resources and create the conditions for better quality of life, especially for their poorest populations. They describe three spheres of development policy and the tasks that governments must carry out to pursue sustainable human development. They critique conventional models of economic growth that primarily emphasize economic adjustment and offer a revised model that focuses on growth with sustainable human development.

The need in developing countries to reduce poverty and enable the poor to participate effectively in economic activities, Hafiz Pasha argues in Chapter 5, is at the crux of achieving the United Nations MDGs and of ensuring more widespread participation in the benefits of globalization. Pasha examines the state's role in enacting and implementing policies for economic restructuring and redistribution. He focuses on the political economy of pro-poor policies that target people who are generally excluded from economic and social progress unless policies channel resources to the places where they live and to the sectors in which they earn their livelihoods. He offers a framework for poverty reduction that requires governments to actively and deliberately focus their development strategies on pro-poor policies.

In Part II of this book, contributors explore ways to increase the capacity of the state to play a catalytic role in creating the structures and processes needed to enhance participation in the global society of the twenty-first century—combating corruption, improving financial management, building social capital through civic engagement, and creating and applying knowledge, innovation, and technology. In Chapter 6, G. Shabbir Cheema contends that countries cannot play a meaningful and sustainable role in a global society unless their governments can strengthen their integrity, combat corruption, and improve accountability and transparency. He describes the forms of corruption that plague both developed and developing countries and how corruption can undermine democratic processes and weaken economic competitiveness. He examines successful reforms in developing countries that help ensure government integrity and offers lessons of experience for governments seeking to combat corruption.

In Chapter 7, Suresh Shende turns attention to the state's crucial role in mobilizing financial resources and efficiently, effectively, and honestly managing tax and expenditure systems. He explores the important roles of domestic and international resource mobilization for meeting the challenges of globalization and attaining the MDGs. He compares alternative sources of revenue generation for developing countries that seek to participate effectively in a global economy and outlines recommendations for strengthening the state's financial management capacity.

The state's role in resource mobilization cannot focus on financial resources alone. In Chapter 8, Khalid Malik and Swarnim Waglé emphasize the need to build social capital in developing countries to facilitate economic, political, and social transactions. They see civic engagement as one of the most important means of building social capital and enhancing people's ability to participate effectively in making policies and implementing programs that affect their livelihoods and standards of living. They explore the concepts and practices of civic engagement and its contributions to building social capital, to economic and social development, and to participatory decision-making.

In an increasingly interconnected global society, the capacity to create and apply knowledge and technology and to innovate in scientific and social endeavors is crucial for countries seeking to achieve sustainable economic and social development. In Chapter 9, Jennifer Sisk outlines the crucial role that Knowledge, Innovation and Technology Systems (KITS) play in economic development and poverty alleviation. She describes the components of KITS, the relationships among them, and the conditions that governments must put in place to make them work effectively. She notes the emerging role of E-government in helping public officials to work more effectively with each other, to broaden access for citizens, and to deliver services more effectively. Governments, she contends, have a strong role in creating the enabling conditions that allow civil society organizations and the private sector to generate and use knowledge and information more effectively in achieving development goals.

Part III focuses on ways in which central governments can collaborate, cooperate, and partner with local governments, nongovernment organizations, and the private sector. In Chapter 10, John-Mary Kauzya defines the elements of good governance, the conditions for effective local governance, and the crucial role they play in eliciting the participation of people at the local level. He extends the concept of local governance beyond strengthening local governments and argues that the institutional capacities of all organizations—international donors, central governments, local governments, nongovernment organizations, civil society organizations, and the private sector—must be assessed and strengthened if people in local communities are to participate more effectively in economic, social, and political decision-making. He offers a framework for assessing and strengthening capacity in a holistic way.

Robertson Work draws on decentralization projects in ten countries carried out through the UNDP to describe the impacts of participation and partnership in delivering services more effectively to the poor. In Chapter 11, he emphasizes the importance of the state's role in creating an enabling environment for decentralization and good local governance, the impacts of decentralization in ten countries on participation and service delivery, and the factors that contribute to the success of decentralization policies. Work offers lessons for governments seeking to design and implement decentralized processes through which national and local governments, civic and nongovernmental organizations, and the private sector can work together with the poor to improve service delivery.

In Chapter 12, Dennis Rondinelli outlines the private sector's increasing role in providing services that, in the past, had been the primary responsibility of governments. Globalization opens new opportunities for private enterprises from around the world to expand access to services and to build infrastructure that contribute to economic and social development. He explores why governments and the private sector are cooperating on service and infrastructure provision, how government and the private sector cooperate with each other, and the conditions necessary to make public-private partnerships effective. Rondinelli notes that public-private partnerships are not panaceas for improving services in developing countries; they provide benefits only when the state plays a responsible role in designing and administering the partnerships and assessing their performance.

In Part IV, Dennis Rondinelli and G. Shabbir Cheema provide an overview and summary of the lessons about the impact of globalization on the roles and functions of the state and the dimensions along which government must be reinvented to meet the challenges of globalization. They review, in Chapter 13, the new responsibilities of governments in promoting economic growth and sustainable human development in an environment of global uncertainty. They cull from authors' recommendations ways to create a "Competent State" that can carry out its responsibilities for economic and social development, reduce poverty, protect natural resources, ensure democratic policymaking, build social capital, and strengthen human resources to provide all citizens with a better standard of living in a globalizing society.

NOTES

1. Dennis A. Rondinelli, "Sovereignty On Line: The Challenges of Transnational Corporations and Information Technology in Asia," in *Sovereignty*

Under Challenge: How Governments Respond, eds. John D. Montgomery and Nathan Glazer (New Brunswick, N.J.: Transaction Publications, 2002), 345–371.

2. United Nations, *World Public Sector Report: Globalization and the State* (New York: United Nations, Department of Economic and Social Affairs, 2001).

3. Stanley Hoffman, "Clash of Globalizations," *Foreign Affairs* 81, no. 4 (2002): 104–115.

4. Dennis A. Rondinelli and Jack N. Behrman, "The Promises and Pains of Globalization," *Global Focus—International Journal of Business, Politics and Social Policy* 12, no. 1 (2000): 3–16.

5. U.S. Central Intelligence Agency, *Handbook of International Economic Statistics* (Washington, D.C.: CIA, 1999).

6. World Trade Organization, *Annual Report 2002* (Geneva: WTO, 2002).

7. World Bank, *World Development Indicators* 2002 (Washington, D.C.: World Bank, 2002).

8. World Bank, *Global Economic Prospects and the Developing Countries* (Washington, D.C.: World Bank, 1994).

9. World Trade Organization, *International Trade Statistics 2001* (Geneva: WTO, 2002).

10. United Nations Conference on Trade and Development, *World Investment Report 2002* (Geneva: UNCTAD, 2002).

11. Organization for Economic Cooperation and Development, *Open Markets Matter: The Benefits of Trade and Investment Liberalization* (Paris: OECD, 1998).

12. N. Crofts, "Globalization and Growth in the Twentieth Century," WP/00/44 (Washington, D.C.: International Monetary Fund, 2000).

13. United Nations Food and Agricultural Organization, *The State of Food and Agriculture 2000* (Rome: FAO, 2000).

14. World Bank, *World Development Indicators* (Washington, D.C.: World Bank), various years.

15. United Nations Development Programme, *Human Development Report 2002* (New York: Oxford University Press, 2002): p. 1.

16. Freedom House, *Freedom in the World 2001–2002* (New York: Freedom House, 2002).

17. OECD, *Open Markets Matter.*

18. United Nations Development Programme, *Human Development Report 2002.*

19. David Dollar and Aart Kraay, "Spreading the Wealth," *Foreign Affairs* 81, no. 1 (2002): 120–133; David Dollar and Aart Kraay, "Growth is Good for the Poor," World Bank Policy Research Paper No. 2587 (Washington, D.C.: World Bank, 2001).

20. World Bank, *World Development Indicators 2002.*

21. H. Nordstrom, "Trade, Income Disparity and Poverty: An Overview," in *Trade, Income Disparity and Poverty,* eds. D. Ben-David, H. Nordstrom and L.A. Winters. Special Studies No. 5 (Geneva: World Trade Organization, 1999): 1–9.

22. Nordstrom, "Trade, Income Disparity and Poverty," 325.

23. Asian Development Bank, "Private Sector Development Strategy," (Manila: ADB, 2000): 3.

Part I

Globalization and Government

2

Globalization and the Role of the State: Challenges and Perspectives

Guido Bertucci and Adriana Alberti

GLOBALIZATION IS A TERM USED to describe and explain many worldwide phenomena. Those who advocate greater economic integration across national borders give it positive connotations, while those who perceive globalization as unfettered capitalism and a threat to social cohesion and the welfare state severely criticize it.[1] The animosity surrounding the debate requires a holistic approach to analyzing globalization, a prismatic phenomenon that should be examined in all its dimensions. What is globalization? What accounts for the unequal distribution of the effects of globalization around the world? What is the impact of globalization on the nation-state? What is the relationship between globalization and inequality? How should we redesign the state so that people can benefit from globalization? What capabilities does the state most need to respond to the challenges of globalization? This chapter will explore the factors that contribute to the successful integration of a country into the world economy.

GLOBALIZATION: A MULTIFACETED PHENOMENON

Globalization is a complex phenomenon that encompasses a variety of economic, social, and cultural dimensions and therefore does not lend itself to easy definition. For purposes of simplicity, we can describe it as the increasing flows between countries of goods, services, capital, ideas, information, and people that produce cross-border integration of economic, social, and cultural activities. It creates both opportunities and costs and, for this reason, should not be demonized or sanctified; nor should it be made a scapegoat for the major problems affecting the world today.

17

Four main driving forces are increasing global interdependence: trade and investment liberalization; technological innovation and the reduction of communication costs; entrepreneurship; and global social networks. Although technological innovation and entrepreneurship are thought to be the main forces behind globalization, these factors alone cannot explain increasing economic integration. National governments have played a pivotal role in allowing greater interdependence and economic integration by adopting domestic and international market-oriented policies.[2] State efforts to promote free trade and lower trade barriers are reflected in the eight successive negotiating rounds of the former General Agreement on Tariffs and Trade (GATT), which culminated in 1995 in the creation of a multilateral trading system administered by the World Trade Organization (WTO).[3]

Thus, economic globalization is not simply a blind force: individual governments set the policies of and rules for the global economy. Economic globalization is, in other words, the result of policy decisions made by governments in individual countries that allow global market forces to operate. It is important to understand the political source of economic globalization in order to avoid interpreting this phenomenon as a deterministic force about which little can be done. The real questions are: Which countries set the rules? Whom do the rules favor? How can the least powerful countries also influence international policymaking and do it in ways that will benefit them? Some countries have less leverage in setting the international economic and political agenda because of significant power imbalances, which are reflected in international institutions.[4]

Governments have played a crucial role in promoting global integration, but increasing interdependence among countries also receives impetus from technological innovation and reductions in transportation and communication costs.[5] During the past decade, two significant developments have accelerated globalization: widespread use of computers and the expansion of Internet technologies. The use of computers has expanded dramatically not only in government and business organizations, but also in households for information retrieval and processing, education, entertainment, and communication. Technological innovations and greater economic liberalization have opened new economic opportunities for transnational corporations and for easier cross-border movements of capital, technology, and management.[6]

Economic globalization is driven by the rapid expansion of international trade, foreign direct investment, and capital market flows. The last fifty years have seen trade expand faster than output by a significant margin, increasing the degree to which national economies rely on international trade.[7] Developing countries received about a quarter of world FDI inflows in 1988–1998, though the share fluctuated from year to year.[8]

Globalization has also fostered and, in turn, has been driven by the emergence of international and regional organizations, nongovernmental organizations (NGOs), and transnational networks based on shared interests. NGOs, however, are by no means an invention of the past few decades. Some notable NGOs, such as Save the Children, were founded at the beginning of the twentieth century, while others such as the International Red Cross were created even earlier. What has changed is the increasing number of NGOs and their growing political leverage. Four decades ago fewer than 1,000 NGOs operated mostly at the local level; at the beginning of the twenty-first century, the United Nations reports that almost 30,000 NGOs operate internationally. Moreover, NGOs are increasingly invited to participate in global meetings such as the United Nations Conference on Financing for Development and the recent World Summit on Sustainable Development.

OPPORTUNITIES AND CHALLENGES OF GLOBALIZATION

Globalization and economic integration generate both opportunities and costs. Greater economic openness, foreign direct investment, and technology transfer offer potential opportunities for economic growth. Free trade allows specialization between different regions, allowing them to produce according to their own comparative advantages, and expands consumption choices by providing increased opportunities to buy goods and services from other countries. In this respect, international trade is not a zero-sum game in which some countries are always winners and others are always losers. Competitive trade can benefit all countries because it enhances consumer choices and the quality of products; it can also lower prices and raise real wages.

Globalization also provides opportunities for developing countries to expand the size of their export markets and attract foreign capital. Foreign investment and technology can also increase productivity. Greater competition among firms benefits consumers who have access to products at increasingly lower prices. Those who gain most from free trade in both developed and developing countries are often the poorest people who, as the result of international trade, can buy goods at more affordable prices. In this sense, by increasing standards of living, free trade can be an indirect way to reduce poverty.

Unfortunately, until now, many developed countries have not lifted their protective barriers in many sectors in which developing countries produce or export goods and services.[9] They have not liberalized sectors such as textiles and agriculture, which could provide real new opportunities for developing countries. Thus while globalization offers many opportunities, it also imposes costs for some groups in countries that are integrating into the world economy. Economic restructuring in developing countries can, for example, lead to short-term unemployment. In this, and other areas, the state must often intervene to help minimize the costs of globalization.

Every change has adjustment costs, and not adjusting can lead to opportunity losses.[10] To turn globalization into an opportunity for all, governments need a new vision for the future, a vision that goes beyond what George Soros calls "market fundamentalism."[11] They must find ways to balance policies for expanding markets with those that support social development and poverty reduction.[12] Although globalization has great potential, without appropriate domestic conditions it can have negative effects for many people. A significant part of humanity does not have the capacity to influence its own living environment, let alone international policies. The impressive technological advances of the past few decades benefit only a small proportion of the world's population. Despite globalization, many of the poorest countries remain marginalized from world trade and investment. Social and economic polarization creates a world in which sophisticated, globalized, and increasingly affluent countries currently coexist with nations composed of a large marginalized underclass.[13]

GLOBALIZATION AND ITS IMPACT ON THE STATE

Lifting trade barriers and liberalizing world capital markets, along with rapid technological progress—especially in information technology, transportation, and telecommunications—has vastly increased and accelerated the movement of people, information, commodities, and capital. It has also broadened the range of issues that spills over national borders, requiring states to become more heavily involved in international norm-setting and regulation, consultation, and formal negotiations on a global or regional scale. Many of the problems afflicting the world today—such as poverty, environmental pollution, economic crises, organized crime, and terrorism—are transnational and cannot be dealt with only at the national level or by state-to-state negotiations.

Greater economic and social interdependence seems to affect national decision-making processes in two fundamental ways: It calls for a transfer of some decisions from the national to the international level and, due to increasing demands for participation, it also requires many decisions to be transferred from the national to local levels of government.[14] The fact that cooperation and regulation are required on many levels due to the complexities and transnational nature of current world issues has led some scholars to predict the "end" of national state power. Some argue that the state can only adjust to globalization but not actively influence it, and thus will become obsolete.

Despite concerns about the loss of sovereignty, the state remains the key actor in domestic and international policymaking. The assumption that the emergence of global civil society and increasing levels of cross-border trade, finance, and investment turns the nation-state into an anachronism is simply wrong. Closer international cooperation among states is, in itself, an exercise of state sovereignty. Concerted action does not necessarily weaken states; rather, it can strengthen them by creating a more stable international environment and by giving them greater scope to expand their international interactions. Moreover, globalization without effective and robust multilateralism is bound to lead to crisis because markets are neither inherently stable nor equitable.[15] Indeed, nation-states drive the entire framework for global interaction.

Thus the image of a borderless world in which the nation-state has little or no relevance is in many ways misleading. In fact, two realities coexist. One is the so-called borderless virtual world where geography does not count and communication and business transactions can occur in a matter of seconds. The other world is that of the everyday life of people, in which borders still count, local realities are still complex, and national and local governments still need to address social and economic problems. Only the state can guarantee through independent courts respect for human rights and justice, promote the national welfare, and protect the general interest. The state's role is essential in operating the intricate web of multilateral arrangements that characterize global economic interaction. States, collectively or individually, still set the rules of the game, enter into agreements with other states, and make policies that shape national and global activities.

At the same time, the problems arising from inadequate state capacity are becoming more pronounced. States with stronger capacity have more political influence in shaping the international agenda. States with weaker capacity, especially developing countries, have a less active role. The debate continues about whether globalization negatively affects the state's capacity to provide social goods and services. According to the findings of the United Nations *World Public Sector Report 2001*, globalization does not reduce the size of the state. Evidence on the relationship between openness and the size of central governments, as measured by expenditure and taxation, shows no conflict between openness and government expenditure. On the contrary, governments of open economies tend to spend a significantly larger portion of GDP and collect more taxes. Participation in the world economy reduces the size of government only if policymakers believe that small government is a condition for open markets. In reality, there is no evidence that openness to the world economy has led to a reduction in the size of government during the 1990s. Neither does evidence support the argument that globalization reduces social welfare programs and social spending.[16] On the contrary, a strong democratic state redistributes the benefits of globalization and minimizes the costs that some segments of the population may bear.

To put it another way, globalization requires the state to improve its capacity to deal with greater openness, but it does not seem to undermine its fundamental national or international roles. The state remains central to the well-being of its citizens and to the proper management of social and economic development. The state is also responsible for adopting policies that facilitate greater economic integration. In brief, globalization does not reduce the role of the nation-state but redefines its functions.

To ensure that all segments of society benefit from globalization, and to minimize its negative effects, governments need to reinforce democratic state institutions. As subsequent chapters point out, governments often need to promote decentralization; strengthen social policies, in particular social safety nets; reinforce social capital; promote an efficient public administration; develop an effective strategy of resource mobilization; and improve tax administration systems. Governments in many countries must build capacity in the public sector to support the creation and application of knowledge, innovation, and technology for development.

REDEFINING THE ROLE OF THE STATE

Globalization has transformed the functions and roles of the state. Overall, the course of change points to a shift of focus away from hands-on management and the direct production of services and goods and toward strategic planning. States must establish, maintain, refine, and reform an enabling framework for private enterprise and individual initiative. A parallel shift has moved the state's center of gravity and, with it, the locus of power. Decentralization, debureaucratization, and deregulation are adding to the importance not only of local government, but also of non-state actors on whom significant functions are devolved or outsourced. At the same time, many tasks and policy decisions traditionally handled by national bureaucracies are transferred to intergovernmental or supra-national levels with the increasing flows between countries of goods, capital, labor, and information. Increasingly, the state is acting as a link in processes of planning, consultation, negotiation, and decision-making involving diverse governmental and nongovernmental organizations at different levels of governance. The state is the hub of activities connecting multiple partners and stakeholders from varied fields, regions, cultures, occupations, professions, and interests.

With the advance of globalization, the state has an important role to play in establishing and preserving an even playing field and an enabling environment for private enterprise, individual creativity, and social action. The state can also contribute to creating and maintaining social safety nets; promoting and facilitating social dialogue at the subnational, national, and international levels; establishing and maintaining mechanisms for dispute mediation and conflict mitigation; and reconciling rival cultures or interests in diversified contemporary societies. Last but not least, strong democratic states are necessary to protect children, the sick, the elderly, and other vulnerable social groups; combat the social exclusion of minorities; and ensure a more equitable distribution of the benefits of globalization.

A democratic state must be proactive and strategic to combat poverty and underdevelopment. Combating poverty, both nationally and internationally, is essential to restoring public trust and rebuilding human capital. More than ever before, a strong democratic state must have institutions that are capable of coping with both domestic and international challenges. Strong democratic institutions are vital in providing a solid framework of political, economic, and social rules and in creating an enabling environment for people's prosperity. To seize the benefits of globalization, developing countries need to strengthen and modernize their democratic institutions and public administration.[17]

The hallmarks of an intelligent, democratic state can be summarized as follows:

- strong institutions of governance and the rule of law;
- credible and independent judicial institutions;
- effective legal frameworks for economic activity;

- an open and competitive economic environment;
- price stability and fiscal responsibility;
- an equitable tax system;
- developed and competitive labor, financial, and capital markets;
- adequate steering, regulatory, and enforcement capacities together with judicious privatization and outsourcing of services to private providers;
- public and private partnerships in business promotion, with emphasis on microindustries and small and medium enterprises;
- access to information; and
- promotion of technological and infrastructure development.

An intelligent democratic state must also be socially proactive, but this does not necessarily imply "big government." Government activities should focus on quality, not quantity. The state should be lean but with strong democratic institutions. The term intelligent, democratic state "emphasizes the capacity to carry out effectively the tasks incumbent on the state internationally, nationally, and locally."[18] An intelligent, democratic state is one that intervenes strategically by creating the conditions that support constructive endeavors for people-centered growth. Its role should be catalytic and supportive, supervisory and regulatory. Recent experience has shown that people may benefit when the state is not the only institution involved in producing goods and services. Greater competition can reduce prices and enhance consumer choice. Inherent in this concept of the state is the critical notion of quality, in particular the quality of its normative, strategic, and steering tasks.

The twenty-first century state will differ in many ways from that of the past. It will depart significantly from the characteristics of the welfare state as we knew it. Still, it might be unwise to talk of the "minimal state" in view of the catastrophic results that concept has produced in many developing countries. We should not forget that the welfare state contributed to social and economic progress in many countries, although arguably it often led to large public debts and to the inefficient use of state resources. Efficiency is widely acknowledged as a critical attribute of good governance. Nevertheless, governments should not pursue efficiency and effectiveness at the expense of legality and promotion of the public interest.

Poorly managed states and exclusionary politics can hold back economic and social development. To be sure, economic growth alone is not sufficient to sustain equitable human development. Providing health care and education, public infrastructure, safety nets for the unemployed, equal opportunities, and the basic human rights are fundamental responsibilities of the state. When the state has a larger distributive role, it can help reduce poverty and promote development and can minimize the negative effects of globalization. In the words of UN Secretary-General Kofi Annan, speaking at the Global Compact meeting in July 2000, "let's choose to unite the powers of markets with the authority of universal ideas. Let us choose to reconcile the creative forces of private entrepreneurship with the needs of the disadvantaged and the requirements of the future generations."[19]

Globalization calls for building robust partnerships between the state and civil society. Such partnerships, however, can only emerge between an intelligent, democratic state and a vibrant civil society. Globalization requires improved channels of participation. The need continues to grow for greater citizen participation and new participatory policymaking. In particular, the state could greatly benefit from weaving stronger social networks. It has been common to see important social and economic problems in developing countries as the exclusive responsibility of the state when, in reality, they might be more effectively solved by civil society or the market.

Civil society can make valuable contributions to solving social problems. Religious communities, labor unions, universities, neighborhood associations, and NGOs set up to provide social services can contribute ideas and invaluable human and financial resources. In developing countries, the power of volunteers is important.

To foster a new relationship between civil servants and citizens, state institutions should be more open, flexible in the face of change, and more accountable to the public. The trend in developing countries toward creating a powerful and pervasive state that favors the rich and influential at the expense of the poor needs to be counteracted. State institutions should work for all and not be seen or act as repressive or unfriendly to the majority of citizens. Therefore, greater emphasis should be placed on ethics and professionalism in government, as well as on anticorruption measures. Governments need to give greater attention to developing a more service-oriented spirit among civil servants and to ensuring effective and transparent mechanisms for citizens to channel their complaints about inefficient or inaccessible public services. Governments should establish or strengthen ombudsman mechanisms because, in many countries, gaining access to public services is difficult for those who lack personal influence or money.

PUBLIC SECTOR CAPACITY BUILDING

If the state is to perform effectively its new role, the public sector will need to adapt to globalization and the new demands of development. Modernizing and reforming the public sector is a key component in promoting the development agenda of any country. Improving and reforming governance systems and institutions, including strengthening public sector capacity, is crucial to achieving the United Nations Millennium Declaration and its development goals of alleviating poverty, making globalization work for all, enhancing citizens' participation, protecting the environment, promoting sustainable development, and preventing and managing violent conflicts. Four main areas of the public sector—institutional reform, human resources development, resource mobilization and financial management, and innovation and information technology capacity building—need to be strengthened to enable developing countries to integrate effectively into the global economy and achieve the MDGs.

Institutional Reform

Institutional reform is a precondition for good governance. Having in place effective and transparent legislatures that can adequately represent and articulate the citizen demands, check the power of the executive through effective oversight, and make consistent and coherent laws is an important step in building a democratic system. Strengthening legislatures and their administrative efficiency ensures that they serve as the main forums for reaching agreements on and solutions to compelling problems.

In most developing countries, institutional capacities of legislatures or parliaments are severely constrained. To perform at their best, legislatures need to be functional, accountable, informed, independent, and representative. Developing countries need to strengthen and institutionalize democratic elections and parliamentary and electoral systems by developing electoral management institutions and mechanisms. They should reinforce the organization and management of national and local legislative bodies by creating a system of legislative offices that assist constituents and by fostering participatory dialogues that facilitate communication between the electorate and their representatives about policy and proposed legislation.[20]

Ensuring an independent and well-functioning judicial system is another important challenge. Reforming the administration of justice is vital to ensuring that the majority does not trample upon the rights of the minority. Such reform can help minimize the impunity that often leads to insecurity, injustice, corruption, and abuse of public office and power, and that discourages long-term investment. An effective system of checks and balances can prevent the concentration of power in the hands of one branch of government and can help protect minority groups.

Reforming the executive branch and the way it operates is also important. Closed bureaucratic systems should be replaced with open, flexible structures that can respond effectively to new demands and challenges. In the light of current trends, bureaucratic structures no longer work effectively. Debureaucratization and decentralization must go in tandem with new approaches to management, exemplifying openness, adaptability, participation, flexibility, diversity, and responsiveness. Many new tasks of governance require public authorities to act as mediators, advocates or promoters, actively seeking partnerships with business and NGOs and engaging civil society in the pursuit of development objectives.

The state must be in the forefront of implementing change and smoothing the path for progress. This requires government to develop enabling policies, promote the use of new technologies, set up performance measurement and evaluation systems, overhaul administrative structures, and design adequate systems for collecting internationally comparable, reliable, and accurate data for policymaking.

Human Resource Development

Reforming the way institutions operate cannot be complete without an appropriate strategy for human resources development. Efficient institutions are of little use without competent people, and vice-versa. Therefore governments should constantly upgrade leadership skills, facilitate change, and foster a new image of the public service by developing new career structures based on merit in recruitment, placement, and promotion and emphasizing mobility, integrity, and professionalism. Competencies needed to meet the challenges of globalization include strong leadership; negotiating skills that enable developing countries to play an active role in international agreements on trade (for example, WTO negotiations) and other relevant matters; knowledge of international treaties, agreements, and laws; and coordination skills.

Information technology (IT) has enhanced the need for highly skilled professionals in government service. Leadership and strategic planning call for sound analytical and diagnostic capabilities; careful scanning of the environment for possible constraints or emerging opportunities; and the ability to mobilize support for organizational change. These capacities are effective only if governments can build a culture of dialogue and mutual accommodation, encompass diversity, find ways of reconciling differences and promote consensus, and manage change peacefully and effectively.

Resource Mobilization and Financial Management

Rules and people are two fundamental components of a well-functioning organization. A third essential element is financial resources. Without adequate resources, even the most courageous reforms will not result in action. At the same time, mobilizing additional resources is not sufficient per se to promote development unless it is supported by strong political commitment, the will to use those funds toward socially desirable objectives, and efficient public financial administration and management.[21]

Efficient and effective administration is a prerequisite for a tax system to fulfill its revenue-producing potential. The best designed system is only as good as its administration. Therefore governments that decide to undertake fiscal reforms should also pursue tax administration reforms and reorganization that achieve the highest possible degree of voluntary taxpayer compliance with efficiency, effectiveness, fairness, and integrity. Strategies for tax administration reform require: simplification (for instance, the number of tax brackets should be reduced and exemptions and deductions eliminated as far as possible); comprehensive reform rather than ad hoc measures; commitment to reform at all levels of government; and technical competence of administrators and staff throughout the tax system.

Innovation and Information Technology Capacity Building

Building public sector capacity in information, innovation, and technology is crucial for seizing the opportunities of globalization. Timely availability of adequate, reliable, accurate, and relevant data has become a sine qua non not only of sound policymaking but also of the measurement, monitoring, and evaluation of public sector performance. Information technology carries the prospect of major reforms in governance and public administration through more efficient and effective public management; more accessible and better information for the public; better service delivery; and building partnerships for interactive and participative governance.

The introduction of IT in the public sector poses many challenges not only in developing countries but also in the developed world. Governments typically face challenges in introducing IT in the public sector; training civil servants; enhancing the efficiency of IT in delivering services; and improving effectiveness, accountability, and citizen participation. They must formulate policies that ensure computer training and affordable access to information technology for disadvantaged groups, encourage on-the-job training and retraining, and promote lifelong learning in the public sector. Governments must also create safety nets for those laid off because of the introduction of IT in the workplace, and—especially in developing countries—build or improve their capacity to access, manage, and exchange the information that is so critical for public sector policymaking. In this activity, as in others, technology and globalization have accentuated the importance of democratic states acting together through international organizations.

CONCLUSION

Good governance is a key element in development and in ensuring that globalization benefits all in society. The state, in partnership with civil society and the private sector, has a major role to play in the quest for peace, greater freedom, social equity, and sustainable development. Improving and reforming public administration and governance is critical to making globalization work for all, alleviating poverty and income inequality, and advancing human rights and democracy. Good governance is also essential for protecting the environment, managing violent conflict, and combating international crime. States can either guarantee people's freedom and a measure of social justice, or they can hold back development. How the public sector is structured, administered, and operated and the policies it pursues have strong impacts on people's well-being.

A better quality of life and the protection of human dignity should be among the benefits of globalization. Globalization cannot simply mean the abandonment of all things to market forces.[22] Basic needs must be satisfied as an end in itself but also as a means to extending the benefits of globalization. This is especially true in developing countries where people can benefit more from globalization if governments can ensure broad access to quality education and health care, improve physical infrastructure—including transport and communication networks, hospitals, and water systems—and reduce poverty. More people can benefit from globalization if governments can narrow the technology gap and provide greater opportunities for individuals to make choices.[23] With the advance of globalization and increased economic volatility, the State must strengthen its capacity to manage change and complexity.

To label globalization in absolute terms as either totally positive or negative is simplistic. Ultimately, globalization benefits people in countries that enjoy some degree of political stability and that have in place adequate infrastructure, equitable social safety nets, and strong democratic institutions. Experience has shown that globalization requires strong, not weak, states. Thus good governance is one of the main preconditions for spreading the benefits of globalization throughout the developed and the developing worlds.

NOTES

1. This chapter draws upon the *United Nations World Public Sector Report 2001* on "Globalization and the State" to which the authors were among the major contributors.

2. Vincent Cable, "The Diminished Nation-State," *Daedalus* 24, no. 2 (1995): 2–18.

3. World Trade Organization, *Annual Report,* 1998 (Geneva: WTO).

4. United Nations Conference on Trade and Development. Tenth session, Bangkok Declaration, Global Dialogue and Dynamic Engagement, 2000.

5. Vincent Cable, "What Future for the State."

6. Commission on Global Governance Report, *Our Global Neighbourhood* (Oxford: Oxford University Press, 1995).

7. World Trade Organization, *Annual Report,* 1998.

8. World Bank, *World Bank Development Indicators,* 2000 (Washington, D.C.: World Bank).

9. Nicholas Stern, "Globalization and Poverty," address at the Institute of Economic and Social Research, Faculty of Economics, University of Indonesia, December 15, 2000.

10. Gerald Karl Helleiner, "Markets, Politics and Globalization: Can the Global Economy Be Civilized?" Tenth Raul Prebisch Lecture, delivered at the Palais des Nations (Geneva: UNCTAD, 2000).

11. George Soros, *Open Society (Reforming Global Capitalism)* (New York: Public Affairs Press, 2000).

12. United Nations, Millennium Report of the Secretary-General, "We, the Peoples: The Role of the United Nations in the Twenty-First Century," A/54/2000 (New York: UN, 2000).

13. Commission on Global Governance Report, *Our Global Neighbourhood.*

14. José Sulbrandt, "Modernización de la gestión y organización del Estado en América Latina y el Caribe," paper prepared for the former Group

of Experts on the United Nations Program in Public Administration and Finance, Fifteenth Meeting (DPEPA/DESA), 2000.

15. United Nations, Millennium Report of the Secretary-General.

16. International Labour Organization, 89th Session, 5–21 June 2000, Report VI.

17. Anthony Giddens, *The Third Way and its Critics* (Cambridge, UK: Polity Press, 2000).

18. Joseph Stiglitz, "Redefining the Role of the State: What should it do? How should it do it? And how should these decisions be made? Paper presented at the Tenth Anniversary of MITI Research Institute, Tokyo, Japan, 1998.

19. United Nations, Global Compact High-Level Meeting. "Executive Summary and Conclusion: High-Level Meeting on Global Compact," 26 July 2000, New York, press release SG/2065/ECO/18.

20. United Nations, Report of the Secretary-General on the Role of Public Administration in the Implementation of the United Nations Millennium Declaration, A/57/262 (New York: UN, 2002).

21. United Nations, Report of the Secretary-General on the Role of Public Administration in the Implementation of the United Nations Millennium Declaration.

22. United Nations, Millennium Report of the Secretary-General, "We, the Peoples: The Role of the United Nations in the 21st Century."

23. Amartya Sen, *Development as Freedom* (New York: A.A. Knopf, 1999).

3

Promoting National Competitiveness in a Globalizing Economy: The State's Changing Roles

Dennis A. Rondinelli

MANY OF THE POLITICAL, ECONOMIC, SOCIAL, AND PHYSICAL ILLS often attributed to globalization plagued the world long before the current cycle of globalization began. As noted in Chapter 1, during the period of globalization beginning in the early 1980s, many of the world's economic, social, and political indicators have improved. The problems often attributed to globalization may in fact be due to the failure of states to create the competitive national market systems that allow individuals and organizations to participate effectively in global trade and investment.

Some economists argue that firms, not nations, compete in international trade and investment. In reality, nations do compete in the sense that they provide locations for trade and investment that are more or less attractive to international firms. Countries with restrictive trade laws and barriers to investment are less likely to be attractive locations for trade and investment than countries with liberal trade regimes and investment-friendly policies. Thus, at least in terms of the trade and investment environment that governments create, they do compete with each other for trade revenue and foreign direct investment in a global economy.

What, then, are the characteristics of national competitiveness that governments need to foster and support? The InterAmerican Development Bank points out that "national competitiveness" is the quality of the economic environment for investment and for increasing productivity.[1] Macroeconomic stability allows a country to integrate with the international economy.

A competitive national economy is based on an open, efficient, and effectively operating market system. A market economy, in its purest form, is one in which individuals and business organizations decide which goods to produce and services to offer, how much and when to produce, and how much to charge for those goods and services, based on market signals without direct interference by nonmarket institutions.[2] To maximize profits, individuals and businesses continually adjust these decisions in response to consumer demands. Prices offer consumers information about how much money they must sacrifice to obtain products or services, and they give producers estimates about the amount of revenue they can earn from their sale. Prices also tell producers the costs of factors of production—technology, labor, raw materials, and capital—that help determine their profit margins.

In a competitive market, economic decision-making is highly decentralized. The market operates through laws of supply and demand. Supply is the number of units of a product offered for sale; demand is the number of units that consumers are willing to buy at a given price. When demand exceeds supply, prices generally rise; when supply exceeds demand, prices generally fall. The market "clears" when supply and demand are in balance. When they are not in balance, self-regulating mechanisms (the "invisible hand") will push producers to adjust either the amount of goods and services offered or the price at which they offer them. Producers who do not adjust prices or output cannot compete with other producers and will eventually go out of business. Competition among producers requires them to gain comparative advantage through adjustment and innovation. Through innovation they find new methods of production, new products, new raw materials and inputs, or new ways of organizing to make better products at lower cost.

In essence, a competitive market economy is a process of exchange through which individuals, households, and businesses—acting in their own perceived interests—exchange money, factors of production, goods, and services. Distribution depends on participants' ability to earn income; that is, for individuals or households to obtain money by selling their labor or by earning interest and dividends on investments, and for business organizations to earn revenue from the sale of goods and services. When a market works effectively it is an extremely efficient means of providing consumers with a wide range of goods and services, creating value and wealth, and allocating resources to their best uses in society. The market provides information on prices and values that allow individuals, households, and businesses to make economically rational decisions. Competition raises the quality of goods and services and lowers prices over time by rewarding participants who act on market signals and by punishing with bankruptcy those who do not. Market expansion generates jobs, providing workers with higher incomes and more re-sources to consume and save.

The factors or conditions that contribute to a competitive national economy are reflected in the evaluations made by international organizations and TNCs. The World Economic Forum, for example, uses a national competitiveness balance sheet that ranks countries on growth competitiveness shaped by information and communications technology, macroeconomic environment, innovation, technology transfer, corruption, and law and contracts; current competitiveness based on sophistication of company operations and strategy and quality of the business environment, and other indicators including technology, public institutions, and macroeconomic environment.[3] Similarly, *The World Competitiveness Yearbook,* published by the Institute of Management Development, ranks the competitiveness of countries on four sets of factors: 1) economic performance, including the soundness of the domestic economy, international trade, international investment, employment and prices; 2) government efficiency, including public finance, fiscal policy, institutional framework, business legislation, and education; 3) business efficiency, including productivity, labor market, finance, management practices, and impact of globalization; and 4) infrastructure, including basic infrastructure, technological infrastructure, scientific infrastructure, health and environment, and value system.[4]

The InterAmerican Development Bank points out that a competitive national economy requires financial market development (financial regulation and supervision, information in financial markets, and micro-financing sources; policies that remove barriers to improved labor productivity; efficient infrastructure) good ports and transport; electricity and telecommunications; the capacity to innovate; and effective industrial and investment policies.[5]

Governments have an important policy role in creating conditions that allow these factors to develop or be strengthened within their countries in order to enhance national competitiveness. The United Nations Conference on Trade and Development (UNCTAD) points out that "the basic policy challenge facing most developing countries remains how best to channel the elemental forces of trade and industry to wealth creation and the satisfaction of human wants."[6] The World Bank contends that competitiveness and economic growth reduce poverty when countries enact and implement policies based on two pillars of development: "building a good investment climate in which private entrepreneurs will invest, generate jobs and produce efficiently, and empowering poor people and investing in them so that they can participate in economic growth."[7]

These and other organizations emphasize that although it is private enterprise and not nations per se that compete in the global economy to create jobs, income, and wealth, governments play a crucial and pervasive role in fostering, maintaining, and supporting efficient markets through which competition takes place. Indeed the most important roles of the state are to enact and implement market-supporting policies and sustain institutions that encourage and promote efficient economic interaction.

THE ROLES OF GOVERNMENT IN FOSTERING NATIONAL COMPETITIVENESS

The most important roles of governments in an era of globalization are to set the rules of the game and to protect vulnerable groups from the ill effects of market failures. The traditional economic roles of government in a market system are to protect the health, safety, security, and welfare of the population; to establish and enforce fair and equitable rules for market behavior; and to ensure open competition. To deal with market failures, governments often intervene in the economy to counter the negative impacts of business cycles, "free riders," social inequities, and spillover effects (the negative impacts on one group of people or territorial jurisdiction from activities in another).

Although in most cases markets can deliver goods and services efficiently, in some countries and at some times the private sector cannot profitably provide socially valued public goods. Personal and national security (police, judicial and penal systems, the armed forces), universal education, health and welfare services, and low-cost housing are often more accessible when they are delivered by governments or nonprofit organizations. Governments sometimes play a strong role in the economy when the private sector cannot or will not offer goods or services at affordable prices to a poor population. In a market system, governments can help assure access to opportunity for and participation in economic activities, although they cannot guarantee equal distribution of benefits. In most countries governments are also significant purchasers of products and services from individuals, households, and businesses.

The most important roles of governments in fostering and promoting competitiveness in a global economy are:

- creating an institutional structure for market competition in countries that previously had government controlled, centrally planned economies or nonfunctioning market systems,

- initiating and sustaining macroeconomic reforms,
- strengthening legal institutions for economic transactions,
- enacting and implementing policies that support private enterprise development,
- improving government efficiency, accountability, and responsiveness,
- providing infrastructure and overhead capital,
- protecting the economically vulnerable, and
- strengthening and supporting civil society organizations.[8]

Creating an Institutional Structure for Market Competition

To gain from participation in the global economy, states must create or strengthen their market processes or maintain the efficacy of existing ones. The fullest participation of countries in a global economy depends on their ability and willingness to structure their political, economic, and social institutions to meet the requirements of global market systems.[9] Institutions are generally defined as rules or norms of behavior, the mechanisms that enforce them, and the organizations through which they are applied so that people can interact effectively in conducting economic and social transactions.[10] In a review of development experience in Asia, Chang found that institutional development was one of the crucial factors driving economic growth.[11] East and Southeast Asian countries were able to grow economically and integrate into the global economy through their institutions of coordination and administration, learning and innovation, and income redistribution and social cohesion.

Creating an institutional structure for market economies and national competitiveness is a long-term process. Market economies developed in Western industrial countries over more than 200 years. Few developing or transitional countries can pursue all of the changes simultaneously and, in many, a new institutional structure may take generations to put into place. Since the late 1980s, however, governments in countries around the world have been under increasing pressure, both from within and without, to accelerate the process of institution-building to create or strengthen their market economies in order to participate more effectively in the global economy. To do so, they must build institutional capacity to support the market attributes described earlier.

Governments often play a crucial role in creating or strengthening institutions that establish ethical norms of behavior and transparency in government and the private sector, set and enforce legal rules, develop and sustain appropriate macroeconomic policies, liberalize trade and finance, protect property rights, and privatize the ownership of state enterprises and land. The World Bank points out that efficient markets require: agricultural institutions that allow ownership and transfer of land, access to financial resources and agricultural technology, and that promote innovation; institutions for the governance of firms and application of business laws; financial institutions that enhance access to investment and operating capital; political institutions that develop policy and promote judicial efficiency and effective regulation; and formal and informal social institutions through which people and groups can interact.[12]

Initiating and Sustaining Macroeconomic Reform

Governments in countries seeking to expand their international trade and investment, create jobs, increase incomes and wealth, and improve the standards of living for their citizens must find ways to create a domestic economic system in which most or all goods are available on the market for purchase or sale. Governments can help make markets competitive by allowing prices to reflect true relative scarcities in the economy, encouraging decision-makers to behave according to rules of the market, and allowing producers to obtain fair profits. In most countries this means finding effective ways of implementing structural adjustment policies, liberalizing trade and investment, creating or strengthening property rights, and developing a legal framework for economic transactions.

Implementing structural adjustment policies. Governments in most countries periodically make structural adjustments that enhance the financial viability of productive enterprises. Such policies aim to establish a system in which private enterprises survive or fall on the basis of profit-making capability rather than on central government plans, bureaucratic controls, and budgetary support, and in which enterprises are penalized for inefficient or unprofitable activities by the possibility of bankruptcy or liquidation.

Macroeconomic adjustment policies encourage the development of market mechanisms that can efficiently and effectively allocate scarce economic resources and set prices for both production inputs and consumer goods. This often requires financial liberalization and the reduction (and eventual elimination) of price controls. Macroeconomic adjustment policies seek to change the economy's structure of production and consumption by increasing the efficiency and flexibility of producers and consumers to respond to market signals.

By encouraging interaction through market competition, macro-economic reforms establish a process in which firms are free to enter and leave the market based on their profitability. Policies promoting market competition should prevent excessive collusion through antitrust laws, reduce barriers to entry, and eliminate marketplace impediments to competition. At the same time, those countries facing serious problems of inflation and decline in national output must enact economic stabilization policies to reduce balance-of-payments deficits, reschedule debt, control the money supply, reducing subsidies, and restrain wage increases.

Liberalizing trade and opening the economy to investment. The effective operation of competitive market economies requires all governments to adjust their trade and investment policies to become or remain competitive. Promoting export competitiveness, as UNCTAD emphasizes, involves "diversifying the export basket, sustaining higher rates of export growth over time, upgrading the technological and skill content of export activity and expanding the database of domestic firms able to compete internationally."[13] Liberalization of trade laws and regulations and the enactment of more favorable investment policies have become crucial aspects of structural reforms. Reforms generally aim at developing the capacity to expand export markets and engage more effectively in foreign trade and investment. This requires liberal trade and investment policies including programs for export promotion, FDI, exchange rate adjustments, and the easing of investment restrictions and trade barriers.

The importance of developing international trade and investment capacity is seen not only in the challenges facing regimes in developing and transitional countries but also in the pivotal role that foreign trade has played in the history of established market economies. In the West, the extension of trade and the freedom of a merchant class to engage in trade substantially expanded economic opportunities.[14] Trade allowed new products and commodities to be introduced into the domestic economy (that were later produced locally or transformed into yet other products that found both domestic and overseas markets) and provided consumer goods for which no local or national source yet existed. Innovation by extension of trade and the discovery of new resources has been a major source of creativity and profitability for enterprises and for their suppliers and distributors in the West and will continue to be a driving force of economic growth in the future.

National competitiveness increasingly depends on governments' willingness and ability to participate in regional trade agreements—free trade areas, customs unions, common markets, or economic unions. Since the 1970s countries have been expanding their international trade by cooperating in regional trade alliances such as the North America Free Trade Agreement, the Association of Southeast Asian Nations, the Arab Common Market, the Southern Africa Customs Union, and the European Union.

National trade policies are influenced increasingly by international trade agreements, international rules of the game by which nations and industries must play in order to build competitive advantage. Standards set by the WTO not only attempt to move toward a freer world trade regime but also assess trade penalties against member nations that violate the agreements. Increasingly a country's international competitiveness is determined by the pace and degree to which national policies conform to international trade and investment rules. The major provisions of the WTO agreements reduce tariffs by member countries, prohibit them from restricting trade through health and safety standards that have no scientific basis, and eliminate import quotas.

Creating or strengthening property rights. One of the most important institutions for market development and national competitiveness is a reliable system of property rights that facilitates property ownership and its transfer. In many developing countries, the lack of property rights results in "common pool" problems: resources or assets are overused and eventually depleted because there are no limitations on their use. Without an effective system of property rights, a country's resources can be allocated inefficiently, private agents can bribe officials to grant them preferential use of property, bureaucrats engage in rent-seeking behavior, intellectual property developed through innovation can be difficult for its creators to protect and common property is often depleted.[15] The lack of enforceable private property rights in many countries allows state-owned (common or collectivized) property to be misused, abused, overused, or unused, leading to inefficient resource allocation.

The institutional components of an effective property rights system include rules for asserting claims of ownership; recording ownership; identifying the types of property that can be publicly and privately owned; settling ownership disputes; and acquiring title to property that has been lost, abandoned, or improperly acquired.[16] An impartial, comprehensive, stable, and efficient body of contract law must be created to institutionalize these rights. Many developing countries are still in the early stages of privatizing state-owned assets and enterprises. They are far from establishing effective rights to both real and intellectual property and its use for productive purposes. Yet without these institutional property protections, achieving the benefits of deep integration from direct foreign investment and the meshing of factors of production around the world is difficult, if not impossible, to achieve.

Strengthening Legal Institutions for Economic Transactions

Establishing and enforcing a rule of law—that is, providing a reliable legal framework for business transactions—gives participants in market economies the guidelines to operate efficiently and effectively and establishes a framework for protecting natural resources and ecological systems. Without a transparent system of business laws, enterprise owners and managers waste time and money negotiating each transaction with government officials—a process that opens the way for bribery and corruption. Business laws provide rules for structuring and organizing corporations, identifying the activities in which they can engage, defining the nature and characteristics of legitimate business practices, and clarifying corporations' rights and obligations. Through national law or international agreement, legal institutions should set the standards for treatment of foreign-owned or multinational corporations.[17] They should determine allowable levels of foreign ownership of joint ventures and identify conditions of business entry and exit, including visa restrictions on noncitizens for doing business in the country, business registration, liquidation and bankruptcy, and import and export requirements.

Markets also depend on legal institutions to establish and enforce product and pricing standards, antitrust laws and regulations on restrictive business practices, securities and exchange regulations, rights of access to credit and capital, regulation of bank operations, and guidelines for viable contracts and adjudication of disputes. Labor laws establishing legal working conditions, hours, minimum wages, and obligations of workers and employers are essential to reduce complaints by governments in other countries of social dumping or exploitation of women and children. In most market economies, the legal system for business also regulates the sale and management of commercial real estate, corporate tax rules and exemptions, and licensing and permitting regulations.

Finally, national competitiveness in international trade depends on a set of legal standards ensuring fair treatment of foreign investors, including rules on admission, entry, and establishment of foreign firms and general standards of fair and equitable treatment. Governments should also create effective mechanisms for the transfer of capital and profits and for dispute settlement through local courts or international arbitration.[18]

Implementing Policies that Support Business Development

Creating or strengthening market economies and national competitiveness requires governments to enact and implement policies that help expand the private sector. Governments can privatize state-owned enterprises; enact policies that facilitate developing small- and medium-size enterprises; and create conditions that attract, develop, and expand TNCs. Enterprises of all sizes must learn to respond to greater market fragmentation, shorter product cycles, smaller production runs, and faster redesign and production of customized goods, because all business processes are affected by technological advances in communications and transportation. The growth of the Internet and electronic commerce requires manufacturing and service firms that wish to compete internationally to become more flexible in their operations; use advanced technology to produce high-quality, reasonably priced goods; adopt speed-to-market methods of operation; use multisite locations; manage just-in-time production and delivery systems; and engage in world-wide sourcing of goods and services.[19]

Privatizing state enterprises. An immediate challenge facing most former centrally-planned economies is to privatize and restructure their state-owned enterprises (SOEs). Privatization of SOEs has become an important instrument of economic transition and development.[20] Privatization became more attractive with increasing evidence that many SOEs were lossmakers rather than revenue generators.[21] The heavy demands of SOEs for capital have squeezed private investors out of capital markets in some countries, and in others have limited the private sector's access to borrowing for investments that could generate jobs, income, and public revenues.[22]

Financially strapped governments in both Western industrial nations and developing countries use privatization to generate revenues and reduce budget deficits. The worldwide value of one form of privatization—public and private sales of SOEs—grew from about $25 billion in 1990, to more than $161 billion in 1997.[23] From 1990 to 2000, SOEs valued at nearly $1 trillion were transferred from government to the private sector.[24] Substantial privatization will continue over the next decade in Central and Eastern Europe, South Asia, Southeast Asia, Central and South America, and Africa.[25] Privatization continues to be an instrument for reducing inflation by promoting investment of savings in SOEs and for reducing external debt by attracting foreign capital investment in privatized firms. In some former socialist countries, privatization is a means of restructuring the political system by separating economic and political decision-making. In many developing countries, privatization is essential for reallocating public resources from SOE subsidies to investment in infrastructure and social programs; for increasing the size and dynamism of the emerging private sector, for distributing SOE ownership more widely, and for promoting both foreign and domestic private investment. Moreover, privatization can generate the revenues needed by the state to create new jobs for workers displaced by industrial restructuring, reduce the state's administrative responsibilities and the burdens of government intervention in enterprise management, and provide consumers with more efficiently produced goods. For all of these reasons, in both economically advanced and developing countries, privatization remains an alternative to expanded government production and distribution of goods and services.

Promoting small enterprise development. Simply making macroeconomic adjustments and privatizing state-owned enterprises do not ensure that market economies flourish or that developing countries become competitive. Market economies require a steady supply of entrepreneurs and small-business owners to produce goods and services. Developing small businesses is crucial for creating competitive economies. However, in many countries new enterprises face overwhelming challenges in surviving and expanding. Studies in thirty-two developing countries indicate that many have highly complex administrative procedures for establishing and operating businesses, which prevents or delays entry of new enterprises and discourages flows of FDI.[26] The International Finance Corporation points out that in many countries governments can play an important role in making the environment more conducive to the expansion of small- and medium-size enterprises, including:

- reducing barriers to entry and eliminating noncompetitive behavior,
- reducing the expense and time required to meet regulatory requirements for licensing and registration,
- reducing official and unofficial levies that undermine small business growth and survival,
- enacting a legal framework for commercial transactions and dispute settlement,

- enforce laws protecting business and intellectual property,
- reform tax structures that discriminate against small enterprises,
- revise government procurement policies that discourage or prevent small firms from bidding,
- reduce labor rigidities that limit small firms' flexibility in hiring and firing workers, and
- provide infrastructure that allows small firms access to information and markets.[27]

The expansion of small enterprises and their ability to generate jobs depends ultimately on national economic growth and on government policies that create an environment conducive to private enterprise development. Governments seeking to strengthen their market economies should therefore implement reforms that allow markets to expand and operate more efficiently, including effective fiscal and monetary policies, legislation that offers investment incentives, efficient market mechanisms and competitive practices, and appropriate pricing policies for basic commodities and services. It is also important to enact incentive-oriented wage policies and merit reward systems, stabilize exchange rates, and enact tax and incentive programs to encourage domestic saving and develop financial markets. Moreover, demand-side policies that increase consumer purchasing power and income, expand subcontracting and piece-rate work between formal and informal sector firms, and give small firms equal footing in public procurement could substantially assist small business development.

Supply-side policies are also important. Governments have a crucial role in providing credit for operating small and microenterprises, training informal sector owners and workers in better management practices, and creating trade organizations and cooperatives to promote the small enterprises interests both in procuring supplies and in selling products. Governments can also help develop technologies used by informal sector firms, pass and implement laws that improve working conditions for informal sector participants, and enhance the prospects for small enterprise expansion. Supply-side and demand-oriented policies must complement and reinforce one another.

In many countries, ambiguous and rapidly changing government policies and regulations are serious obstacles to small enterprise expansion. The World Bank's survey of 3,600 firms in developing countries found that entrepreneurs in some countries live in constant fear of "policy surprises."[28] A majority of firms in Central and Eastern Europe, Latin America, and Africa reported serious negative business impacts due to unpredictable policy changes made by governments that did not consult with or inform businesses before the changes were made. In many developing countries, registering small enterprises can take months, forcing them to operate in the informal sector and inhibiting their ability to expand. Although governments and international development agencies recognize the importance of SMEs in job creation and wealth generation, most international assistance programs remain inadequate, poorly designed, and ineffectively implemented.

Developing, attracting, and retaining transnational corporations. Market development and national competitiveness depend heavily on attracting the investment of TNCs and on creating a business climate that encourages privatized enterprises and small- and medium-size businesses to become more actively involved in international trade and investment. Studies in Central and Eastern Europe indicate that increases in FDI by TNCs help developing countries integrate into international production and marketing networks, provide opportunities for small- and medium-size companies to become suppliers to international companies, and bring technology and managerial experience that can spread throughout the industry.[29] As the UNCTAD points out, "[as] the competitive advantage of resource-intensive, low-cost, low-skill activities declines, countries must be able to attract higher value FDI. If they fail to do so, they will pay the price in terms of slower economic growth."[30]

All enterprises, large or small, that do business across national borders are transnational. The more TNCs a country has and the more successful they are in trade and investment, the more globally competitive the national economy is likely to become and the more likely it will be to grow. As noted earlier, TNCs play a critical role in international trade and investment, global economic integration, and national economic development in many industrialized and market-oriented developing countries. The strategies of parent firms often progress from simple integration strategies in which affiliates provide inputs to the parent firms, to stand-alone strategies that involve one-way links based on ownership, finance, and technology, and to complex integration in which parent firms and affiliates benefit from economies of scale, increasing revenues from exports, and increasing market share by locating business activities in many countries around the world.

Attracting TNC investment requires a business climate that is liberal, open, and relatively unrestrictive. International business experts emphasize that the most important investment conditions sought by

TNCs in foreign countries include economic and political stability, certainty in the rules affecting foreign investors, low barriers to trade and financial movements, and a significant role for domestic private enterprise vis-a-vis state-owned enterprises. TNCs prefer countries in which there is a minimum of government intrusion in business operations and decisions and reasonable protection against foreign competition. They seek countries in which governments provide appropriate infrastructure and priorities for development and accept international business and investment laws.

Improving Government Efficiency, Accountability, and Responsiveness

The roles of government in creating the institutional structure for market systems are clear. The Asian Development Bank points out that good governance rests on fundamental principles: accountability, transparency, predictability, and participation.[31] The emerging global market economy requires governments to provide high quality services through responsive organizations that meet citizens' needs with a minimum of corruption. In established market economies, the public demands better services at lower cost. In countries seeking to increase the competitiveness of their businesses and industries in world markets, political leaders must respond to increasing demands for stronger business support services and infrastructure. As a result, governments in many countries are attempting to control corruption and establish ethical norms for economic transactions, undertaking extensive administrative and civil service reforms, and decentralizing and democratizing administrative and political institutions.

Controlling corruption and establishing ethical norms. Among the most important market economy institutions are those that disseminate, inculcate, and reinforce ethical norms of behavior. The absence of appropriate ethical norms undermines the operation of market economies, which depend ultimately on public trust and responsible behavior in business transactions.[32] Although individuals and enterprises in market systems are expected to act self-interestedly to maximize profits, the effective functioning of markets also requires participants to act responsibly toward one another. In open economies, companies that cheat their customers and suppliers, attempt to eliminate their competitors, and abuse their employees are quickly driven from the market. Governments or societies that condone or protect socially irresponsible behavior undermine public confidence in both the political and economic systems. Socially and culturally determined rules and ethical norms generally define the limits of acceptable behavior and, unless those rules are clearly established and effectively enforced, the presumption of trust on which market interactions depend quickly erodes. Transparency International's *Corruption Perceptions Index 2002* found that 70 percent of 102 countries surveyed (90 total) did not achieve a score above five on a ten-point scale (ten equals least corrupt, one equals most corrupt).[33]

Widespread corruption in public and private transactions in many developing country institutions indicates that methods for enforcing ethical norms are weak. Corruption can include bribery, extortion, influence-peddling, nepotism, kick-backs, rake-offs, speed-money, compliance fees, fraud, falsification of reports or applications, conflicts of interest, extravagance with public funds, favoritism in purchasing contracts, collusion, protection rackets, smuggling, and thievery.

Widespread, unchecked corruption seriously weakens or destroys people's trust in public policies and market operation because it undermines the arm's length relationship and the checks and balances between government and the private sector on which market system transactions should rely.[34] Pervasive corruption has toppled governments or tainted ministries. Although developing countries have no monopoly on corruption they, unlike most Western countries, often lack the institutional arrangements for uncovering and punishing it or for keeping it in check. Corruption is so pervasive in the government bureaucracy and in the private sector of many developing countries that the World Bank and the International Monetary Fund (IMF) have attempted to calculate its costs as a means of persuading governments to take more effective countermeasures. The IMF estimates the amount of money involved in only one form of corruption, money laundering, is equivalent to two to five percent of world's GDP.[35] Corruption wastes resources and seriously damages the prospects for economic progress in the developing world. Widespread corruption hampers efficient market decisions, reduces returns to investment, and impedes foreign capital inflows. It makes public investments in infrastructure more expensive and skews the assignment of tax revenues toward economically nonproductive and socially inequitable activities.

Studies of corruption in countries transitioning to market economies have found that it can be reduced by lowering barriers to entry of new businesses, improving the effectiveness of the legal system, and increasing competitiveness of services provided by infrastructure monopolies. Strong market institutions, clear and transparent rules, fully functioning checks and balances, fair enforcement of regulations, and a competitive environment reduce the opportunities for corruption. Local NGOs can also help identify the sources of corruption, publicize them, encourage transparency and accountability, and create alliances with international organizations to carefully observe government decisions that involve potential corruption. Ultimately, however, ethical norms must be established, disseminated, accepted, and reinforced through politically accepted legal institutions and social organizations, and then enforced by government.

Making public administration more responsive. Creating or strengthening a market economy often requires governments to change the way they operate. In a market economy, governments cannot monopolize political power or service provision. Usually they must rely heavily on the participation of private entities and NGOs to provide services effectively and efficiently. The rapidity of changes resulting from globalization and technological advances require government agencies to restructure and manage in less bureaucratic fashion. Governments organized by function are often too inflexible and isolated to respond effectively to public needs. Government agencies must collaborate with other institutions and delegate operational responsibilities to lower organizational levels. Governments also must persuade and motivate citizens to secure their allegiance and act as consensus makers to get stakeholders to work together in common cause.[36]

Market development and national competitiveness require effective public administration and civil service systems. Such systems must be able to attract qualified, competent, honest, and realistically paid individuals into public service. If domestic and international investors are to have confidence in a country's economy, the government must have a civil service system that relies on merit-based recruitment and promotion, incentive-based compensation, and clearly defined, reward-oriented career paths. The civil service must be able to attract and retain a corps of professionals who are responsible for formulating and implementing economic policies and must then support them with good training, an appropriate degree of independence, and professional reward structures. Professional civil servants must be protected from inappropriate political interference as they carry out their responsibilities. The civil service should also be given enough flexibility to facilitate communication between the public and private sectors.

To achieve these goals and make government more responsive to changing needs and demands, the civil service must recruit using common selection criteria and appointments based on merit, and provide protection from inappropriate political influence. Senior officials should have adequate authority to manage their responsibilities for delivering services and providing policy advice to political leaders. Managers should also be given adequate authority to make appropriate technical and administrative decisions without central approval; create and abolish positions; appoint, promote, and transfer staff; and deal directly with most other personnel management issues in their departments. Although difficult and slow to change in most countries, civil services in market economies must become more efficient, effective, responsive, and accountable if governments are to play a positive role in economic development.

Strengthening judicial institutions. In many countries governments must not only strengthen their administrative and legislative branches but must also establish an effective judiciary. The promulgation of business laws without strong enforcement or judicial institutions renders legal guidelines meaningless. The World Bank found, in a survey of 3,600 developing country firms, that 80 percent of entrepreneurs in Latin America, Sub-Saharan Africa, Central and Eastern Europe, and the former Soviet Union expressed "a lack of confidence that the authorities would protect their person and property from criminals."[37] More than 70 percent of the entrepreneurs complained that "judicial unpredictability was a major problem in their business operations." Strong judicial institutions assure that private citizens and corporations have equal access to legal procedures for redressing grievances and obtaining reasonable and timely resolution of disputes. Judicial institutions enforce business and civil laws, offering adequate remedies for wrongs determined through litigation. Strong, independent judicial institutions have competent and impartial judges; adequate physical facilities, management, and records maintenance for courts; and court procedures that are balanced, fair, and guided by principles of due process, rules of evidence, and discovery of evidence. Creating and enforcing a set of legal standards ensuring fair treatment of foreign investors—including those for rules on admission, entry, and establishment of foreign firms and general standards of national treatment—facilitate a country's participation in international trade and investment.

Decentralizing government. Creating or strengthening market systems requires governments to democratize the political system and expand managerial capacity in public institutions. Economic problems often arise from the central bureaucracies having too much control over public services and infrastructure. Some countries require more decentralized administrative and political systems in order to perform their functions and implement economic development policies more effectively.[38] The extent to which their enterprises and industries are able to compete successfully in global markets and generate profits depends on the availability and quality of support services and physical infrastructure; thus highly centralized governments may be less effective in creating a conducive business environment than governments that are more decentralized and able to respond quickly to changes in local needs and conditions. Governments in industrial, transitional, and developing countries all face challenges in determining the appropriate allocation of functions and responsibilities among central governments, local governments, and the private sector. Governments in transitional and developing countries have the opportunity to strengthen administrative capacity through decentralization.

Administrative decentralization seeks to redistribute authority, responsibility, and financial resources for providing public services among different levels of government.[39] Administrative decentralization can be defined as the transfer of responsibility for planning, management, and raising and allocating resources from the central government and its agencies to field units of government agencies, subordinate units of government, semiautonomous public authorities or corporations, or area-wide, regional or functional authorities.

Most governments in developing countries decentralize through deconcentration or delegation. Deconcentration redistributes decision-making authority and financial and management responsibilities for providing services and facilities among different levels of the central government, that is, to central government officials posted in regions, provinces, or districts.[40] Delegation is a somewhat more extensive form of decentralization. Through delegation, central governments transfer responsibility for decision-making and administration of public functions such as education or health services to semiautonomous organizations not wholly controlled by the central government, but ultimately accountable to it. Governments delegate responsibilities when they create public enterprises or corporations, housing authorities, transportation authorities, special service districts, semiautonomous school districts, regional development corporations, or special project implementation units. Usually these organizations have a great deal of decision-making discretion. They may be exempt from constraints on regular civil service personnel. They may be able to charge for their services and may be operated like private corporations, using business practices and procedures.

In most countries seeking to create an efficient and competitive market economy, national governments must strengthen the administrative, financial, and legal status of local governments, especially those of cities. This may require devolution, another form of decentralization. When governments devolve functions, they transfer authority for decision-making, finance, and management to autonomous units of local government with corporate status. Devolution involves transferring responsibilities for services to municipalities that elect their own mayors and councils, raise their own revenues, and have independent authority to make investment decisions.

Providing Physical and Technological Infrastructure

Modern and efficient physical and technological infrastructures are preconditions for national, regional, and local economic growth and channels through which private enterprise participates in domestic and international trade. Experience suggests that physical infrastructure is a necessary but not a sufficient condition for promoting economic diversification and strengthening productive enterprise. Economic infrastructure and the services it provides include: public utilities (power, telecommunications, piped water supply, sanitation and sewerage, solid waste collection and disposal, and piped gas); public works (including roads and major dam and canal works); and other transport facilities (including urban and interurban railways, urban transport, ports and waterways, and airports). More important, in a global economy driven by technological innovation, governments must play an increasingly crucial role in establishing and sustaining technological infrastructure.

The Commission of the European Communities concludes that among nations and regions having similar location, population concentration, and sectoral structure endowments, those with better physical infrastructure achieve higher levels of income, productivity, and employment.[41] Insufficient or poor quality infrastructure creates bottlenecks for development and limits the capacity of local enterprises to benefit from location advantages or to change the sectoral mix of the regional economy. Investments that improve infrastructure can also overcome some of the limitations of unfavorable location or low population concentrations.

An efficient system of services and infrastructure also enhances the efficiency of private capital. Entrepreneurs and managers are more likely to be attracted to regions with better social services and physical facilities where they can use the other production factors more effectively.

Regions with insufficient infrastructure suffer not only from bottlenecks, but also from not being able to attract and maintain mobile factors of production or pay competitive remuneration for entrepreneurs
and labor.

Relentless technological innovation, especially in globally interconnected digital communications, transportation, and business logistics
systems, has spawned the rapid growth of service and manufacturing
industries linked through virtual networks and supply chains. This innovation is increasing the demand for rapid delivery of high quality goods,
services, and information in North America, Europe, Asia, and Latin
America. Rapid advances in information technology and electronic commerce are fundamentally changing the demands on businesses and revo-
lutionizing the way they conduct transactions.[42] Advances in digital
communications technologies are driving down the costs of and increasing capacity for exchanging information. As technology-based manufacturers increasingly adopt advanced computer systems and robotics to
do simulated product design, virtual prototyping, concurrent or simultaneous engineering, and motion planning to reduce design and production cycles and increase their flexibility in meeting customer orders,
they need more advanced communications infrastructure, such as local
area networks and wide area networks.

Globally competitive businesses require more than analog switched,
copper line–based telephone systems; they increasingly have come to
depend on infrastructure that allows mid-band and broad-band access for
a wide range of communications and Internet equipment. Fiber-based
cable, satellite, and cellular communications infrastructure will be essential to connect companies to their customers and suppliers and to their
own branches, offices, subsidiaries, and partners. Communications and
transportation infrastructure offer more firms and industries the capacity
to develop larger markets that extend beyond national borders to satisfy
worldwide demand for new products and services. To cope with the rapidly changing trends in the international economy, governments must
provide the infrastructure and services that businesses of all sizes need to
respond more quickly to their customers' rapidly changing needs.

Protecting the Economically Vulnerable

Governments in market economies have a vital role in protecting economically vulnerable segments of the population from catastrophic
impacts, at least until they are able to participate productively in market

activities. By the mid-1980s studies began to show that IMF and World Bank prescriptions for structural adjustment had mixed impacts on the economies of developing countries and short-term negative effects for the poorest populations.[43] Although the transformation to a market-oriented economy brought great economic and political benefits to many former planned economies, the transition also resulted in relatively high levels of unemployment, especially among lower-skilled, less-educated and long-time employees of state enterprises, and drastic declines in GDP ranging up to 40 percent in some countries in the years immediately following macroeconomic reforms. Transitional countries saw an increase in poverty that was related both to unemployment and unfavorable temporary economic conditions. Many countries experienced a deepening of income inequality as private entrepreneurs and professionals gained in income and wealth relative to the rest of the population.

Some of the most serious problems arose because governments and international assistance organizations paid little attention to the social consequences of the reforms. As state enterprises were privatized and restructured, their modernization brought drastic changes in the conditions of employment, especially in former socialist countries. Wages became more closely linked to individual and group performance rather than to occupational classifications, employees had to become more flexible in their work times or accept part-time work, and advancement depended on developing multiple skills and a willingness to take on multiple tasks required in companies that had to adjust rapidly to customer demands.

From the transition experience in East and Southeast Asia, the Asian Development Bank concluded that governments seeking to provide social protection to the economically vulnerable segments of the population during transition and cyclical downturns should focus on five areas: 1) labor market policies that help generate employment and ensure efficient operation of labor markets; 2) social insurance programs that mitigate some of the risks associated with unemployment, disability, ill-health, and old age; 3) social assistance and welfare service programs for those groups such as single mothers, the homeless, or physically and mentally challenged people who have no other adequate means of support; 4) micro- and area-based projects that address causes of vulnerability within communities by providing access to microinsurance, agricultural insurance social funds, and disaster relief; and 5) child protection programs that ensure healthy and productive child development.[44]

Among the most important components of a social safety net policy for protecting the economically vulnerable is protecting the pension systems that form the primary or sole source of cash income for those too old to work. It is also important to create or maintain reasonable unemployment benefits for workers who are released from their jobs in state enterprises, laid-off because of restructuring after privatization, or in the process of changing employment. Governments must also help establish and maintain a system of private health and social insurance to replace those provided by state enterprises for workers who face loss of short-term income because of health contingencies and in maintaining social assistance programs for the disadvantaged who are adversely affected by economic transition.[45]

To create an efficient and effective system of social benefits, eligibility requirements must be carefully designed to protect all in the most vulnerable groups. Benefits must be set within the limits of available government resources and at levels that foster development of the private sector and competition.

Governments in most developing countries also face strong challenges in alleviating widespread poverty, which undermines social cohesion, political stability, and economic productivity. Market economies require a productive workforce drawn from a healthy, educated, and skilled population. The UNDP notes that to alleviate poverty, governments and the private sector must prepare the poor to participate effectively in the economy.[46] This requires increasing their access to basic education and health services.

Governments must also enact agrarian reform policies that give the rural poor a more equitable distribution of land and agricultural resources and open access to credit by changing creditworthiness criteria and decentralizing credit institutions. Governments can play an important role in expanding productive employment opportunities and sustainable livelihoods for those who are unemployed or underemployed and in increasing the participation of the poor in developing and implementating poverty-alleviation policies and programs to assure that they are needed and appropriate. In developing countries it is especially important for governments to provide an adequate social safety net to protect those excluded temporarily or permanently from the market, while pursuing policies that promote economic growth and increased productivity so that new opportunities are available for the poor to improve their living standards. As development accelerates, government can work closely with the private sector to increase people's capacity to use resources in a sustainable and environmentally-beneficial manner.

Strengthening and Supporting Civil Society Institutions

Globalization has had a strong impact on strengthening organizations of civil society in many countries with previously authoritarian regimes, according to studies carried out by the Economic and Social Commission for Asia and the Pacific (ESCAP).[47] "Certain aspects of globalization greatly favor the creation of new associations and interest groups in societies as well as networks of them to offer mutual support and resources," ESCAP points out. "Such cooperation is particularly visible in fields such as environmental protection, equality for women and human rights."

While globalization facilitates the development of civil society organizations, promoting a robust network of social and civic institutions—commonly referred to as "social capital"—seems to be essential in most countries to the effective operation of markets, national competitiveness, and economic growth. Social capital has powerful consequences because civic networks and norms ease the dilemmas of collective action by institutionalizing social interaction and reducing opportunism, by fostering norms of social reciprocity and social trust, and by facilitating political and economic transactions.[48] Well-developed civil institution networks also amplify the flows of information and help transmit knowledge of people's reputations that lower economic and social transaction costs. They offer channels for reliable political, economic, and social collaboration.

Among the most important institutions of civil society are employers organizations; industry associations; commercial associations; labor unions; employee groups; professional associations; policy and advisory groups; a free press, television, and radio; gender, language, religious, and other social-interest groups; and community and neighborhood groups. As societies become more complex, people also need the help of consumer groups, charitable and philanthropic organizations, and social organizations that bring them together to participate in a wide range of activities from sports and recreational endeavors, to music, art, handicrafts, hobbies, or other forms of social interaction. All of these groups, by bringing people together in common cause, provide them with mechanisms for contributing to the quality of life in their communities and countries.

Institutions of civil society can make powerful contributions to life support systems, especially in countries where civic networks were not encouraged and social capital was allowed to decay. Civic organizations can help offset or mitigate the adverse effects of market weaknesses and market failures. Institutions of civil society also play crucial roles in providing functions and services that the market cannot offer. They have especially strong impacts on economic, political, and social development when they cooperate with each other, the government, and the private sector. They can contribute to economic development by helping create an entrepreneurial milieu so essential to sustaining a market economy, by working with other institutions in developing human resources, by protecting the economically weak segments of the population from the potentially adverse effects of economic transformation, and by participating in activities that help alleviate poverty.

CONCLUSION

Market systems are the engines of national economic growth and the means through which private enterprises become competitive in a globalizing economy. To operate effectively, however, market systems require a strong institutional framework. Globalization and the technological innovation that drives economic, social, and political interaction across national boundaries can bring substantial benefits to people in countries where governments focus on enacting and implementing market-supporting policies and on creating and sustaining the institutions needed to make markets open, equitable, and competitive. Studies of countries that have transitioned from closed, planned, controlled economies to open market systems indicate that successful transformation requires not only economic policy reforms but also political liberalization.[49] Creating the institutions and policies that support efficient market systems and facilitating national competitiveness requires long-term political commitment by governments with strong developmental orientation.

States seeking to participate in and benefit from a global market economy must create and sustain institutions that promote or strengthen the following seven underlying attributes of market systems that make them more open to domestic and international transactions:[50]

- economic motivation—market systems depend on society's acceptance of material gain and the need for business organizations to make profits as a primary motive for individual production and investment
- private productive property—in market systems governments must protect private ownership of income and wealth to reward those who produce goods and services

- freedom of enterprise—to employ private property effectively, owners must be permitted to mobilize the resources needed to make it more productive
- market-based decision-making—in market systems, economic and business decisions must be made by market signals, that is, primarily through consumer decisions affecting supply and demand
- competition—a basic attribute of market economies and the primary motivator for individuals and producers to divide labor, specialize, develop comparative advantages, improve quality, cut costs, and innovate
- equality of opportunity—"free" markets require institutions that assure all individuals and groups of the opportunity to engage in economic activity through the ownership of property and the formation of enterprises, or fair sale of their labor for income
- societal rule setting and guidance—for markets to operate efficiently and effectively, participants must establish and adhere to institutionalized rules of the game, and government must establish a rule of law and enforce regulations within which markets can function efficiently.

When they operate fairly, effectively, and efficiently, market economies facilitate competitiveness and stimulate economic growth, create jobs, raise incomes, provide opportunities for saving and investment, and give people the chance to improve the quality of their lives. Competitiveness in the global economy can generate the income needed for people, businesses, and governments to protect their environment and conserve natural resources, reduce poverty, and enhance human assets. Properly guided, economic growth enables organizations of civil society to work closely with business and government to strengthen the life-support systems that improve the human condition and protect the global ecosystem.

NOTES

1. InterAmerican Development Bank, *Competitiveness: The Business of Growth* (Washington, D.C.: IDB, 2001).

2. A. J. Isacksen, C. B. Hamilton, and T. Gylfason, *Understanding the Market Economy* (Oxford, U.K.: Oxford University Press, 1992).

3. Klaus Schwab, Michael E. Porter, and Jeffrey D. Sachs (eds.) *The Global Competitiveness Report 2001–2002* (New York: Oxford University Press, 2002).

4. Institute of Management Development, *The World Competitiveness Yearbook 2002* (Lausanne, Switzerland: IMD, 2002).

5. InterAmerican Development Bank, Competitiveness: The Business of Growth.

6. United Nations Conference on Trade and Development, *Trade and Development Report 2002* (New York: UNCTAD, 2002): iv.

7. World Bank, *World Development Indicators 2002* (Washington, D.C.: World Bank, 2002): 273.

8. Dennis A. Rondinelli, "Capacity Building in Emerging Market Economies: The Second Wave of Reform," *Business & the Contemporary World* 6, no. 3 (1994): 153–167.

9. Jack N. Behrman and Robert. E. Grosse, *International Business and Governments: Issues and Institutions* (Columbia, S.C.: University of South Carolina Press, 1994).

10. Douglas C. North, *Institutions, Institutional Change and Economic Performance* (Cambridge, U.K.: Cambridge University Press, 1990).

11. Ha-Joon Chang, "The Role of Institutions in Asian Development," *Asian Development Review* 16, no. 2 (1998): 64–95.

12. World Bank, *World Development Report 2002* (Washington, D.C.: World Bank, 2002).

13. UNCTAD, *World Investment Report 2002:* 11.

14. N. Rosenberg and L. E. Birdzell, Jr., *How the West Grew Rich: The Economic Transformation of the Industrial World* (New York: Basic Books, 1986).

15. Andrei Shleifer, "Establishing Property Rights," *Proceedings of the World Bank Annual Conference on Development Economics* (Washington, D.C.: World Bank, 1994): 93–117.

16. D. Orr. and T. S. Ulen, "The Role of Trust and the Law in Privatization," *The Quarterly Journal of Economics and Finance* 33, Special Issue (1993): 135–155.

17. R. M. Sherwood, G. Shepherd, and C. Marcos De Souza, "Judicial Systems and Economic Performance," *The Quarterly Review of Economics and Finance* 34, Special Issue (1994): 101–116.

18. United Nations Conference on Trade and Development, *World Investment Report 1994* (New York: UNCTAD, 1994).

19. Dennis A. Rondinelli, "Making Metropolitan Areas Competitive and Sustainable in the New Economy," *Journal of Urban Technology* 18, no. 1 (2001): 1–21.

20. Dennis A. Rondinelli and Max Iacono, *Policies and Institutions for Managing Privatization: International Experience* (Geneva: International Labor Office, 1996).

21. Raymond Vernon, "Introduction: The Promise and the Challenge," in *The Promise of Privatization,* ed. R. Vernon (New York: Council on Foreign Relations, 1988), 1–22.

22. World Bank, *Bureaucrats in Business* (New York: Oxford University Press, 1995).

23. M. Baker (ed.), *Privatisation International Yearbook, 1998* (London: IFR Publications, 1998).

24. L. Mahboobi, "Recent Privatization Trends," *Financial Market Trends* 79 (2001) 43–56.

25. Henry Gibbon (ed.), *Privatization International Yearbook 2001* (London: IFR Publishers, 2001).

26. Jacques Morisset and Olivier Lumenga Neso, "Administrative Barriers to Foreign Investment in Developing Countries," World Bank Working Paper No. 2484 (Washington, D.C.: World Bank, 2002).

27. Kristin Hallberg, "A Market-Oriented Strategy for Small and Medium-Scale Enterprises," IFC Discussion Paper No. 40 (Washington, D.C.: International Finance Corporation, 2000).

28. H. G. Broadman and F. Recanatini, "Seeds of Corruption: Do Market Institutions Matter?" Working Paper No. 2368 (Washington, D.C.: World Bank, 2000).

29. Barlomiej Kaminski and Beata K. Smarzynska, "Foreign Direct Investment and Integration into Global Production and Distribution Networks," Working Paper No. 2646 (Washington, D.C.: World Bank, 2001).

30. United Nations Conference on Trade and Development, *World Investment Report 2000* (New York: UNCTAD, 2000).

31. Asian Development Bank, "Governance in Asia: From Crisis to Opportunity," *Annual Report 1998* (Manila: ADB, 1998): 15–36.

32. John H. Dunning, "Whither Global Capitalism?" *Global Focus—International Journal of Business, Economics and Social Policy* 12, no. 1 (2000): 117–136.

33. Transparency International, *Corruption Perceptions Index 2002* (Berlin, Germany: Transparency International, 2002).

34. Thomas Wolf and Emine Gurgen, "Improving Governance and Fighting Corruption in the Baltic and CIS Countries," Economic Issues Paper No. 21 (Washington, D.C.: International Monetary Fund, 2000).

35. M. Camdessus, "Money Laundering: The Importance of International Countermeasures," (Washington, D.C.: International Monetary Fund, 1998).

36. M. Massè, "Economic, Financial, Political and Technological Pressures Shaping Public Sector Reform," in *Proceedings of the Canada South-East Asia Colloquium: Transforming the Public Sector,* ed. Claire E. McQuillan (Ottawa, Canada: Institute on Governance, 1992): 3–7.

37. Broadman and Recanatini, "Seeds of Corruption: Do Market Institutions Matter?"

38. G. Shabbir Cheema and Dennis A. Rondinelli (eds.) *Decentralization and Development: Policy Implementation in Developing Countries* (Beverly Hills, Calif.: Sage Publications, 1983).

39. Dennis A. Rondinelli, "What is Decentralization?" in *Decentralization Briefing Notes,* eds. Jennie Litvack and Jessica Seddon (Washington, D.C.: World Bank Institute, 1999): 2–5.

40. Dennis A. Rondinelli, James McCullough, and Ronald W. Johnson, "Analyzing Decentralization Policies in Developing Countries: A Political-Economy Framework," *Development and Change* 20, no. 1 (1989): 57–87.

41. D. Biehl, *The Contribution of Infrastructure to Regional Development: Final Report* (Luxembourg: Commission of the European Communities, 1986).

42. Dennis A. Rondinelli, "Technology Policies and Regional Economic Development: Strategy for the Twenty-First Century," in *Knowledge for Inclusive Development,* eds. P. Conseicao, D. Gibson, H. Heitor, G. Serilli and F. Veloso (Westport, Conn.: Quorum Books, 2002): 301–322.

43. Dennis A. Rondinelli and John D. Montgomery, "Managing Economic Reform: An Alternative Perspective on Structural Adjustment Policy," *Policy Sciences* 23, no. 1 (1990): 73–79.

44. Asian Development Bank, "Social Protection: Reducing Risks and Increasing Opportunities" (Manila: ADB, 2002).

45. Sanjeev Gupta and Robert Hagemann, "Social Protection During Russia's Economic Transformation," *Finance & Development* 31, no. 4 (1994): 14–17.

46. United Nations Development Programme, *Human Development Report 1994* (New York: Oxford University Press, 1994).

47. United Nations Economic and Social Commission for Asia and the Pacific, *Sustainable Social Development in a Period of Rapid Globalization* (Bangkok, Thailand: ESCAP, 2002): 17.

48. Robert Putnam. "Comment," in *Proceedings of the World Bank Annual Conference on Development Economics 1994* (Washington, D.C.: World Bank, 1995): 198–199.

49. M. Reiser, M. L. Di Tommaso, and M. Weeks, "The Measurement and Determination of Institutional Change: Evidence from Transition Economies," Working Paper No. 29 (Cambridge, U.K.: Cambridge University Department of Applied Economics, 2001).

50. Jack N. Berhman and Dennis A. Rondinelli, "The Transition to Market Oriented Economies in Central and Eastern Europe: Lessons for Private Enterprise Development," *Global Focus—Journal of International Business, Economics and Social Policy* 11, no. 4 (1999): 1–13.

4

Making Globalization and Liberalization Work for People: Analytical Perspectives

Manuel R. Agosín and David E. Bloom

IN THE CLOSING YEARS OF THE TWENTIETH CENTURY, most developing countries adopted increasingly liberal economic development strategies. They opened domestic markets to international trade, gave market forces greater play in the allocation of resources, and privatized many state-owned enterprises. There was also a sea change in policies toward FDI, with liberalizing measures far exceeding restrictive ones throughout the 1990s.[1]

However, liberalization has not always delivered the expected rates of economic growth, and the gap between rich and poor countries has continued to grow. The breakdown of the WTO meeting in Seattle crystallized concerns about the direction of globalization, among both proponents and opponents. Strongly liberal voices such as *The Economist* described the breakdown as "a global disaster" and claimed "the poor will be the real losers."[2] Others welcomed what they saw as the humbling of the WTO, arguing that "globalization is hurting too many and helping too few," and that "the forces behind global economic change—which exalt deregulation, cater to corporations, undermine social structures, and ignore popular concerns—cannot be sustained."[3] Meanwhile Claude Smadja, Managing Director of the World Economic Forum, has warned of the danger of a backlash against globalization, which "may put at risk the benefits that globalization has brought to both the developed world and the emerging-market economies."[4]

A longer version of this chapter appears in *Solving the Riddle of Globalization and Development*, eds. Manuel Agosín, David Bloom, Georges Chapelier, and Jagdish Saigal (forthcoming). Published here by permission of UNCTAD-UNDP Global Programme.

From a developing country perspective, it is now clear that a passive policy of liberalization is no longer sufficient and that a range of active policies is needed. From an economic perspective, these policies recognize that liberalization offers economies opportunities that will be successfully exploited only if sufficient capacity is developed to enable a range of actors to engage successfully with the new market conditions. Furthermore, a broader perspective reminds us that economic growth is only a means to the more significant goal of human and social development. Human capital, social capital, and economic growth are all intricately bound in a set of complex relationships. Each has the potential to support the other, but equally deficits in one area can lead to deterioration in the others. Virtuous and vicious spirals are therefore possible, indicating the need for a balanced approach to development. At the same time there is some evidence that a policy environment emphasizing human development, described by the UNDP as "the process of widening people's choices and the level of well-being they achieve,"[5] is more likely to lead to a virtuous spiral than is one focusing more narrowly on economic growth.[6]

THREE SPHERES OF DEVELOPMENT POLICY

This chapter discusses three complementary policy spheres: integration into the global economy and liberalization of markets; promotion of fast economic growth; and development of human and social capital. The three policy spheres can be characterized as intersecting circles (see Figure 4.1). Confining policy initiatives to a single sphere tends to deliver disappointing results. Sustained development (economic, human, and social) is most likely to be achieved at the intersection of the three spheres. Democratic governments, while striving for electoral support, must therefore develop a balanced policy portfolio likely to contribute to virtuous development spirals. They must be aware of the extent of their power to promote change in any area and of the possibility that government intervention may inhibit action by other actors. In many cases, civil society and the business sector may be able to play a significant and increasing role in promoting broad-based development.

For aid organizations operating at national or international levels and other multilateral actors, there is a strong case for a more broad-based approach to providing development assistance. The World Bank, for example, has come up with its Comprehensive Development Framework, which aims to promote partnership between different institutions and maintain progress along a number of fronts. There are still unanswered

Figure 4.1 Three Spheres of Development Policy

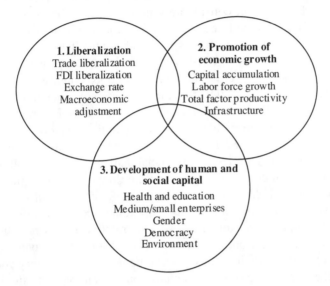

1. **Liberalization**
Trade liberalization
FDI liberalization
Exchange rate
Macroeconomic
adjustment

2. **Promotion of economic growth**
Capital accumulation
Labor force growth
Total factor productivity
Infrastructure

3. **Development of human and social capital**
Health and education
Medium/small enterprises
Gender
Democracy
Environment

questions about whether this approach will increase the effectiveness of development assistance and how to reconcile the agendas of different national and multinational actors. Nevertheless a growing body of evidence and analysis is available to policymakers seeking to develop a framework in which liberalization and globalization deliver enhanced benefits to people while simultaneously ameliorating some of the harsher impacts of these processes.

Sphere 1: Integration into the Global Economy

For most developing countries, openness to the international economy provides a strong environment for stimulating growth. Many developing countries are small, and inward-looking economic strategies can therefore quickly come up against demand constraints. Countries that export are able to grow much faster, especially if they can diversify the products they bring to international markets. Openness, of course, also involves increased investment in imported capital equipment, which combines capital accumulation with access to modern technologies to improve productivity. At a time when markets are developing quickly, closed economies are becoming increasingly less viable.[7]

Openness in developing countries is composed of a number of policies:

1. *Trade liberalization.* Most developing countries have significantly lowered their trade barriers, with average tariff levels down, and tariff dispersion considerably narrowed. Countries joining the WTO, in line with their new international obligations, have dismantled a variety of subsidies and nontariff barriers to trade. Many countries have also signed free trade agreements with neighbors and occasionally with developed countries.

2. *Liberalization of FDI.* Most developing countries have liberalized their FDI regimes. Indeed, some now have FDI regimes that are distinctly more liberal than those in the developed world.[8]

3. *Freeing of non-FDI capital flows.* Many developing countries now look to international financial markets to supplement investment from domestic saving, and the flow of capital to the developing world has increased, though with uneven results.

4. *Macroeconomic adjustment.* Inflationary conditions discourage investment, weaken the ability of relative prices to guide resource allocation, and seriously discourage the private sector. Recently, inflation rates have come down almost everywhere in the developing world, and many countries have made significant progress in balancing their budgets.[9]

Achieving these reforms has not been easy, and there is now a vast literature analyzing the obstacles societies face in adopting policies that encourage openness. Much less attention has been paid, however, to the fact that even as openness is achieved, many developing countries are still failing to generate strong economic growth. There is, of course, no single explanation for these failures. The international economy is fast-moving and demanding. Thus it is not sufficient for countries simply to dismantle inefficient industries. Developing-country firms and industries must engage in a continual search for new competitive advantage, and countries must strive to develop capacity in high-productivity sectors. Coherent price signals are therefore needed to steer resources toward promising new export sectors. Exchange rate policies are extremely important in this respect. Often trade liberalization is accompanied by capital inflows that appreciate the exchange rate. This ends up stimulating the production of nontradables rather than encouraging nascent exports.

The experience of the successful Asian countries is instructive. For more than two decades, while their exports grew at unprecedented rates, the Republic of Korea and Taiwan (Province of China) were able to stabilize their real exchange rates through active management of the market. This clearly contributed to their export performance. On the other hand, experience shows that countries using the exchange rate as an anchor for domestic prices have found that real exchange rate appreciation is very difficult to avoid, with adverse effects on the growth of new exports.

However, even when price signals are strong, supply responses to price signals are weak in many developing countries. Markets are often segmented regionally and labor may be geographically immobile as well as uninformed about risks and opportunities. Small producers are unable to seize new opportunities due to poor levels of education or health, a lack of organizational or technological capabilities, or inadequate access to financial markets. Poor quality management can also leave larger enterprises unable to respond rapidly to changing market conditions. Meanwhile, with FDI, investors look for resources relevant to their needs before committing themselves to investing in a particular country. With the emergence of increasing numbers of high-value industries, human assets have become a crucial factor for investment decisions. Thus the capacity, flexibility, and initiative of a country's human resources are at the heart of many, if not most, investment decisions.

Finally, increased capital flows can pose serious threats to the stability of a country's economy. While direct investors are likely to have at least a medium-term stake in a country's future, portfolio investors and foreign creditors have tended to exhibit herd-like behavior. Waves of enthusiasm in emerging markets have given way to waves of panic.[10] The result has been extraordinary booms followed by deep recessions, which have had demonstrable effects on human and social development. The East Asian financial crisis not only had economic effects such as bankruptcies, increased poverty, and rising unemployment, it has also led to reduced schooling, diminished public services, and increased social stress and fragmentation.[11] While the Asian economies are now recovering, the adverse social effects are proving long-lasting.[12] Meanwhile, there is little evidence that countries have increased their ability to manage foreign capital flows or reached consensus on the features of "a new international financial architecture."[13] In sum, the liberalization of markets appears to be close to a necessary condition for rapid, sustainable human development–centred growth. But it is highly insufficient, for two reasons. First, it must be adequately managed at the national and international levels. Second, countries must ensure strong supply responses to new price signals from a wide variety of actors, especially the poor, as will be discussed further in Sphere 3.

Sphere 2: The Promotion of Fast Economic Growth

Liberalization offers great economic development opportunities to a country, but active policies are needed to ensure those opportunities are taken up. Coherence in policymaking is also needed to promote fast and sustained economic growth. By establishing growth-friendly policies, policymakers not only increase international confidence in their countries' development prospects, they also enhance domestic confidence that the future can offer rising levels of prosperity.

Economic growth depends upon factor accumulation and improvements in total factor productivity. In recent years our understanding of factor accumulation has been broadened by a wider appreciation of the nature of capital. Physical capital has become relatively less important, as knowledge- or information-based products and services grow in value. Even in traditional industries, a growing information element may come to constitute the core of competitive advantage and be the source of most profit.[14] The "knowledge economy" is thus increasingly reliant on the accumulation of social and human capital.

The accumulation of physical capital depends on the rate of investment in an economy. While FDI and other international capital flows can contribute to financing investment, domestic rates of saving remain crucial. In East Asia, for example, saving rates have been exceptionally high (averaging over 30 percent for decades), enabling these countries to achieve the level of investment necessary to sustain rapid growth. In other regions, however—Latin America is a good example—saving rates have been much lower. In most developing countries, including those introducing economic reforms, investment rates have rarely surpassed 20 percent of GDP. This is well below the 25–30 percent needed to raise growth of income per capita to more than 5 percent per year over the long term.

Many factors depress domestic saving. Excessive government involvement in financial markets and inflation both discourage saving, as does lack of public confidence in the soundness of domestic financial systems. Rather than providing a sound prudential regulatory framework, many governments engage in unjustified intrusions into financial markets that distort financial resource allocation.

Further, it is not enough for markets merely to attract savers. They must also be able to deliver capital to those in need of credit. Micro-enterprises and small firms are typically cut off from financial markets. For those who do have access, in many developing countries, the spread between the rates of interest paid to lenders and those demanded of borrowers is notably high, reflecting lack of competition, inefficiency, and the high-risk nature of their financial markets.

Policymakers therefore need to facilitate a well-functioning financial sector by offering a stable and predictable macroeconomic environment as well as a regulatory environment that upholds the rule of law, respects private property, and enforces legitimate contracts. Prudential oversight of the banking system to ensure, for example, adequate bank capital, reserves for defaulted or risky loans, and restrictions on loans to related parties are also needed to inspire confidence in the system. Without such confidence, financial markets will be less active, and savings will be concentrated offshore.

Private and public investments are often complementary. For example, without roads and energy systems (both typically built and maintained by governments), private investment for large markets is just not feasible. There are, however, a large number of constraints to efficient public investment. Budget cuts due to macroeconomic adjustment policies have tended to fall disproportionately on public infrastructure investment. In other cases, governments have attempted to do too much at the same time, overestimating their capabilities to carry out investment projects efficiently.

Sphere 3: Development of Human and Social Capital

The case for giving increased priority to human and social capital development has been advanced on many fronts in recent years. Two main arguments have been made. First, development of human and social capital is the ultimate end of the development process, with economic growth simply representing an important means to that end. This view has been strongly advanced by the UNDP, which opened its first *Human Development Report* with the following statement: "The real wealth of a nation is its people. And the purpose of development is to create an enabling environment for people to enjoy long, healthy and creative lives."[15] This simple but powerful truth is often forgotten in the pursuit of material and financial wealth. Second, there is growing evidence that, as well as being the main objective of broad-based development, human and social capital development is also an exceedingly powerful instrument of economic growth and development. It is recognized increasingly as an economic input, not simply an output, and powerful evidence indicates that these forms of capital are becoming more important for economic development.

In discussing human and social capital, we note the importance of both as legitimate ends to development but also explore their role as a vital instrument in the development process itself.

Human capital. The study of human capital, i.e., the skills and knowledge embodied in people, focuses on the role of people in society, with increases in human capital improving the opportunities that people enjoy.[16] Education, for example, increases social mobility, enhances participation in a range of social activities, and has well-documented effects on health and perceptions of quality of life. It is also an important determinant of economic growth, offering clear private and public economic benefits.[17] The better educated are more productive and have greater opportunities to succeed in the labor market. With the knowledge economy demanding ever-greater skills from its workers, educated people are better equipped to respond to changing market signals. This is especially important when an economy must restructure. Asian countries with a strong developmental record during the latter half of the twentieth century all strongly emphasized improving both the quantity and the quality of their educational systems.

If education offers people opportunity, then health provides them with security—and its importance is increasingly being recognized.[18] The burden of poor health falls most squarely on the poor. Not only do they have the weakest access to quality healthcare, but they also rely most on their labor, and poor health reduces people's ability to work. A health shock can quickly wipe out the savings of a poor or middle-income family in a developing country, while simultaneously decreasing investment in other forms of human capital (as a child is removed from school, for instance, both to save money and to act as a caregiver). Again, better health has measurable effects on the economy. Healthy people are better able to work as well as more likely to save for their retirement and invest in their (healthier) children's education.[19] Improvements in health can significantly enhance the opportunities of the poorest in society.

A related factor is demographic change, which offers many developing countries favorable economic opportunities in the years to come. Demographic change can be seen as a link between certain key aspects of human and social capital development (better health and education, poverty reduction, gender equality) and faster economic growth. Demographic change can be impeded by poverty, lack of education, and inadequate access to health care. Conversely, improved education and health can speed up demographic change and can help countries reap a growth-enhancing demographic dividend.[20]

As infant mortality declines and life expectancy increases, there is a lag before people start to choose to have fewer children. However, once fertility declines, it does so steeply (though how steeply varies from country to country) as people choose to invest more resources in fewer children. This demographic transition is at the heart of the development process. When large families are common, universal education is difficult to provide. Further, rural families look to their children to become productive on the land from a young age. The role of women also changes rapidly when smaller families are common. They are more likely to receive education and to become more active outside the family. This in turn increases the opportunities available to children, who tend to receive better education and more access to resources as their mothers become more highly educated.

Research shows that these processes can be accelerated by policies that actively promote women's capability and autonomy and that seek to protect them from discrimination and physical abuse. Thus there is a clear positive relationship between the protection of gender equality, other elements of social development, and economic growth.

Demographic transitions clearly have economic effects. Reductions in mortality initially affect infants and children most and set forces in motion that create a bulge (or baby boom) in the age distribution. More specifically, the mortality decline creates the leading edge of the bulge while the trailing edge is formed by the subsequent decline in fertility. Once this enlarged cohort has been educated, they become available to the labor market, causing a sharp rise in the ratio of workers to dependents. If these workers can be gainfully employed, then a country has an opportunity to seize a substantial demographic dividend. This dividend is intensified by the likelihood that the baby-boom generation—with higher life expectancy and fewer children—will save more if supportive policies are in place.[21] This generation may also be more entrepreneurial in its attitudes, as a consequent shift from country to town and city promotes more individualistic attitudes.

Social capital. The concept of social capital broadens human capital's focus on individuals to explore the importance of relationships among individuals. More specifically, social capital refers to the premise that networks between citizens have value. "Specific benefits," according to Robert Putnam, "flow from the trust, reciprocity, information, and cooperation associated with social networks."[22] In a civic society, citizens participate in their communities and work together to solve social problems and provide public goods. By contrast, in an uncivic society, citizens lack the trust in others that characterizes a cohesive community. Such lack of trust leads them to focus on the pursuit of individual goals, which tends to prevent them from exploiting the many natural benefits of collective action.

Democratic government balances the rights and responsibilities of citizens and seems to be the form of government most attuned to the modern world.[23] The strength and effectiveness of a democracy—and popular confidence in and support for its survival—has important implications for the quality of life people enjoy. Democracies also seem most suitable for fostering values relevant to successful modern economies. The myth that pro-market reform can only be implemented under dictatorships has now been dispelled. Democratic governments have demonstrated that they are capable of designing and implementing far-reaching economic reforms, and that their politicians can build popular support for such reforms. In fact, without democracy, economic reform lacks legitimacy and can easily be turned back. It is also easier to foster widespread entrepreneurial attitudes within a democracy, as individuals enjoy the risks and benefits of taking responsibility for their own actions.

Strong democracies rely on institutional strength, which is also vital to economic development and the efficient functioning of markets, as the disastrous experience of the former USSR shows. Russian democratization and market liberalization were accompanied by rapid deterioration in almost all institutions and, as a result, the country faces economic decay, increasing poverty, and a precipitous decline in health status.[24] Even countries with well-functioning institutions cannot afford complacency, as a rapidly evolving environment (owing, among other things, to integration into the global economy) requires appropriate institutional responses. Many institutions find this process of continual reform difficult to achieve. Rich and poor countries alike struggle with a reliance on outmoded institutions that continue to offer poor value and levels of service.

Social capital describes more than the formal relations in society, however. Indeed, many have argued that it is best confined to describing informal relations. For example, Fukuyama argues that "social capital can be defined simply as a set of informal values or norms shared among members of a group that permits cooperation among them," but warns that sharing values and norms does not automatically produce social capital.[25] Some cohesive groups, for example organized criminal gangs, may substantially diminish a society's stock of social capital. For numerous reasons, social capital is harder to analyze and measure than human capital. It is also much more difficult to say which social changes are likely to contribute to increasing social capital.

Social capital may be interpreted as the degree to which society promotes the involvement of individuals with its institutions. This involvement works best when social institutions reward individual effort in a fairly equitable manner. In other words, a minimum degree of equality of opportunity must be present. Thus in its broadest sense the accumulation of social capital lessens conflicts of interest and channels the efforts of individuals toward goals in which individual enhancement is aligned with the common good. This positive outcome requires that individuals perceive they have a stake in their society and will, therefore, want to work to promote its development.

INTERACTIONS

None of the three policy spheres can be developed in isolation. Rapid economic growth is exceedingly difficult to achieve in isolation from global markets. Technology now advances too rapidly for any country to proceed alone, and knowledge shows little respect for national borders. Policies to encourage openness, however, are difficult to sustain without economic growth. Global markets change quickly and are relatively unforgiving of economies that are not responsive to their signals. Sluggish economies will not experience sufficient benefits from liberalization to offset the inevitable costs. The consequences for all societies, and especially for democracies, will be growing protectionist pressures and reversals of liberal policies.

Nor can economic development be seen in isolation. Human development is the ultimate aim of development policy, but it is also a vital route to economic development and to enabling a society to benefit from openness. While it is possible for a society to get richer without its poorest people seeing their prospects improve, it is uncommon for large numbers of people to escape poverty while the economy as a whole remains stagnant or suffers reverses. Equally, an open society offers many advantages to those trying to achieve human development. Enhanced communication and a greater awareness of living conditions in other societies is a fundamental threat to repressive regimes—and liberal policies stress individual responsibility, which is impossible to achieve when human and social capital have been diminished.

By working at the intersection between the policy spheres—and creating a balanced policy portfolio—policymakers can seek to set up a positive feedback loop between different policy elements. By delivering sustained improvements in health, for example, policymakers will create a direct effect on demography, investment in education, physical capital accumulation, and labor productivity. The resulting smaller families spend more on the health of their children, creating the beginning of a self-reinforcing cycle of health and development. And just as the educated are better able to extract benefits from health systems, as well as be more receptive to preventive health messages, so do those with productive jobs spend more on nutrition and healthcare.

Similar interactions can be seen across all policies. Formal analysis, for example, has been used to explore the interaction between demography and openness to trade. A country whose working-age population grows at 3 percent a year (and twice the pace of overall population growth), can reap a demographic dividend three times as large if its economy is open. In other words, a rate of growth of the working age population of 3 percent boosts output growth by 2.1 percent in open economies, as compared to only 0.7 percent in economies that are not open to world trade.[26] Policymakers should therefore strive to achieve virtuous spirals whereby interactions among policy elements generate a set of positive and reinforcing development benefits.

Conversely, policymakers must also act quickly and decisively to tackle a serious deterioration in any policy area, as this risks starting a vicious spiral causing declines across other indicators. In Sub-Saharan Africa, for example, the AIDS epidemic is having a dramatic effect on life expectancy, the productivity of the workforce, and parents' ability to invest in their children's future. As a result, the region's wider prospects are deteriorating rapidly.

The differences between the conventional approach to development and an sustainable human development–centred approach can be visualized with the assistance of Figures 4.2 and 4.3. Figure 4.2 outlines the conventional approach to development policy. This approach emphasizes, in one way or another, a trickle-down model of human development, which is viewed as the end result of policies that first promote growth. As shown in Figure 4.2, the accumulation of capital and productivity improvements lead to higher growth, which raises wages and increases tax revenues. These in turn induce an increase in both public and private expenditures in health and education, both of which lead to an improvement in well-being (human capital development, in our scheme).

The view of development from a human development perspective is quite different, as illustrated in Figure 4.3. For illustrative purposes, we concentrate here only on efforts to raise public expenditures on health and education, but we could have taken any other point of departure (for example, efforts to promote greater gender equality and poverty reduction). Improvements in people's access to good health and education have a number of positive effects on human development directly and on an economy's capacity to grow. Better health and education by themselves

Figure 4.2 The Conventional Approach

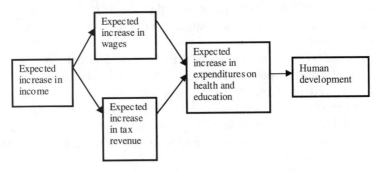

Figure 4.3 The Vision from Sustainable Human Development

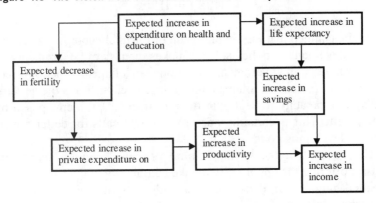

broaden people's choices: they live better and longer lives, and these, in their own right, must be counted as important development achievements. In addition, they have positive effects on growth. First, women who expect to live longer and are better educated prefer a smaller number of children with a higher quality of life. Therefore fertility rates decline, and families spend more of their own incomes on the health and education of their children. The enhanced private and public expenditures on health and education have positive effects on productivity and competitiveness. In addition, as people live longer, they increase their savings for retirement, which also has a favorable impact on long-term growth.

These flowcharts can be superimposed to show the many pathways that link human development and economic growth, as well as the many entry points into this complex system.[27] The resultant composite framework illustrates the powerful outcomes that can be obtained from working at the intersection of policy spheres. Of course, the positive effects of enhancing human development-related variables will be greater in an open economy than in a closed one. In an open economy, people have the entire world as potential suppliers of their needs and as potential users of their products. But they must be given the proper tools to respond productively to the stimuli they receive from the broader world into which they are integrating. They must also be protected against the traumas likely to arise during the transition to a more internationally integrated economy.

ACTION POINTS

It could be claimed that this emphasis on three highly complex and multifaceted development policy spheres makes the task of governments all but impossible. Can governments act at once in a large number of directions? One of the basic problems of developing countries is the government's poor capacity to deal with the multifaceted problems posed by development. This is certainly one problem that calls for better governance in developing countries.

The concept of the virtuous spiral provides a route out of this impasse, offering the opportunity to take complexity into account, act in a limited number of directions, and adopt a number of different approaches. Instead of advancing on all fronts, governments can identify strategic points of entry that can be used to push the spiral into action. If governments succeed in identifying the strategic points of entry, they can set in motion virtuous spirals, with effects on variables in other policy spheres. However, as the first benefits are released, it is important to ensure that governments shift their attention to other areas of the policy portfolio. Balance, in other words, is most practically achieved as a dynamic process, rather like the way a cyclist stays upright—by continually adjusting to a permanent state of disequilibrium.

One consequence of this approach is to sound a long overdue death knell for the single model of development. Whatever the idea may be, it usually claims dogmatically to be the only fruitful approach to the development problem. Of course, the "right model" changes with the intellectual fashion du jour. It is increasingly recognized, however, that multiple models can deliver results (although many more models are unlikely to be successful). There is also some evidence that a bias toward human development is more likely to start the spiral moving than a bias toward short-term economic growth. Ramírez, Ranis, and Stewart argue that countries displaying "human development lopsidedness" moved to virtuous spirals in about one-third of the cases, while all cases of "economic growth lopsidedness" resulted in only temporary gains.[28] They also suggest that models need to change as progress is made, with basic health and education favored in the earliest phases but with resources gradually being shifted toward science, technology, and more advanced education. They also note that labor-intensive rural employment may be an initial priority, but economic growth in higher-productivity sectors will be essential to sustain growth.

Another consequence is to emphasize the need for cooperative actions between developed and developing countries. It is now amply clear that development will not likely occur unless developing countries pursue a portfolio of policies that leads to human development and growth at the same time. It is also clear that the international environment must be helpful to the efforts of developing countries to promote their own development. Otherwise such efforts will fall on barren soil.

To date governments have been less than successful in shielding the most vulnerable groups in society from the disruption of pro-market reform. Reforms are therefore threatened by rising inequality. Measures to tackle social exclusion have two aims. The first is to increase the security of the socially excluded through safety nets protecting the vulnerable members of society from the inevitable social side effects of a liberalized market economy.[29] These safety nets should be structured to encourage individuals and groups to take an active approach to improving their lives, rather than simply encouraging dependency (as, for example, have many developed country welfare systems). The second aim is to enhance opportunities by offering the excluded a range of ways to increase their participation in society, through education, support for small businesses, microcredit facilities, and so forth. Active government action to combat discrimination against women, members of particular ethnic groups, and religious minorities can also be key.

Inequality can also be a sizeable drag on society, especially in countries where a significant minority, or a majority, of people lives in poverty. Poverty is associated with higher fertility, which impedes the demographic transition. It also diminishes the demand for education. Large numbers of poor people also make a country more vulnerable to natural disasters and to internal wars. Sri Lanka, for example, is frequently praised for the priority it has given to human development. But poverty levels remain high, a civil war has cost tens of thousands of lives, and few would claim that the country has made broad development gains in recent years. Pro-poor growth should focus on achieving and ensuring the maintenance of full employment; removing antipoor biases from macroeconomic policies;[30] investing in the capabilities of poor people; ensuring poor peoples' access to resources, including credit; increasing the productivity of small-scale agriculture and small businesses; and promoting labor-intensive industrialization. These approaches to development policy are very much in line with UNDP's emphasis on sustainable human development.

Currently it is possible to identify a number of strategic points of entry that offer policymakers an opportunity to make significant development progress. Examples include:

Support for small business. The small business sector is increasingly important to modern economies, but many small businesses—especially in developing countries—suffer from low productivity, lack of skills, and archaic production methods. In fact, many such businesses are no more than a symptom of disguised unemployment. Action to strengthen the small business sector can help reduce unemployment by transforming underemployed workers into self-employed entrepreneurs (who may eventually employ others), while improving skills, increasing access to technology, and providing access to credit for working capital and investment.

Recent experience shows that a particularly useful point of entry is support for financial institutions catering to the needs of micro- and other small enterprises. A large number of successful financial institution experiences in the developing world rely on innovative credit programs for delivering services to microenterprises and small firms. The most famous example is, of course, the Grameen Bank in Bangladesh. But there are many others, including Banco Sol in Bolivia, Fundación Calpiá in El Salvador, and Bank Rakyat Indonesia Unit Desa.[31] These innovative institutions allow poor people and small firms to help themselves by enabling them to become entrepreneurs. Policies to promote these institutions are an example of working at the intersection of policy spheres: they are welfare-enhancing in their own right and thus promote human development, and they also foster growth by enabling people to raise output and investment. Such efforts need the support of the international community.

Action targeted at potential entrepreneurs is effective even when people move into other forms of employment, helping to create employees with the "intrapreneurial" attitude that modern businesses value.

Most exciting, today's first generation entrepreneurs may breed a second generation with vastly increased ambition and scope.

Higher education. Higher education has become, in many ways, the basic education of the knowledge economy. Yet in developing countries, resources for higher education, and indeed higher education systems themselves, remain inadequate. Urgent action is therefore needed to expand and diversify as well as to build systems that will meet the requirements of tomorrow's world. Enhanced higher education will not only lead to better-trained graduates, it will also provide developing countries with important points of contact with the global economic "commons" as well as exerting upward pressure on education quality throughout the rest of the education system.[32]

Action on health. As argued above, improved health is crucial to combating poverty.[33] As successful immunization programs have shown, action on health is especially suitable for international cooperation. There are many areas where renewed action is needed. In Eastern Europe and the former Soviet Union, for example, deteriorating health (along with the breakdown of governance) is a significant contributor to the disastrous performance of many countries.[34] HIV/AIDS, meanwhile, can be (partly) tackled through education and the effective marketing of health messages (as the examples of Uganda and Thailand show). A renewed global campaign, with substantial private sector involvement,[35] could have a huge impact on the prospects of much of the developing world.

An especially contentious area needing international discussion and action is access to pharmaceuticals. Once a drug is developed and patented, the cost of producing it is often low, and there may be scope to establish drug pricing schedules that are indexed to country per capita incomes to ensure wide access.[36] Imaginative solutions to this problem could form the basis for a future international agreement on health. A start has already been made through pharmaceutical companies that have developed drugs for AIDS and are willing to market them in developing countries at a fraction of their price in developed countries.

SOME FINAL THOUGHTS

In a global economy, there is a need for strong international institutions as well as for action to equip national institutions to engage more effectively within the global system. The disastrous WTO negotiations in

Seattle demonstrated how much work is yet to be done. The negotiations revealed widespread public disillusionment with globalization, highlighting either how poorly policymakers have articulated the case for openness or the complex mix of benefits and costs experienced by many countries. They also revealed damaging splits between developed and developing countries. Developing countries have been told that liberalization is the best policy, but they have not always found markets in developed countries opening for them. Many developing countries also lack the capacity to negotiate effective agreements. Technical and financial assistance is also clearly needed to help countries implement new trade rules and to adapt to new requirements imposed by the North. While such requirements may be intended to improve consumer protection, they are all too often seen from the South's perspective as examples of covert protectionism.

Improved governance is needed at the international level in other realms as well. International finance has the first priority on the list. The financial and economic crisis that occurred in East Asia in the late 1990s revealed that the globalization of finance has proceeded at a much faster speed than the capacity of the international system to govern international finance to ensure that it contributes to development. The crisis and its aftermath showed that financial crises can inflict enormous harm on fragile countries and that an urgent need exists to design and implement an international financial system that serves the needs of people everywhere.

Poised on the threshold of a new century, policymakers across the world have the opportunity—and the responsibility—to help define this new epoch. The last century delivered a number of major improvements to the lives of many of the world's poor, disadvantaged, and excluded but much work needs to be done. New technology has profound implications. It can help disseminate decades of developmental knowledge capital and open up an incredible range of new opportunities. Equally profound, however, is the responsibility of all to help ensure that those opportunities are used to deliver a decent future for all of our planet's inhabitants.

NOTES

1. United Nations Conference on Trade and Development, *World Investment Report 2000* (Geneva: UNCTAD, 2000).

2. See various articles in *The Economist*, 11 December 1999.

3. Jay Mazur, "Labor's New Internationalism," *Foreign Affairs*, January/February 2000: 79–93. Jay Mazur is Chair of the American Federation of Labor

and Congress of Industrial Organizations (AFL-CIO) International Affairs Committee, as well as President of the Union of Needletrade, Industrial, and Textile Employees.

4. Claude Smadja, "Time To Learn From Seattle," *Newsweek International,* January 17, 2000: 7.

5. United Nations Development Programme, *Human Development Report, 1997* (New York: UNDP, 1997).

6. The Human Development Index, according to UNDP, reflects "the most basic human capabilities—leading a long life, being knowledgeable and enjoying a decent standard of living." These are measured through life expectancy at birth, educational attainment (adult literacy rate and combined primary and secondary enrolment ratio), and income per capita. The concept of human development also acknowledges other, more difficult to measure, capabilities including political freedom and participation, the development of the family, the rights of women, and social cohesion (especially the avoidance of crime and corruption).

7. However, openness also tends to involve increased imports of consumer goods. Insofar as these compete with local production, difficult political and economic issues may arise.

8. M. R. Agosín, "Liberalization and the International Allocation of Foreign Direct Investment," Working Paper No. 8 (Center on International Economics and Development, Universidad de Chile, Santiago, 1999).

9. United Nations, *World Economic and Social Survey 2000* (New York, UN, 2000).

10. S. Radelet and J. D. Sachs, "The East Asian Financial Crisis: Diagnosis, Remedies, Prospects," *Brookings Papers on Economic Activity* vol. 1 (1998): 1–90; J. Furman and J. E. Stiglitz, "Economic Crises: Evidence and Insights from East Asia," *Brookings Papers on Economic Activity* vol. 2 (1998): 1–135.

11. See David E. Bloom, Patricia Craig, and Pia Malaney, *The Quality of Life in Rural Asia* (Hong Kong: Oxford University Press, 2001).

12. United Nations Development Programme, *Human Development Report, 1999* (New York: UNDP, 1999).

13. B. Eichengreen, *Toward a New Financial Architecture—A Practical Post-Asia Agenda* (Washington, D.C.: Institute for International Economics, 1999); J. A. Ocampo, *La Reforma del Sistema Financiero Internacional: Un Debate en Marcha* (Mexico City and Santiago: Fondo de Cultura Económica, 1999); M. R. Agosín and J. A. Ocampo, "La Arquitectura Financiera Internacional: Hacia la Creación de un Marco Propicio para la Estabilidad de los Mercados Financieros y Cambiarios" (CEPAL, unpublished, November 2000); M. S. Ahluwalia, *Reforming the Global Financial Architecture* (London: Commonwealth Secretariat, 2000).

14. P. Evans and T. S. Wurster, "Getting Real About Virtual Commerce," *Harvard Business Review,* November–December 1999: 84–94.

15. United Nations Development Programme, *Human Development Report, 1990* (New York: UNDP, 1990).

16. This is the perspective taken by Amartya Sen, *Development as Freedom* (New York: Knopf, 1999), Nobel Prize winner in Economics for 1998. Sen

prefers the expression "human capabilities" to the more conventional one of human capital. We retain the term "human capital" but give it the scope of Sen's "human capabilities."

17. See David E. Bloom and Joel E. Cohen, "Education for All: An Unfinished Revolution," *Daedalus*, Summer 2002, 84–89.

18. D. E. Bloom and D. Canning, "The Health and Wealth of Nations," *Science*, February 2000: 1207–1209.

19. See David Bloom and David Canning: "Health as Human Capital and Its Impact on Economic Performance," *The Geneva Papers on Risk and Insurance* 28: 2 (April 2003), 304–315.

20. See David E. Bloom, David Canning, and Jaypee Sevilla, *The Demographic Dividend: A New Perspective on the Economic Consequences of Population Change* (Santa Monica, Calif.: RAND Corporation, 2002).

21. D. E. Bloom, D. Canning, and P. Malaney, "Demographic Change and Economic Growth in Asia," *Population and Development Review*, 2000; D. E. Bloom, D. Canning, D. Evans, B. Graham, P. Lynch, and E. Murphy, "Population Change and Human Development in Latin America," background paper prepared for Inter-American Development Bank, *Economic and Social Progress in Latin America, 1999–2000 Report* (Washington, IDB, 2000); D. Bloom and J. D. Sachs, "Geography, Demography, and Economic Growth in Africa," *Brookings Papers on Economic Activity* vol. 2 (1998): 207–295; and David E. Bloom, David Canning, and Jaypee Sevilla, *The Demographic Dividend: A New Perspective on the Economic Consequences of Population Change* (Santa Monica, Calif.: RAND Corporation, 2002).

22. Robert D. Putnam, *Bowling Alone* (New York: Simon & Schuster, 2000).

23. The number of democracies increased rapidly in the last decades of the twentieth century. For a more detailed discussion, see R. A. Dahl, *On Democracy* (New Haven: Yale University Press, 1998).

24. C. Becker and D. E. Bloom (eds.), *The Demographic Crisis in the Former Soviet Union*, Special Issue of *World Development* (November, 1998).

25. F. F. Fukuyama, *The Great Disruption: Human Nature and the Reconstitution of Social Order* (New York: The Free Press, 1999).

26. D. E. Bloom, et al., "Population Change and Human Development in Latin America."

27. See David E. Bloom and David Canning, "Demographic Change and Economic Growth: The Role of Cumulative Causality," in *Population Matters: Demography, Growth, and Poverty in the Developing World*, eds., Nancy Birdsall, Allen C. Kelley, and Stephen Sinding (New York: Oxford University Press, 2001): chapter 7.

28. G. Ranis, F. Stewart, and A. Ramirez, "Economic Growth and Human Development," *World Development* 28, no. 2, 2000: 197–219.

29. For a similar view, see D. Rodrik, *Has Globalization Gone Too Far?* (Washington, D.C.: Institute for International Economics, 1997).

30. It is a well-known fact that macroeconomic adjustment programs often include cuts in expenditures that benefit the poor.

31. J. Morduch, "The Microfinance Promise," *Journal of Economic Literature* 37 (1999): 1569–1614.

32. See Task Force on Higher Education, *Higher Education in Developing Countries: Peril and Promise* (Washington, D.C.: The World Bank, 2000). See also David E. Bloom, "Mastering Globalization: From Ideas to Action on Higher Education Reform," in *Globalisation Universities, Private Linkages, Public Trust*, eds. Gilles Breton and Michel Lambert (UNESCO, IAU and Presses de l'Université Laval, 2003).

33. David E. Bloom and David Canning, "The Health and Poverty of Nations: From Theory to Practice," *Journal of Human Development* 4, no. 1 (March 2003): 47–71.

34. See C. Becker and D. E. Bloom (eds.), *The Democratic Crisis in the Former Soviet Union.*

35. See David E. Bloom, Lakshmi Reddy Bloom, and River Path Associates, "Business, AIDS, and Africa," in *Africa Competitiveness Report 2000/2001* (New York: Oxford University Press, 2000): 26–37. See also David E. Bloom, Ajay Mahal, and River Path Associates, *HIV/AIDS and the Private Sector: A Literature Review,* Dorset, UK: River Path Associates, June 2001.

36. David E. Bloom and River Path Associates, "Something to be Done: Treating HIV/AIDS," *Science* 288, no. 23 (June 2000): 2171–2173.

5

Pro-Poor Policies for Development

Hafiz A. Pasha

THE UNITED NATIONS MILLENNIUM DECLARATION places poverty reduction at the center of the development process. It is, therefore, essential to search for national development strategies that achieve secure, sustainable, and equitable human development and that empower people. In the Millennium Declaration passed by the UN General Assembly in 2000, more than 160 heads of state or government pledged their commitment to achieving the Millennium Development Goals (MDGs). First among these goals is reducing the incidence of global poverty by half (compared to the 1990 level) by 2015. Other goals such as the elimination of hunger, universal access to primary education, mortality reduction, and gender equality all support the goal of reducing poverty.

The concern for pro-poor policies is the consequence of a deep-rooted disillusionment with the development paradigm that placed exclusive emphasis on the pursuit of economic growth. During the 1950s and the 1960s, the primary target was raising levels of investment in developing countries, initially by the injection of foreign savings (aid), in order to achieve rapid growth. The expectation was that the trickle-down effect, largely through higher employment and real wages, would alleviate poverty. In this paradigm, there were no explicit pro-poor policies, only pro-growth policies that would ultimately lead to poverty reduction. However, in many situations, the process of growth raised inequality such that the trickle down effect was either weak or nonexistent.

Given this failure of growth to mitigate poverty, the focus shifted initially to the design of targeted antipoverty interventions in the form of social safety nets to tackle poverty. The objective of this strategy was to reach those groups that remain excluded from or marginalized by the process of growth. This is the implicit philosophy behind the Poverty

Reduction Strategy Papers prepared by developing countries for concessional financing by international financial institutions such as the IMF and World Bank. The macroeconomic framework embodied in the papers continues to focus on stabilization leading to growth, with targeted interventions superimposed to manage any negative fallout from the strategy on the poor. However, the basic problem is that if the country's growth strategy spreads impoverishment, a separate poverty program can do little to reverse the trend.

The need to go beyond social safety nets and focus directly on providing jobs and raising incomes of the poor through explicit policy interventions is now widely recognized. Experience suggests that, generally, countries that have been most successful in reducing poverty have combined policies promoting equity and growth. Public policies need to influence both the generation and distribution of income in such a way as to disproportionately benefit the poor. In other words, the focus now is on pro-poor growth.

The importance of growth, however, cannot be forgotten. A strategy that focuses primarily on reducing inequality through redistribution of assets or incomes but ignores or sacrifices growth is unlikely to lead to a sustained reduction of poverty. In addition, in the absence of growth serious constraints to finding the resources necessary to finance targeted antipoverty interventions will arise.

Therefore growth needs to be rapid enough to significantly improve the absolute condition of the poor as well as their relative position. This can be achieved either by ensuring greater equity at the start of the growth process, for example, through land reform (as in Korea and Japan), or it can be achieved by decreasing inequality during the growth process (such as making low-skilled jobs more readily available and thereby pushing up wages among the poor, as was achieved initially by East Asian economies such as Thailand, Korea, and Malaysia through export-led growth in labor intensive manufactures). However, efforts to improve assets or income distribution should not retard growth by either dislocating economic activity or adversely affecting the investment climate or by distorting resource allocation.

The objective of this chapter is to identify pro-poor policies that, while directly affecting poverty, do not have unfavorable consequences for growth, and may even promote it. The chapter describes the key elements of such policies, analyzes different types of policies in terms of their effectiveness in contributing to poverty reduction, and provides a framework for tackling poverty at different levels.[1]

THE NATURE OF PRO-POOR POLICIES

Is growth with equity possible? There are many examples of countries in which this has been the case, at least during certain periods. Perhaps one of the best examples is China. During the early 1980s, China's agriculture-led development strategy sparked a historically unprecedented reduction in poverty. Unlike many countries, China gave favorable treatment to farmers, dividing the land equitably among them, raising the prices of their output, and giving them the incentive to benefit directly from harder work. Farmers also benefited from earlier state investment in rural physical infrastructure and basic health and education. The consequence was a surge in pro-poor growth. The resulting rural prosperity directly propelled the growth of nonfarm township and village enterprises, further boosted employment and incomes, and created a virtuous circle of growth and poverty reduction.

During the 1990s, Vietnam followed the same strategy with similar, though less dramatic, results. Recently the Democratic Peoples Republic of Korea also announced a policy of exiting from food ration quotas at subsidized prices to market-determined prices of agricultural produce, along with higher wages. It remains to be seen whether this will impact favorably on poverty by raising food production.

When China shifted in the 1980s to a development strategy oriented toward exports and FDI (mostly in the richer coastal region) growth became notably less pro-poor, and poverty reduction slowed. It has become essential to launch an antipoverty program for the more backward western regions.

Similarly, in India the increase in the aggregate growth rate in the 1990s coincided with a major economic reform involving a degree of external trade liberalization along with convertibility of the rupee; deregulation of industry, including relaxation of past restrictions on domestic and foreign investment; and some financial sector reform. However, the rate of decline in poverty, from 36 percent to 26 percent, associated with relatively high growth was low.

Reasons the growth process in India was less pro-poor include, first, its sector composition, especially the relatively poor performance of agriculture, which did not help rural areas where much of the poverty is concentrated. Second, the pattern of growth was skewed—it did not occur in the states where it would have the most impact on poverty nationally. Third, the problem of adverse initial conditions undermined the strategy. States that lagged behind in terms of initial rural development and human development faced not only limited prospects of overall growth but also of pro-poor growth.

During the 1980s when the overall growth rate was somewhat lower, the reduction of poverty in India was more spectacular (from 51 percent to 36 percent), due mainly to the agricultural breakthrough. Similarly, Bangladesh reduced poverty substantially in the 1980s (from 70 percent to 48 percent) by improving food production.

The general principle that can be derived from these examples is that for growth to be immediately poverty-reducing, it should direct resources disproportionately to: sectors in which the poor work (such as agriculture); areas in which they live (such as underdeveloped regions); factors of production that they possess (such as unskilled labor); and outputs that they consume (such as food). This implies that a strategy of pro-poor growth consists primarily of employment generation combined with relative price stability of essential goods and services, such as food, in the consumption basket of the poor.

Based on these general principles, there are four policies to reduce poverty: macroeconomic policies, microeconomic or microsector policies, restructuring policies, and redistributive policies.

Macroeconomic Policies

The key macroeconomic ingredients of pro-poor growth are high levels of employment and low rates of inflation. However, in the sense of the classic Phillips' curve, there can be a trade-off between these two objectives. That is, achieving price stability requires restricting the aggregate level of demand, with its adverse implications on the level of output and employment. Alternatively, raising the level of employment necessitates stimulating demand, which can spill over into inflationary pressures. This trade-off can be mitigated, however, if there is excess capacity in the economy or if efforts are made to augment factor productivity.

The traditional Washington Consensus on macroeconomic stabilization supported by the international financial institutions overemphasizes low inflation, frequently at the expense of growth and development. In particular, the obsession with eliminating fiscal deficits (and, thereby, current account deficits), if achieved through cutbacks in public expenditure on development activities and public services, has retarded the process of growth and created more poverty. Contrary to the view that higher fiscal deficits crowd out private investment by raising interest rates, there is persuasive empirical evidence that if higher fiscal deficits are caused by larger public investment outlays, then this may actually "crowd in" private investment on a net basis by removing physical bottlenecks of infrastructure and thereby raising the factor pro-ductivity of private investment. In addition, larger public outlays on education and health raise the productivity of the poor and better equip them to get out of the poverty trap.

Therefore the question is, what is the optimal point in the inflation–unemployment trade-off from the viewpoint of poverty reduction? The experience seems to indicate that there is a case for tolerance of larger fiscal deficits to stimulate investment and growth. As long as inflation is moderate, it need not dampen growth. Moreover, growth stimulated by fiscal expansion can help finance government deficits—as long as they are not excessive—through faster growth in tax revenues. The larger levels of public investment made possible in this strategy should focus on activities that stimulate private investment, develop human resources, and reduce poverty.

Pakistan's economic performance in recent years is a prime example of the stabilization process gone too far, under the aegis of an ongoing IMF program, which has substantially retarded growth and led to rapid increases in unemployment and poverty (from about 20 percent in the early 1990s to over 33 percent currently). During the 1990s, public sec-tor development expenditures were cut from almost 10 percent of GDP to less than 3 percent. Now that a degree of stabilization exists, the cur-rent account deficit has been converted into a surplus, and foreign exchange reserves have increased sharply. Favorable developments include resumption of grant assistance by the United States, debt rescheduling on favorable terms, and larger inflows of home remittances.

However the growth rate has plummeted to about only 3 percent. Private investment has declined in recent years as stabilization policies have led to high real rates of interest, higher relative costs of imported capital goods (due to high real exchange rate depreciation), significant excess capacity due to low levels of aggregate demand, and the absence of complementary public investment in infrastructure. Fiscal stabiliza-tion has proved elusive and the budget deficit has remained high (at close to 7 percent of the GDP) due primarily to the failure of tax rev-enues to grow in the presence of a stagnant economy.

Microeconomic or Microsector Policies

For growth to be strongly poverty reducing, it has to contribute to employment generation in excess of the increase in labor force and to stability in prices of essential items. This implies that growth has to be concentrated in sectors that are major sources of livelihood for the poor or produce goods and services that they consume.

The main sector that meets both these criteria is agriculture. Agricultural development—in particular enhanced food production and more broadly speaking rural development—are likely to make the biggest contribution to alleviating poverty, especially since most of the poor live in rural areas. Of course, the extent of the impact depends on how unequal the initial distribution of land is and on the nature of the particular strategy for achieving agricultural development. The rise in rural poverty in Pakistan in the 1990s during a period of rapid agricultural growth (over 4 percent annually) and the resulting attainment of food self-sufficiency highlights the importance of these factors. The rise in rural poverty is attributable both to a high level of inequality in rural landholdings and to changes in the land tenure system whereby share-croppers have been converted into wage labor.

The experience with pro-poor agricultural growth is that it depends on appropriate technical progress, for example, the dissemination of high yielding varieties of seed for increased food, as happened during the Green Revolution in the 1960s. It also requires larger investments in rural infrastructure, for example, in secondary and tertiary irrigation networks, farm-to-market roads, electricity, and basic social services. Removing farm price repression has helped stimulate farm employment and production through improved incentives. However, governments should weigh this against the adverse consequences for the urban poor and the fact that in many developing countries even the rural poor are mostly net food buyers. Greater farm mechanization, facilitated by expanded provision of credit, has contributed to a more unequal distribution of output gains and led to eviction of small farmers and greater landlessness.

Another sector that comes closest to meeting these criteria is construction, especially if it focuses on shelter for low-income families and on providing pro-poor infrastructure in urban slums and squatter settlements or to villages in the more backward areas. Rapid growth of the construction sector can absorb a significant proportion of unskilled labor. Many countries have included a public works program as an important component of their poverty reduction strategy for purposes of absorbing seasonally unemployed agricultural workers and unskilled migrant workers in urban areas.

Restructuring Policies

In the 1980s and 1990s, economic restructuring policies increasingly focused on diminishing the state's role as the leading agent of development and of integrating countries more closely into the global economy. This has involved a standard set of measures such as privatization and deregulation, financial sector liberalization, trade liberalization, and capital account convertibility.

Lessons from recent experience highlight the need for the proper sequencing and pace of reform. The financial crisis that hit the East Asian countries in 1997 demonstrates clearly the need for stronger regulation of domestic capital markets and banking sectors. This crisis, which also triggered a collapse of the real economy, led to dramatic reversals of poverty reduction in countries such as Indonesia and Thailand. Overnight, these financial crises wiped out poverty reduction gains.

Problems of incorrect sequencing are visible in countries such as Pakistan where financial sector liberalization, involving a move to market-based interest rates prior to fiscal reform, has exacerbated the problem of large fiscal deficits due to the resulting explosive growth in debt-servicing liabilities. This has crowded out development expenditures and led to substantial underinvestment in human development.

Privatization has had ambiguous impacts on poverty. Where it contributed to greater efficiency, it conferred consumer benefits by either reducing prices or limiting price increases in basic utilities. However, where it led to the formation of quasi-monopolies, it restricted access for the poor by removing cross-subsidies and phasing out loss-making services. In addition, privatization involving substantial downsizing of labor has led to more unemployment and poverty in the absence, first, of buoyant private investment for creating new employment opportunities for displaced labor and, second, of adequate social safety nets for access to credit and retraining mechanisms.

Policies for enhancing private sector participation in the provision of basic social services such as elementary education and curative health services have led to a dual structure of provision. The rich gained access to higher quality private services and the poor saw falling standards of service. The retreat from service provision by the public sector diverted highly skilled personnel such as doctors and teachers to the more remunerative private facilities. Although a case can be made for privatization of industry and trade on the grounds of efficiency, the government retains a crucial role in maintaining the poor's access to basic utilities and services.

During the 1990s, trade liberalization became a basic strategy by which developing countries could benefit from globalization and achieve faster export-led growth. In countries where the initial level of trade repression was high (for example India and Bangladesh) opening up their markets did confer significant gains in the early- to mid-1990s. Most countries have continued to bring down their import tariffs, phase out their quantitative restrictions, and move toward market-based exchange rate regimes in an effort to encourage investment in export promotion rather than in import substitution. Simultaneously, attractive fiscal incentives opened more sectors to FDI. But the optimism has gradually faded in the face of overall recession in the world markets in recent years. Developed countries raised barriers to labor-intensive exports through export quotas (as in textiles) and enormous subsidies (especially to agriculture) to domestic producers. FDI remains largely concentrated in middle-income countries.

Meanwhile the reduction in import tariffs had several deleterious consequences, especially on poverty reduction. Many industries died because of their inability to compete with cheaper imports. For example the indigenous artisan and crafts sector of India, employing large numbers of people in cottage and home-based industry, is facing extinction due to the availability of mass-produced basic consumer goods from abroad. Sectors that have benefited from trade liberalization and foreign direct investment in India, such as the information technology sector, have essentially emerged as export enclaves with few backward or forward links with the domestic economy.

The conclusion from current research is that developing countries should attempt to engage with the world economy, but cautiously and on their own terms. Premature opening can lead either to immediate displacement of economic activity and loss of growth or to an uneven distribution of the gains. Only if governments appropriately sequence trade and capital account liberalization can globalization favor the poor. Domestic investment strategy should seek to initiate an indigenous growth process before opening up to the global economy. Simultaneously, efforts must be made to raise levels of human development to face the competitive pressures of globalization and to tackle the institutional constraints—such as the absence of adequate arrangements for marketing, quality control, transfer of technology, and research and development—that hinder export sector development.

One of the implications of trade liberalization that has seldom been examined is its adverse implications for human development via the impact on public revenues. Most developing countries rely heavily on international trade taxes for revenue because they are relatively easy to collect. Scaling down import tariffs as part of trade liberalization has caused sizeable revenue losses due to the inability to substitute custom duties with more effective taxation of domestic incomes, production, and transactions that require more sophisticated tax administration. The revenue shortage can lead to large cutbacks on human development at a time when developing countries need more expenditure in these areas.

Redistributive Policies

A recent study by the World Institute for Development Economics has shown that inequality has increased in two-thirds of countries for which reliable data are available. Several explanations are offered for this including skill-based technological change, the weakening of labor unions, trade liberalization, and the skewed distribution of FDI. Globalization has not only contributed to greater inequality among countries but also to greater inequality within countries. Growth of the world economy during the 1990s was, therefore, less pro-poor.

Governments must find inequality-reducing policies that can also contribute to growth or are at least neutral. One key area of reform is redistributive policies that alter public resource allocation through changing the pattern of expenditure and taxes. Many countries have hidden or perverse subsidies or tax expenditures that benefit the rich. For example, in Pakistan, subsidies on services consumed by the rich add up to as much as 4 percent of GDP; the corresponding estimate for India is even larger at close to 7 percent of GDP. Underpriced, pro-rich services include irrigation, electricity, and higher education. Proper pricing policies for these services could generate additional revenues to cross-subsidize basic services for the poor.

Tax expenditures, in the form of exemptions to or concessions in the application of tax laws (especially relating to direct taxes), are rampant in many countries. In Pakistan, they cost almost 4 percent of GDP in terms of foregone revenue and include favored tax treatment of unearned income, including income from capital gains or interest; low effective rates of taxation on real estate; tax-free privileges to high-level government functionaries; and tax exemption of agricultural income. One effective way of broadening the tax base is to withdraw these tax expenditures along with simultaneously reducing the rates of indirect taxes, which are generally regressive in nature and affect the poor more adversely.

Another major area of reform in public expenditure is to change its composition. For example, defense outlays in many South Asian countries substantially exceed social expenditures. Efforts at achieving greater peace and stability in the region could yield a substantial dividend in terms of larger spending on health and education.

Another area where redistributive policies could be effective is in the allocation of bank credit. This would involve orienting the banking sector toward microcredit for low-income households and to loans for small and medium enterprises. The emphasis should be on increasing access rather than on subsidized credit. The experience of financial institutions like Grameen Bank of Bangladesh is that this emphasis can keep intermediation costs lower through group-based lending while sustaining repayment performance at high levels, even at near-market rates of interest, through peer group pressures and the prospect of repeat borrowing. In contrast, large borrowers are more likely to be prone to willful default due to the system of political patronage and crony capitalism, especially in state-run banks. In addition, credit made available to small borrowers can contribute to substantially larger income and employment multipliers and, thereby, help reduce poverty.

Finally, the case for land reform is strong in countries where the distribution of land is highly uneven. For example, in Pakistan and the Philippines, the top 2 to 3 percent of farmers own more than one-third of the land. The issue of land reform is, however, contentious from the viewpoint of impact on agricultural productivity. Nevertheless much of the empirical evidence highlights the absence of a positive relationship between farm size and productivity. It appears that while larger farms can use capital and nonfactor inputs more intensively, small farms are likely to be characterized by higher land use, cropping, and labor intensities. Altogether, land reform coupled with expanded credit and better marketing arrangements can fundamentally alter the position of the rural poor.

THE POLITICAL ECONOMY OF PRO-POOR POLICIES

What is the feasibility of adopting pro-poor policies and under what conditions are they likely to be adopted? Even in supposedly democratic societies we see evidence of state capture by the elites, whereby public policy and the allocation of public resources are biased in favor of the rich and powerful. Pro-poor economic policies are not likely unless the politics and the governance process are more pro-poor. For economic policies to focus on poverty reduction, governance structures need to be effective in achieving this objective. To make such structures effective, broad pro-poor coalitions are necessary.

The choice and implementation of pro-poor policies clearly depend upon the political economy implications of the process. Who are the gainers and losers? The basic question is whether effective coalitions can be organized to thwart attempts by powerful vested-interest groups to block change and preserve the status quo. If interest groups see change as a zero sum game, with well-defined gainers and losers, then they are more likely to resist. This is why attempts at once-and-for-all inequality reduction, such as progressive land reform, are extremely difficult to implement. Opposition to this reform is intense not only because of potential economic losses but also because of the fundamental impact on the rural power structure. Therefore, land reform has usually come in the aftermath of a cataclysmic event (for example, war, as in Japan or following the partition of India) or when the problem of poverty and the resulting social breakdown have become so serious that radical governments have emerged with an agenda involving major structural change. The recent experience of Nepal reveals that, in the face of a Maoist insurgency, the government was compelled to announce major land reforms, although they have remained largely unimplemented to date.

Pro-poor policies are more likely if vested-interest groups see them as a positive sum game. This is the case when incomes are generally increasing rapidly and it becomes possible at the margin to distribute a disproportionate part of the income gains in favor of the poor. For example, Malaysia was able to pursue a strong affirmative action program in favor of indigenous Malays who were poorer than Chinese or Indian residents, during a period of strong economic growth. This is why it is important to demonstrate that pro-poor policies are also pro-growth and that the development strategy seeks to tackle poverty during the process of growth.

What the key elements of governance are likely to support the adoption of pro-poor policies? Systemic and institutional changes that enable the poor to have a stronger voice in the formulation and conduct of public policy are important and include:

- *Rule of Law.* The interests of the poor can be subverted either by the presence of inherently inequitable laws—such as those relating to property rights or to the discriminatory treatment of minorities and women—or by the inequitable application and enforcement of laws. Broadly speaking, a proper and judicial system is required that promotes stable and higher economic growth while respecting property rights, guaranteeing the sanctity of contracts, and lowering transactions costs.
- *Transparency and Accountability.* Serious problems with economic governance include the overcentralization of decision-making and

the lack of stakeholder involvement that permit patronage or powerful special interests and high levels of corruption. Clearly, policymaking will have to be more transparent and accountable, and the bureaucracy must be more responsive. Elected parliaments should have stronger oversight functions to monitor the allocation and use of public expenditure. Independent accountability institutions must also be set up to detect and punish the worst corruption.

The development of an appropriate legal and fiscal framework is also essential for providing a suitable environment for strong NGOs. Civil society can play a major role in articulating the concerns of the poor, and NGOs can be effective in targeting and delivering services to the poorly served segments of the population. Simultaneously, a free and vibrant press can contribute to greater transparency and accountability in the system.

• *Decentralization.* Decentralization and devolution can increase peoples' participation and empower the poor. There is currently a wave of decentralization in the Asia and Pacific region, with major efforts at strengthening local governments in diverse countries such as India, Pakistan, Nepal, Indonesia, Thailand, and China. However, for this reform to lead to a more pro-poor allocation of resources, governments must strengthen the process. They can do that by averting local elite capture by giving special representation to disenfranchised groups such as peasants, workers, women, and minorities; political education that organizes the poor, creates awareness of issues, fosters local leadership, and promotes higher voter turnout; genuine fiscal decentralization that transfers significant resources to the lower tiers of government on the basis of objective and transparent criteria and permits the exercise of true fiscal autonomy; and building the capacity of local governments.

In most countries, the challenge is to improve the process of governance in such a way that public policy fundamentally protects the general public interest rather than holding it hostage to vested interests.

FRAMEWORK FOR POVERTY REDUCTION

To attain the Millennium Declaration target of reducing poverty by one-half by 2015, average per capita income growth in developing countries will have to be faster, about 4 percent per annum as compared to the past average of 3 percent. At the same time, inequality will have to fall sharply within countries, such that the rate of decrease in the percentage of poor is at least 50 percent faster than the rate of growth.

To achieve these ambitious targets, pro-poor policies will have to be implemented at global, regional, national, and local levels. Globally, policies for allocation of official development assistance will have to target more effectively countries that have a high incidence of poverty and that demonstrate a strong commitment to attaining the MDGs. In addition, trade restrictions must be relaxed to provide greater access to the least developed countries, especially in agricultural commodities and labor-intensive manufactures. In addition, international organizations must expand debt relief along with greater technology transfer and investment by multinational corporations.

Regionally, recognition of the need to reduce war tensions and move toward peace and stability will allow the diversion of defense expenditures to fight the real war against poverty. This, along with the emergence of effective regional trading arrangements, can lead to more intraregional trade and can better equip countries to face the challenge of globalization. Developing regional trunk infrastructure such as transport, gas, and hydroelectric systems and tackling the problem of cross-boundary spillovers such as drug trafficking and environmental hazards may require new special institutional arrangements.

Nationally, governance reforms are needed that allow the adoption of the appropriate mix of pro-poor macroeconomic policies, sector policies, restructuring policies, and redistributive policies. Governments must design and effectively manage social safety nets for targeting the chronically poor.

Locally, governance reforms and social mobilization will be necessary to stimulate wider participation and the empowerment of people. This requires stronger local governments and community-based organizations.

Poverty will have to be tackled at all levels—global, regional, national, and local—through pro-poor policies for development if the more than one billion poor people of the world are to be given a real chance to get out of the vicious poverty trap and lead their lives with a semblance of human dignity and security.

NOTES

1. The analysis and conclusions in this chapter are based on the author's research on poverty in South Asia, especially in his country, Pakistan. A

comprehensive program for tackling poverty has been articulated in his recent book, *Social Development in Pakistan: Towards Poverty Reduction* (Oxford University Press, 1999). Insights on the feasibility and effectiveness of pro-poor policies have also been gained in his role of policymaker in different governments of Pakistan as the federal minister for finance, planning, commerce, and education. The author more recently studied a large sample of countries in his capacity as Director of the Regional Bureau of Asia and Pacific of the UNDP. Given this experience, most of the examples presented in the chapter are from the Asia and Pacific Region.

Part II

Enhancing State Capacity

6

Strengthening the Integrity of Government: Combating Corruption Through Accountability and Transparency

G. Shabbir Cheema

ACCOUNTABILITY, TRANSPARENCY, AND INTEGRITY are essential elements of democratic institutions and processes. They apply not only to public institutions but to private and civil society organizations as well. The accountability of public officials, the transparency of public decision-making, access to information, and the implementation of enforceable ethical standards and codes all have significant impacts on democratic institutions and poverty reduction strategies.

This chapter defines the concepts of integrity, ethics, and corruption. It discusses the forms, magnitude, and causes of corruption in developing countries and the impact on the quality of democratic institutions, economic development, and poverty reduction. It also presents case studies of some useful practices for combating corruption and analyzes core issues of policy reform.

ACCOUNTABILITY, TRANSPARENCY, AND INTEGRITY

Accountability is the pillar of democracy and good governance that compels the state, the private sector, and civil society to focus on results, seek clear objectives, develop effective strategies, and monitor and report on performance. It implies holding individuals and organizations responsible for performance measured as objectively as possible. It has three dimensions. Financial accountability implies an obligation of the persons handling resources, public office, or any other position of trust to report on the intended and actual use of the resources. Political accountability means regular and open methods for sanctioning or rewarding those who hold positions of public trust through a system of checks and balances among the executive, legislative, and judicial branches. Administrative accountability implies systems of control internal to the government including civil service standards and incentives, ethics codes and administrative reviews.

Transparency promotes openness of the democratic process through reporting and feedback, clear processes and procedures, and the conduct and actions of those holding decision-making authority. It makes information understandable and keeps clear standards accessible to citizens. Integrity completes the continuum of accountability and transparency.[1] It is synonymous with incorruptibility or honesty and requires that holders of public office should not place themselves under financial or other obligations to outside individuals or organizations that may influence them in the performance of their official duties.

FORMS OF CORRUPTION

Corruption has many facets and nuances in different cultures and societies. It is universally recognized as the behavior of public officials that deviates from accepted norms in order to serve private ends, and behavior in the private sector that breaches the public interest to gain special personal advantages. Corruption can be viewed from at least five perspectives:

1. The moralist–normative perspective defines corruption as inherently bad, as a lack of moral commitment and integrity among officials and focuses on the negative effects of corruption on public morality, institutional discipline, and public trust of officials.
2. The functional perspective views corruption as an ever-present quality of every society that changes and adapts to the circumstances. Thus the concept of corruption differs in accordance with cultural heritage, political and institutional structures, level of socioeconomic development, political culture, and the period of transition.[2] In transitional periods, for example, political and bureaucratic institutions that are unable to cope with increased demands made upon them by entrepreneurs, businessmen, foreign investors, and others may allow corruption.
3. The public office–legalistic perspective stresses the importance of creating legal institutions and making laws. Corrupt behavior is thus based on deviation from rules against the exercise of

authority for personal gain. One of the limitations of this approach in developing countries is the inability to enforce laws against the abuse of authority by those in power.

4. The public interest–institutionalist perspective seeks to explain how institutions shape individual officials and how collective and nonpecuniary goals are as much a part of corruption as interest-maximizing pecuniary corruption for personal gain. Thus the prospects of corruption by the individual official are limited by the norms, structures, and capacity of the institution to which the individual belongs and, therefore, the individual acts corruptly because of the fixed norms and conduct within the institution.

5. The market-centered perspective views every official as self-maximizing and entirely bent on personal gains. Self-interest drives officials to avoid their responsibilities and to use the rules to serve their own ends. The individual officeholder converts political resources into goods necessary to initiate and maintain corrupt relationships with those outside the formal political decision-making process. This perspective, however, ignores the collective pressure on an institution and other limits of action and behavior by institutional norms and structure.

Political corruption has been defined as a "transaction between the private and public sectors such that collective goods are illegitimately converted into private-regarding payoffs."[3] The most common forms of political corruption concern campaign finance, the award of government contracts on the basis of political support or affiliation, donations to political campaigns with the expectations of later benefits in the form of political appointments, the use of political position to leverage kickbacks or illicit payments, and appointment to high office on the basis of patronage. Large-scale bureaucratic corruption is more likely to take place in the privatization of public enterprises, distribution of land, implementation of public works projects, or awarding of major government contracts. It can take many forms: to obtain contracts or assets; to gain access to benefits; to avoid paying taxes, duties, or levies; to obtain permits and licenses; to influence legal and administrative outcomes; or to speed up or slow down government processes. It can also involve outright theft, as when government revenues and resources are simply stolen, salaries are charged for work not performed, and legitimate taxes are collected but not passed on to the government.

In many cases, bureaucratic and political corruption coexist and reinforce each other. In societies characterized by concentration of economic and political powers in a few hands, political and private sector elite are closely linked. In such circumstances, it becomes extremely difficult to ensure accountability of the ruling groups even though the country might have a democratic structure.

Some of the recent cases of corruption in high places in Thailand, India, the Philippines, and Indonesia that made the headlines in the national and international news media show the complicity of political and economic interests. In developed countries too there have been numerous cases of corruption involving influential politicians.

CORRUPTION AND THE QUALITY OF DEMOCRATIC PROCESS

Systemic corruption is very much a political issue because it affects the relationships between the state and society and because it affects political processes and outcomes. On the one hand, corruption significantly influences politics because most forms of corruption lead to misuse of political influence. It results in bypassing due process, weakening civil rights, and "blocking off legitimate channels of political access and accountability while opening up (and concealing) illicit new ones."[4] It can also lead to the weakening of political institutions and the loss of the people's trust in the political system. In many cases, military regimes use high levels of corruption in society to justify the overthrow of governments. Corruption has adverse effects on the quality of political process because it ignores three key elements of the democratic process: representation, debate, and choice.

On the other hand, politics affects the types and magnitude of corruption in many ways. Corruption can be used in contentious and politicized ways that sometimes make it difficult to differentiate corruption from partisan scandals. Political opponents who are discouraged from criticizing the existing government might find corruption useful as a way to challenge government without threatening its claim to political power.[5] In democratic regimes, the parties in power also consider public perceptions about the extent of corruption. In new and old democracies alike there is a general sense of alienation of people from politicians because of the expanding role of money in politics and their increased awareness about lack of transparency in governance.

Corruption appears as several syndromes. Johnston has identified four of these. In the interest group bidding syndrome, the elite are more accessible than autonomous, and there are more economic opportunities than political ones. Interest groups resort to their economic resources such as campaign contributions to influence political decisions. This is typical of liberal democracies such as the United States, the United Kingdom, and Germany. In the elite hegemony syndrome, an "entrenched political elite facing little political competition and few meaningful demands for accountability dominates and exploits economic opportunities, manipulating political access (a scarce and valuable commodity) in return for further economic gains."[6] Examples include China, Nigeria under military regimes, and South Korea. In the fragmented patronage and extended factionalism syndrome, the elites are accessible but need to seek power in the situation of intense political competition and scarcity of resources leading to fragmented politics. The elites are politically insecure and usually not able to sufficiently reward their followers through patronage. Examples include Russia and pre-Fujimori Peru. Because countries in such situations tend to be politically unstable, there are much greater chances for extreme corruption. Under the patronage machine syndrome, the elite manage to control political competition by manipulating scarce economic rewards through systematic use of patronage, lending to the concentration of political power in a few hands. Patronage is used to keep control of the degree of corruption inherent in such circumstances. Examples of this type include Mexico and Indonesia before the democratic reforms in those countries.

Quantifying the impact of corruption on political change is difficult because of a lack of data. Corruption can lead to systemic political change or breakdown of the political process or to major shifts in political power (such as in Liberia, Niger, Nigeria, the Philippines, the former Soviet Union, and Sudan). Or it can lead to regime change and "realignment of political competition" such as in Argentina, Bangladesh, Indonesia, Mexico, Pakistan, South Korea, and Thailand.[7]

Even though corrupt politicians can be voted out of power in a democratically elected government, democracy—especially during early stages—is not necessarily a cure for corrupt practices. In many developing economies, corruption at high levels of government coexists with democratic reforms. As developing countries pass through a transition period, consensus-building and legitimacy remain problematic. One important aspect of political legitimacy is the use of state power by officials in accordance with prearranged and agreed-upon rules. Where civil servants exercise considerable power, as in most of the new nations, they may themselves take the initiative in seeking legislative authorization for what they wish to do. When such legislation is adopted, it does not represent political control over bureaucracy.

The prevalence of corruption in a country may indicate the extent to which civil servants are able and willing to violate laws or permit their violation. Bribes may be given to induce officials to perform their duties—as in granting licenses and permits—or to overlook nonperformance. A constitution is expected to provide the foundation for effective rule. When laws cannot be enforced, however, public apathy and disillusionment turn against the institutions. When the constitution rests upon a precarious base of support, the system is discredited and easily overthrown. Consensus fails to develop and a crisis of legitimacy persists, opening the system to corrupt practices.

In countries where political corruption is pervasive, its corrosive effects undermine the functioning electoral bodies, parliaments, the judiciary, and other government institutions. It creates a negative political environment less hospitable to the institutionalization of democratic processes and practices. The parliaments in developing countries are much less powerful than other organs of government, particularly the executive branch. Government agencies are subject to weak accounting controls and do not face serious scrutiny by the legislature or legal institutions. In some cases, the judiciary is perceived as incapable of taking action on cases concerning government misuse of funds or abuse of power.

The need to make elections free and fair has been on the national agenda of many countries, but corrupt influences on election outcomes have become widespread. In many developing countries, elections are marked by violence, massive fraud, vote buying, and electioneering under government auspices. In Pakistan, for example, four elections were held in quick succession between 1988 and 1997, and each time the loser raised questions about their fairness and impartiality. The allegation of rigging in the 1977 elections led to the military takeover. In Bangladesh, successive elections have led to serious disputes between the ruling and opposition parties about the outcome, leading to a constitutional amendment that provides for an interim government three months before a national election is held to ensure that the ruling party does not misuse its power during the election. Because modern political campaigns require more resources than old style contests and because many candidates in developing economies use their own funds in the absence of public funding, politicians assume a successful outcome will lead to financial returns either through corrupt practices or through legitimate political patronage.

Furthermore, elections in developing countries have become more expensive. Because money invested in elections has to be paid back and most candidates use their own funds, the incentives for corruption can be seen at two levels—to be elected and to remain in power. As the case of the Philippines shows, rising election campaign expenses result from massive spending on media, advertisements, transport, public relations and a semisecret "kitty" to buy votes.[8] Elections therefore have been increasingly understood in terms of access to the spoils system, which in practice opens the way for elected representatives to tap into public money, in many cases without proper safeguards against abuse.

In the absence of organized and disciplined political parties, legislatures in developing countries tend to be weak and unable to perform their constitutionally guaranteed powers. Parliaments in many countries do not provide an effective forum for public debate on policy issues of national importance. The executive branch, with the support of civil servants, monopolizes power and usurps the roles and functions of parliament and political parties. This excessive discretion and weak accountability of the executive branch lead to yet more corruption. In the absence of an adequate system of checks and balances, disincentives against the diversion of public funds are not enforced. Many political parties tend to become personal devices of politicians to gain power rather than vehicles for debate on national policies and programs. A common trend is to join the winning party after every election in the hope of getting favors. The involvement of legislators in the design and implementation of development projects is one of the mechanisms to get favors from the ruling party. In 1990, for example, the Eighth Congress of the Philippines created the countryside development fund for infrastructure projects. In Pakistan, the legislators were provided development funds worth Rs. 5 million each in 1986.[9] The executive branch sometimes uses special budgetary funds and political patronage to purchase legislators' votes to gain a vote of confidence in the parliament.

An independent and well functioning judiciary is a central pillar of the rule of law. Corruption reduces public confidence in the rule of law. Corrupt officials strengthen the hold of criminal elements in society. Furthermore, the lack of public faith in the judiciary leads to the decline of ethical standards and dilutes public integrity. In many countries, the judiciary fails to take action on cases concerning government misuse of funds or against politicians of the incumbent government. Poorly paid and overworked judges and court officials are left vulnerable to offers of bribery or misuse of patronage as well as assaults or intimidation. In Ukraine, for example, judges largely remain dependent on local authorities for their housing, and those who rule against city officials appear to be susceptible to delays in getting houses.[10] Corruption in the judiciary allows the wealthy to buy justice directly by bribing judicial staff and indirectly through their access to the best lawyers. Bribes can be used to speed up court decisions in countries with serious case delays and backlogs.

Political corruption can be entrenched in democratic systems of both developing and developed countries. When the campaign finance rules are not enforced and the judiciary is too weak to hold corrupt politicians accountable, a group of politically well-connected middlemen collects bribes in return for misuse of political patronage by those in power, and some serve as specialized "party cashiers" to collect money for the party coffers from sources such as the construction industry.

IMPACT ON ECONOMIC DEVELOPMENT AND POVERTY ERADICATION

Corruption lowers investments, decreases efficiency, and becomes an additional tax on business. Furthermore, it misallocates scarce resources by diverting them to private pockets and reduces expenditures for development projects and social safety nets. High corruption levels lead to expansion of the unofficial economy. Corruption renders government regulations ineffective by allowing evasion of public health and safety requirements, disregard for regulations, and avoidance of environmental pollution penalties.

Corrupt practices can distort resource allocation and weaken government performance. Although the "impact of corruption on a country's economic health will obviously depend on what bribery is buying," argues Susan Rose-Ackerman, "cross-country research suggests that high corruption levels are harmful to economic growth."[11] Her review of the literature on relationships between economic growth, levels of corruption, and the efficiency of legal and government institutions points to several conclusions. The policy environment affects patterns of export and import substitution; ineffective public enterprises and regional development policies and programs have negative impacts on productivity; and public policies can have unanticipated consequences of creating incentives for illegal activities. Strong and stable government institutions including an independent judiciary and low levels of corruption have beneficial effects on economic growth; high levels of corruption are related to low levels of investment measured as a share of GDP. In brief, more competitive economies tend to be less corrupt.[12]

Studies of the impact of corruption on government procurement policies in several Asian countries reveal that these governments have paid from 20 to 100 percent more for goods and services than they would have otherwise.[13] The example of East Asia is often cited to show that high levels of corruption and impressive growth rates can take place at the same time and that the result of high levels of corruption depends on what the payoffs are used to purchase. However, as Wei argues, corruption works like a tax on FDI. Therefore, reducing corruption and inside dealings would have further improved the performance of the East Asian economies. The magnitude of the harmful effects of corruption on economic growth is unclear. "Because corruption is tied to other features of government structure," argues Rose-Ackerman, "reducing corruption without a more fundamental change in the behavior of public institutions is unlikely to be successful in promoting growth."[14] Another interesting aspect of the relationship between corruption and economic growth is that as long as the economy is expanding rapidly, corruption is more tolerable because everyone can benefit directly or indirectly. However, as Chhibber argues, a regime is vulnerable during economic downturn because it is not able to satisfy all groups that expect a share in the spoils.[15] The Algerian Front de Libération Nationale, he notes, lost power because a serious fiscal crisis led to a takeover by Front Islamique du Salut, a religious party that was strongly supported in the 1990 elections by the small business sector and public sector employees. These groups were negatively affected by downsizing and partial market opening that resulted from the end of the oil boom. To deal with the budget deficits, the government introduced reforms aimed at overturning the centralized, industry-based socialist programs. Political corruption increased in the 1980s, raising costs for the middle class and the public employees who were less politically powerful than the industrial class.

The poor suffer from corruption in many ways.[16] First, because of their weak ability to pay, the poor suffer the most in an illegal price system, receiving a lower level of such social services as public housing, education, and health. Second, state officials prefer to design large-scale public sector projects that provide high levels of payoff and less chances of detection. Thus the infrastructure investments are biased against projects that provide direct benefits to the poor. Third, in countries with high levels of corruption, the poor face higher tax burdens or fewer services because of their inability to pay off tax collectors. Fourth, the poor suffer losses in selling their agricultural produce when corrupt officials create monopolies, such as agricultural marketing boards, to extract personal gains. Fifth, corruption in state regulatory and taxing apparatus severely impedes the growth of indigenous, small-scale enterprises in towns and cities. Finally, petty corruption is a source of income for lower grade civil servants who, though not poor, must support their immediate and distant relatives. Thus while large-scale bribery by senior officials enriches the wealthy, the less wealthy civil servants also accept bribes. Grand corruption is usually not visible. However, petty corruption—such as a policeman asking for a bribe for a legitimate service—is more visible and affects people's day-to-day lives.

MAGNITUDE OF CORRUPTION

It is difficult to measure the magnitude of corruption because of data scarcity and the varying economic, political, and social impacts that corruption has on developing countries. Many studies have been done, however, on the magnitude of corruption in developing countries. A report by the Asian Development Bank points to some staggering figures.[17]

- As much as $30 billion in aid for Africa has ended up in foreign bank accounts. This is twice the GDP of Ghana, Kenya, and Uganda combined.
- Over the last twenty years, one East Asian country is estimated to have lost $48 billion due to corruption, surpassing its entire foreign debt of $40.6 billion.
- In another Asian country, over the past decade, state assets have fallen by more than $50 billion, primarily because corrupt officials have been deliberately undervaluing them in trading off big property stakes to private interests or international investors in return for payoffs.
- Corruption can cost governments as much as 50 percent of their tax revenues. When customs officials in a Latin American country, for example, were allowed to receive a percentage of what they collected, there was 60 percent increase in custom revenues within a year.
- A $2.5 million bribe by a civil servant of the ministry of defense of a European country has caused an equivalent of $200 million in financial damage. This analysis was conducted by Transparency International, which cited that the cost of losses included jobs at the factory that failed to gain the orders, higher than necessary prices, and defective outputs.[18]

Although there are significant variations among countries concerning the magnitude of corruption, the problem is serious enough for governments in developing and developed countries, civil society organizations, the private sector, and bilateral and multilateral development partners to join forces in an international movement to combat corruption. Many governments in developing countries—Uganda and Nigeria, for example—and financial institutions including the World Bank and IMF have initiated specific programs to combat corrupt practices.

CAUSES OF CORRUPTION

Fundamental causes of corruption are economic structures, institutional incapacity to design and implement reform strategies, and the lack of political will. Economic reforms including liberalization and privatization and independent anticorruption bodies are necessary. However it is the lack of political will to combat corruption that further expands illegal practices, especially in transitional economies.

Corruption is a problem of poor governance. It is a symptom of something that has gone wrong in the management of the state. It also indicates that institutions designed to govern relationships between citizens and the state are used instead for personal enrichment of public officials and the provision of benefits to the corrupt.

The basic cause of corruption is monopoly and discretion without adequate accountability. This implies that the expanding role of government in development has placed the bureaucracy in a monopolistic position and has enhanced the opportunities for administrative discretion. Corruption results from excessive regulation, increased bureaucratic discretion, and lack of adequate accountability and transparency systems. The state intervenes in the economy to provide a framework for economic and social activities—protection of personal and property rights, provision of public goods not supplied by the market, redistribution of income, and the provision of opportunities for education, health, and employment. State intervention, however, is also likely to expand the discretion of public officials to make decisions. The misuse of this discretion is one of the primary causes of corruption.

Since the discretion of public officials is needed to promote innovations and respond to specific problems, in the final analysis, effective accountability makes it possible to increase the discretion of public officials.

The causes of corruption are both economic and political. A recent UN study identifies five main causes.[19] First, payments are made for goods and services that are available below the market price. Examples

include when producer goods were sold in China both at the state subsidized prices and on the free market, when prices of oil were set artificially low in Nigeria, when payoffs were needed to get credit in Russia
and Eastern Europe, and when South Africa's twin currency system was
a source of payoffs. When the service is scarce, those with the ability
to pay the highest are able to get the service.

Second, bribes can serve as incentive payments for government
officials to undertake their tasks effectively. Firms and individuals are
willing to pay in order to avoid delays, for example when the government department does not pay its bill on time, when such services as
telephone connection and driver's licenses are delayed, and when fees
have to be paid for even routine services. Continuation of such practices, however, undermines the legitimacy of the state.

Third, bribes can reduce costs for the firms when governments impose regulations, levy taxes, and enforce criminal laws. Payoffs would
reduce the regulatory load. When a state has many inefficient regulations and imposes high taxes on businesses, bribes to avoid regulations
and taxes may raise the firm's efficiency. Thus firms make an alliance
with tax collectors or others responsible for public regulation and
enforcement to lower the cost for the firm, dividing the benefits between the firm or taxpayer and the public official. Such practices result
in savings for the firm, but the revenue losses for the state are enormous, limiting its ability to perform its tasks effectively.

Fourth, payments to obtain major contracts, concessions, and privatization of state-owned enterprises are the main cause of grand corruption that can have significant impacts on government budgets. Illegal
payments could be made by a firm to be included in the list of prequal-
ified bidders, to gain inside information, to structure the bidding specifications to favor the firm giving bribes, to win the contract, or to avoid
quality controls. Examples of grand corruption are found both in developing and developed countries: allegations of up to $7.1 million against
senior ministers in Zimbabwe and a Swedish telecommunications company for the circumvention of local tender board procedures; allegation
of bribes in an airplane deal between the Republic of Korea and several
US companies, with the national security advisor to former President
Roh Tae Woo acknowledging receiving money from businesses involved in the contract; bribes paid to win contracts to build Terminal 2 at
Frankfurt airport leading to an increase in the prices of 20 to 30 percent.[20] The privatization of state-owned enterprises increases opportunities for corruption in ways similar to large-scale infrastructure projects.

Fifth, bribes are also used to buy political influence and votes. Corrupt practices sometimes fund political parties, election campaigns, and vote purchasing by politicians. In some cases those in power also use state resources, patronage jobs, and other favors, thus denying the legitimate recipients of these benefits. Business domination of the political process can lead to political parties losing their ideological focus, as the studies of political systems in France and Italy show.[21] In Japan, some businesses were asked by former Prime Minister Tanaka Kakuei to fund and elect selected candidates.[22] Finally, the business climate is negatively affected where the judiciary is perceived to be corrupt and the legal and regulatory framework is not enforced. Businesses seek private arbitrators and use other mechanisms such as protection provided by organized crime to operate in the country.

Without political will, government promises to reform the civil service and promote transparency and accountability remain unkept. Governments often emphasize political will in their public policy statements to combat corruption and reinvent the relationship between government, the private sector, and civil society to bolster the image of political leaders. "The principal challenge in assessing political will," argues Kpundeh, "is the need to distinguish between reform approaches that are intentionally superficial and designed only to bolster the image of political leaders and substantive efforts that are based on strategies to create change."[23]

Six indicators demonstrate genuine political will: the extent to which the causes and context of corruption have been rigorously examined and accurately understood; the degree to which strategy design is participatory, incorporating, and mobilizing the interests of many stakeholders; a focus on strategic issues based on the assessment of costs and benefits of a particular reform to achieve the stated objective of the political leader; positive incentives and sanctions to ensure compliance; the creation of an objective process to monitor the impact of the reforms and incorporating those findings into policy goals and objectives; and the extent of structural competition in economic and political activities.[24]

There are other causes of domestic corruption, including loopholes in laws defining it, conflict of interest on the part of those directly involved in making decisions, inadequate funding for the civil service, and weak government auditing and monitoring systems. Domestic corruption is also likely to increase where the press is not free to expose misuse of authority and public resources, where civil society organizations are not actively engaged in holding those in power accountable for their actions through advocacy and public awareness, and where political opposition is too weak to expose corrupt practices through the parliamentary and other forums.

Corruption has emerged as a truly global political issue requiring a global response. The driving forces for this change include increasing levels of education and political awareness around the world, availability of more information, and the proactive role of the media, all of which have forced political leaders to ensure greater accountability for their actions. The end of the cold war and the wider democratization of developing countries have accelerated government responses to cross-border corruption. Globalization offers new development opportunities because of rapid movement of capital, people, information, and enterprises from place to place. The emergence of an integrated international economy has also contributed to the perception of corruption as an issue with global ramifications. Corruption among officials in Latin America, for example, is linked with drug-inspired crime in American cities. However, it is extremely difficult to obtain evidence of corrupt activities and to ensure accountability of the actors involved in cross-border corruption because of their ability to do business almost anywhere and because "governments of developing states and international organizations with their finite resources and limited mandates may be no match politically or economically for powerful interests, often working in secret, that hold the leverage underlying cross-border corruption."[25]

Domestic and cross-border corruption are closely related.[26] Economic policies can encourage cross-border corruption. This is particularly the case with excessively open economies and those economies going through rapid transition such as Russia and many countries in Eastern Europe. Some economic policies such as multiple exchange rates and systems of price controls could "encourage the growth of unofficial markets and extensive corruption."[27] Countries dependent on foreign technology and expertise or on the export of natural resources in the global market are more vulnerable to the pressures of outside speculators and middlemen. Furthermore, where property rights and contracts are not guaranteed, foreign firms might pursue other, sometimes illicit, means to protect their interests.[28]

The responsibility for cross-border corruption is shared between local partners and multinational corporations, requiring reforms both domestically and internationally. Multinational firms have an obligation to refrain from bribing public officials in the developing world and thus to reduce illegal payoffs in international trade and investment because sometimes these firms have strong market power and leverage that can have serious negative impact on socioeconomic and political development in developing countries.

COMBATING CORRUPTION: COMPONENTS OF REFORMS

The need to combat corruption is widely recognized by policymakers in developing countries and international organizations such as the UN agencies, the European Union, and the OECD. Financial institutions such as the World Bank and the IMF and regional development banks also recognize corruption as a serious problem negatively affecting their work.

When corruption is endemic, piecemeal reforms are not likely to make a difference. Partial solutions can offer some help to countries with strong and relatively clean government traditions. Other countries need more comprehensive reforms. There are no quick fixes. Experience suggests several rules for successful reform:[29]

- Create strong political will, a critical starting point for sustainable and effective anticorruption programs,
- Focus on prevention and changing systems through changing values, creating a culture of professionalism and training, providing adequate pay, and ensuring deterrence,
- Identify government activities most prone to corruption and review both substantive law and administrative procedures,
- Enforce accountability mechanisms and learn from good practices and examples of others,
- Enact comprehensive anticorruption legislation,
- Establish broad ownership of reforms, among others, by creating strong partnerships with civil society and the private sector, and
- Make corruption high risk and low profit.

Some countries have enacted and implemented successful anticorruption policies. In Hong Kong, an Independent Commission Against Corruption (ICAC) was established in 1974, reporting to the governor and working independently of the police force. ICAC was empowered to investigate and prosecute corruption cases and to promote public education and awareness. ICAC employees were paid more than other government agencies to ensure their independence. ICAC received a large number of complaints from the people, and its effectiveness was enhanced by the appointment of a person of high integrity as head. ICAC focuses on three-pronged strategy—investigation and prosecution, prevention, and communication. Its initial strategy was to investigate and prosecute some of most influential people in Hong Kong. Surveys show that the level of corruption was reduced as a result of ICAC's activities.

ICAC's success was due to the strong political will and long-term commitment of the government, the independence of ICAC, the resources at its disposal to pursue the investigation and prosecution of those involved in corrupt practices, and public education programs and active participation of an informed public. ICAC's ability to extradite and convict the former chief superintendent of police increased its public credibility. Oversight committees and an independent judiciary provided a system of checks and balances on ICAC's activities. The Hong Kong model shows the effectiveness of an independent commission reporting only to the head of government to combat corruption.

In Singapore, the People's Action Party made anticorruption policy one of its priorities in 1959, when it came to power. The government strengthened the powers of the existing Corrupt Practices Investigations Bureau that has been reporting directly to the prime minister since 1970. The bureau requires government ministries and departments to review their internal processes to reduce incentives for corrupt practices. The government has undertaken several steps to reduce incentives for corruption, including increasing wages of civil servants and improving their working conditions, rotating officials, and increasing supervision.[30]

In 1994, Botswana established the Directorate on Corruption and Economic Crime (DCEC) based on the Hong Kong model and staffed by former members of the Hong Kong agency and by the local personnel. The DCEC is operationally independent, though officially under the president. It can investigate and prosecute offenders, prepare strategies to combat corruption, and provide public education and training. With a high conviction rate and collection of fines in excess of its operating costs, DCEC is perceived in the region to be a good practice of combating corruption in a democratic country. Many factors account for Botswana's success in combating corruption. Operational independence and prosecution powers of the DCEC enabled it to get involved in the cases involving politically influential people. Focus on strong enforcement provided deterrence against future abuses. Financial independence and viability gave DCEC more operational independence to pursue its objectives. Botswana's success was also based on some structural factors: a favorable political climate, state capacity to govern, effective civil service reforms, macroeconomic stability, a strong resource base, and the government's record-keeping capacity.[31]

In South Korea, the Seoul City Government adopted the Integrity Pact (IP), an agreement between it and companies submitting bids that bribes will neither be offered nor accepted in public contracts.[32] All bidders for the city's construction projects, technical services, and procurement are required to sign the pact to fight corruption. During the bidding stage, the IP is explained to bidders and only those who agree with the "Bidders' Oath to Fulfill the IP" are qualified to register their submissions. A related government official also submits "the Principal's Oath to the IP." During the contract's concluding and execution stage, both parties must sign a "special condition for contract." Provisions are made to protect and reward those reporting inside corruption. The violators of the IP are disqualified by the city for submitting bids or face termination of contracts. They are banned from bidding for other contracts for six months to two years. The IP is being implemented in two stages— the first stage for projects at the head office and project offices, and the second stage in the twenty-five autonomous district offices in Seoul.

The IP ombudsman will monitor the process of implementation. Specific guidelines were issued for the bidders' submissions, employees of bidders, encouragement of the company code of conduct and the principal's oath to fulfill the obligations of the IP. Guidelines were also issued concerning the termination of the contract for violation of the IP, three-stage public hearings on the contract process, and publicizing the information on the bidding procedures. The IP ombudsmen—a team of five persons appointed by the mayor of Seoul with one of them acting as chief ombudsman—were appointed to monitor the process of implementation. The functions of the IP ombudsmen were to review and inspect all documents for construction projects valued at US$4,200,000 or above, organize public hearings at different stages, ask for an audit on specific issues, and participate in the IP Operational Committee. The IP ombudsmen were not allowed to hold a concurrent job at the National Assembly, a local assembly, a political party, or any company participating in the bids for public projects.

Components of Reforms

Four components of reforms are essential for combating corruption: prevention, enforcement, public awareness and support, and institution building.

Prevention. Simplifying government programs and procedures and minimizing or eliminating discretion can prevent corruption. Prevention also requires civic education to raise the public's awareness of its rights and obligations, compensating public service with decent wages, and rewarding good performance. One of the most effective preventive measures is to end corrupt programs and modify laws that have loopholes for corrupt practices. If subsidy programs and price controls are eliminated, the bribes that result from them will also disappear. If a corrupt parastatal organization is privatized, for example, the level of corruption should go down. Yet it is not always possible or even desirable to end all government social programs and leave them entirely to the market. In such situations, it is essential to repeal or modify relevant laws to eliminate loopholes. In general, reforms that increase the competitiveness of the economy can help reduce corruption, but privatization in developing countries can itself be a source of corruption and may require reforms that remove rent-seeking incentives after a state enterprise is privatized.

Enforcement. Many countries with high levels of corruption do have formal statutes but they are not effectively enforced. It is essential to establish independent investigators, prosecutors, and adjudicators who will perform professional duties independently. The provision of adequate powers of investigation and prosecution should be consistent with international human rights norms. Other elements of enforcement are the development of channels for effective complaint-making or whistle-blowing, and the imposition of powerful incentives for the would-be corrupt, including civil penalties and blacklisting.

Public awareness and support. It is extremely important to determine public perceptions in order to provide baseline information against which to measure the progress of anticorruption reforms. A free press, a dynamic civil society, and freedom of information laws are essential for increasing public awareness and support.

Institution building. In implementing anticorruption policies, the first step should be to establish an independent commission against corruption with broad investigative, prosecutorial, and public education powers. The commission should have strong support from the top political leadership, operational independence in making decisions based on facts, and adequate resources. Public support is likely to be stronger when someone with a reputation for integrity heads the commission.

Establishing an independent commission is necessary but not sufficient; other institution-building measures are essential, including:

- Strengthening oversight institutions such as an office of the Auditor General and ombudsman office,
- Improving performance and quality of public service through civil service reforms aimed at improving wages and working conditions of civil servants; increasing competitive pressures within the government to lower the bargaining power of individual officials; public awareness of the payers; a merit-based, transparent system of selecting civil servants; and effective monitoring to ensure compliance with the regulations,
- Establishing an independent and impartial election commission to ensure legitimacy of the electoral process and redesign the electoral process to reduce incentives for giving voters personal benefits,
- Creating public accounts committees,
- Strengthening police capacity to function effectively as a frontline investigation agency and enable it to work closely with other oversight bodies,
- Improving access to justice and strengthening capacity and independence of the judiciary; and
- Instituting a system of checks and balances including multiple veto points to ensure the consent of a series of institutions representing different constituencies, the ability of citizens and media to obtain information about government operations, protection of the rights of individuals against the state, and using the leverage of international organizations to promote anticorruption strategies.

Experience suggests that an increase in salaries and wages of civil servants, the promotion of democracy and political liberty, and the enactment of economic reforms such as privatization and liberalization do not guarantee that corruption will be reduced. Equally important are the implementation of anticorruption programs and changes in the social and political environment in which they are carried out.[23]

NOTES

1. United Nations Development Programme, *Country Assessment in Accountability and Transparency* (CONTACT) (New York: UNDP, 2001).

2. R. Sandbrook, *The Politics of Africa's Economic Stagnation* (Cambridge: Cambridge University Press, 1985): 59.

3. Arnold J. Heidenheimer, Michael Johnston, and Victor T. LeVine (eds). "Introduction" in *Political Corruption—A Handbook* (New Brunswick, Canada: Transaction Publishers, 1997).

4. Michael Johnston, "Public Officials, Private Interests, and Sustainable Democracy: When Politics and Corruption Meet" in *Corruption and the Global Economy,* ed. Kimberly Ann Elliot (Washington, D.C. Institute for International Economics, 1997): 83.

5. Michael Johnston, "Public Officials, Private Interests, and Sustainable Democracy," 64.

6. Michael Johnston, "Public Officials, Private Interests, and Sustainable Democracy," 72.

7. Michael Johnston, "Public Officials, Private Interests, and Sustainable Democracy," 67.

8. Isgani de Castro, "Campaign Kitty," in *Pork and Other Perks: Corruption and Governance in the Philippines,* ed. Sheila S. Coronel (Metro Manila: Philippine Centre for Investigative Journalism, 1988): 218.

9. Mohammad Waseem, *The 1993 Elections in Pakistan* (Lahore: Vanguard Books, 1994): 85.

10. World Bank, *World Development Report, 1997* (New York: World Bank, 1997): 100.

11. Susan Rose-Ackerman, *Corruption and Good Governance* United Nations Development Programme, Discussion Paper 3 (New York: UNDP, 1997).

12. Susan Rose-Ackerman, *Corruption and Good Governance.*

13. Asian Development Bank, *Anti-Corruption Policy* (Manila: ADB, 1998).

14. Susan Rose-Ackerman, *Corruption and Good Governance:* 40.

15. Pradeep Chhibber, "State Policy, Rent Seeking and the Electoral Success of a Religious Party in Algeria" *Journal of Politics* 58 (1) 1996: 126–48.

16. Susan Rose-Ackerman, *Corruption and Good Governance:* 45–47.

17. Asian Development Bank, *Anti-Corruption Policy* (Manila: ADB, 1998).

18. Jeremy Pope, *Transparency International Sourcebook* (Berlin, Germany: Transparency International, 2002).

19. Susan Rose-Ackerman, *Corruption and Good Governance:* 6–34.

20. Susan Rose-Ackerman, *Corruption and Good Governance:* 24–25.

21. Yves Meny, "Fin de Siecle' Corruption: Change, Crisis and Shifting Values," *International Social Science Journal* 149 (1996): 309–20; and Donatella della Porta, "Actors in Corruption: Business Politicians in Italy," *International Social Science Journal* 149 (1996): 349–64.

22. Steven R. Reed, "Political Corruption in Japan" *International Social Science Journal* 149 (1996): 395–405.

23. Sahr J. Kpundeh, "Political Will in Fighting Corruption" in *International Social Science Journal* 149 (1996): 98.

24. Sahr J. Kpundeh, "Political Will in Fighting Corruption," 90–100.

25. Michael Johnston, "Cross-Border Corruption: Points of Vulnerability and Challenges for Reform," in *Corruption and Integrity Improvement Initiatives in Developing Countries* (New York: UNDP and OECD Development Centre, 1998): 13.

26. Michael Johnston, "Cross Border Corruption," 14.

27. Michael Johnston, "Cross Border Corruption," 19.

28. Michael Johnston, "Cross Border Corruption," 19.

29. This section builds on the work of Transparency International, especially *Transparency International Manual* (Berlin: TI, 2000).

30. Susan Rose-Ackerman, *Corruption and Good Governance;* and Phyllis Dininio with Sahr Kpundeh and Robert Leiken, *USAID Handbook for Fighting Corruption* (Washington, D.C. Center for Democracy and Governance and USAID, 1998).

31. Susan Rose-Ackerman, *Corruption and Good Governance;* Alan Doig and Stephen Riley, "Corruption and Anti-Corruption Strategies: Issues and Case Studies from Developing Countries" in *Corruption and Integrity Improvement Initiatives in Developing Countries* (New York: UNDP and OECD, 1998).

32. Seoul Metropolitan Government, *Integrity Pact* (Seoul: SMG, 2000); Seoul Metropolitan Government, *Clean and Transpararent* (Seoul: SMG, 2001).

33. Alan Doig and Stephen Riley, "Corruption and Anti-Corruption Strategies: Issues and Case Studies from Developing Countries," 45–62.

7

Mobilizing the State's Financial Resources for Development

Suresh Narayan Shende

THE UNITED NATIONS MILLENNIUM DECLARATION resolved to create an environment that is conducive to development and the elimination of poverty. Success in meeting these objectives depends on good governance; on transparency in financial, monetary, and trading systems; and on removing obstacles that developing countries face in mobilizing financial resources. Primary responsibility for achieving stable growth and equitable development, however, lies with the developing countries themselves. This responsibility includes creating the conditions that make it possible to secure the needed financial resources for investment. The actions of domestic policymakers largely determine the state of governance and the condition of the financial system. Achieving such a positive environment is not simply a matter of political will. Capacity building and institutional development are an essential complement to finance in improving the living standards of the poor. Most developing countries, usually the poorest ones, still lack institutions capable of implementing the necessary actions and will need to focus national efforts on capacity building.

The generation of domestic resources to save and invest productively is the essential foundation of sustained development.[1] A low domestic savings rate is the major structural weakness in most developing countries. But there will not be enough domestic savings, or enough high quality national investment, without macroeconomic discipline. Economic policy must be designed to make inflation and the current account balance consistent with sustained growth. For countries with high inflation, this implies that monetary policy should aim to reduce inflation over time, and once it has reached a low level, to hold it there. Monetary policy also needs to be consistent with the chosen exchange rate regime, which must give reasonable assurance that the country will avoid an unsustainably large current account deficit.

Fiscal discipline, too, is required to keep deficit financing small enough to avoid inflation and excessive accumulation of public debt and to ensure that government borrowing does not crowd out private sector investment. Almost everywhere the most potent way to empower the poor to integrate themselves into the market economy—and hence to contribute to and benefit from economic growth—is to make public investments in broadly accessible education, health, and nutrition, in other basic social programs, and in rural areas, where large proportions of the poor typically live. These programs need to have the first call on government resources—they should not be treated as marginal programs whose budgets can be slashed as economy measures when times are difficult.

DOMESTIC RESOURCE MOBILIZATION

Developing countries and countries with economies in transition are currently confronting unsustainable fiscal deficits, unabated debt-service charges, and declining external assistance that seriously affect their development. They need to overhaul their domestic and external financial resources mobilization strategies; adopt tax and nontax instruments that are fair, equitable, and create minimal disincentives for economic efficiency; and initiate tax reforms that simplify and rationalize the tax structure.[2] Nontax revenues include social security contributions, grants from foreign governments and international organizations, property income, interest, dividends from state enterprises, rents from government property, fines, penalties and forfeits, and sale of goods and services. Governments should emphasize improving the efficiency and effectiveness of revenue administration, strengthening the institutional framework, selecting administratively feasible and realistically collectible taxes and duties, widening the tax base and integrating the informal sector into the mainstream of the national economy.

Measuring development by indicators of economic growth remains valid, although over the last decade the concept of development has broadened to include social and environmental dimensions. Without economic progress, however, the financial and other resources needed to achieve social goals would not be available. Thus economic growth is a necessary but not sufficient condition for development. In fact, the development of a country is determined by many factors, including its natural resource base, its human resources, the state of its physical infrastructure, the technology available, the government development strategy, and its openness to the outside world.

Development, or economic growth, can be considered a direct function of the investments made in a country. Care must be taken in the allocation of investments across sectors to avoid or minimize waste and leakage. When investment decisions are made on the basis of market competition, the relative rates of return over time should determine the allocation. Market imperfections, however, arising from inadequate information flows, complications due to the structure of industry (monopoly, oligopoly, imperfect competition), and positive or negative externalities make reliance on relative rates of return as the main determinant of intersectoral allocation problematic.

Broadly speaking, investment resources can be divided into two types: domestic and foreign.[3] Domestic resources comprise household, corporate, and government savings. Some of the factors that influence domestic resource mobilization include the level and growth of per capita incomes, savings preferences of individuals in the society, the degree of development of and confidence in financial intermediation, demographic structure, and fiscal and monetary policies. Transforming these resources into investment in productive activities depends on the quality of the macroeconomic fundamentals including fiscal and monetary prudence, the structure of the financial market including the regulatory and supervisory framework of the banking sector, the size and quality of the securities and bond markets, and the continuity of a consistent investment policy.

Other factors such as the law and order situation, the availability of an appropriately skilled workforce, the state of physical infrastructure development, and property rights also weigh on decisions to convert intermediate savings into investment. The promotion of exports allows countries to generate foreign exchange to pay for import needs, many of which are investment related. Exports are often crucial to pay for the import of new technologies, capital goods, and raw materials not produced at home to improve the productivity and efficiency of investment as well as to take advantage of economies of scale.

Discussion of fiscal architecture is crucial in identifying the revenue capacity of different types of taxes.[4] No single tax system fits all countries. The fiscal architecture presents a range of alternatives for policymakers to consider in raising revenues to fund government operations. The degree of tax compliance also helps policymakers in designing tax policy. In many countries, tax administration strongly influences tax policy.[5] The structure of the economy of developing countries makes it difficult to collect some types of taxes. Finally, countries can no longer effectively design their tax systems in isolation. The increased mobility of capital and labor requires policymakers to consider the tax systems of other countries. Globalization threatens two major sources of tax revenue for developing countries: trade taxes and corporate income taxes. The challenge facing many countries is finding ways of replacing those lost revenue sources with taxes that do not disproportionately burden the poor.[6]

FOREIGN FINANCIAL RESOURCES

Foreign investment resources include funds from the international banking system (commercial short- and medium-term loans), from international capital markets (foreign private portfolio investments), from corporations (FDI), and ODA from bilateral donor governments and from multilateral financial institutions such as the World Bank and Asian Development Bank. The factors influencing the size and composition of private external inflows are similar to those influencing domestic private savings, although economic factors in the rest of the world—particularly the funds' country of origin, its relative growth prospects, interest rates, and tax regimes—are also relevant.

The political and strategic interests, relative level of development, and the amount of funds allocated to aid budgets by donor countries affect foreign official inflows to developing countries. In addition, national efforts to mobilize resources are related to external economic and financial environment. Adverse developments in prices of exports, sharp fluctuations in key exchange rates, or instability in the international financial system can severely constrain such efforts. In general, a country's degree of economic security is crucial to its success in raising resources to finance its development. Political and economic factors affecting saving and investment decisions include government leadership, the risk of external conflict, corruption, the rule of law, racial and ethnic tension, political terrorism, civil war, the quality of the bureaucracy, repudiation of contracts and expropriation risks, and political rights and civil liberties.

Although evidence of the quantitative impact of globalization on public revenues is still limited, indications are that it may reduce tax revenues due to increased tax competition among jurisdictions to attract FDI, exponential growth in electronic commerce, increased mobility of factors of production, and growing importance of off-shore and non-cooperative tax jurisdictions. A decline in revenues can further aggravate budget deficits in fiscally stretched economies. Globalization may also create pressures for increased spending for education, training, research and development, environment, economic and social infrastructure, and for institutional changes aimed at improving efficiency. While these expenditures are consistent with the state's traditional allocation role, globalization may create additional financial requirements for social protection in the form of unemployment benefits to unskilled labor facing retrenchment due to the closing of noncompetitive domestic industries. To the extent that globalization worsens a country's income distribution, it may increase the need for governmental intervention while, at the same time, reducing its financial capacity to intervene.

Official development assistance in recent years has totaled US$50 billion to $60 billion a year. Debt relief under the Heavily Indebted Poor Countries (HIPC) Initiative was US$1.4 billion in 2001. At the same time, trade-distorting policies have prevented the creation of incomes far in excess of these amounts. Estimates of the welfare gains from eliminating all barriers to merchandise trade are substantial, ranging from US$250 billion to US$680 billion annually, of which one-third would accrue to developing countries. These benefits would derive in part from the elimination of access barriers to industrial country markets, but also in good part from reform of the trade regimes of developing countries themselves. Opening markets is a win-win proposition in which both industrial and developing countries gain.

In some cases, the current trade policies of industrial countries directly neutralize the effectiveness of aid. The dumping of agricultural surpluses, in the form of nonemergency food aid or with the help of export subsidies, has damaged farm production in a number of developing countries, some of which had been carefully nurtured under assistance programs. In other cases, tariff peaks and escalation frustrate efforts by developing countries to diversify their exports. Greater coherence between aid and trade policies is therefore essential. In particular, reducing or eliminating biases against developing country products in industrial country import and agricultural regimes would make aid—including debt relief—and trade more effective in promoting development.

Foreign aid has dwindled in the budgets of many donor countries during the past several years, but it continues to loom very large for recipients. In many developing countries, foreign aid receipts are an important source of revenue and thus constitute a key element in fiscal policy. Aid may be an indispensable source of financing, in particular, for expenditures in health, education, and other public services that are essential to raise the living standards of the poor in developing countries. Given that aid is limited, it is particularly important to use it wisely. This requires not only establishing appropriate systems to manage aid funds with a view to avoiding corruption and mismanagement, but also designing aggregate fiscal policy to take proper account of the macroeconomic implications of aid-financed spending. Both aspects are essential to maximize the benefits for recipients and thereby convince donors that aid is money well spent.[7]

Despite the declining share of aid in donor country budgets, aid continues to play an important role in many developing countries. While the impact of aid is typically divided between supplementing domestic saving and contributing to consumption, there is less agreement on the potential effects of aid on growth. The impacts of large aid inflows on the relative prices of traded and nontraded goods are well known, as are those of real exchange rate appreciation on the decline of the traded goods sector in developing countries. But in a dynamic economy, the effects of aid depend on how aid-financed spending affects productive capacity. Several empirical studies suggest that aid tends to enhance growth, but they also indicate that the link is neither direct nor automatic and depends very much on the environment that influences the use of aid.

MOBILIZATION OF GOVERNMENT FUNDS

Governments in developing countries and economies in transition have been, and still are, an important agent of development.[8] While in most of these countries govenments' role in owning and operating productive enterprises has been declining, mainly through the privatization of state-owned enterprises, they remain suppliers of crucial public goods of various sorts, of physical and social infrastructure, and maintenance of law and order. The mobilization of sufficient resources by governments to carry out these functions has always been rather problematic, and many have run up sizeable fiscal deficits. While these countries have not generally suffered prolonged bouts of hyperinflation or fiscal profligacy through the rampant printing of money, they have not yet reached a stage where regular payment of taxes through voluntary compliance is seen as a social responsibility. This tends to complicate the task of raising resources for the government.[9]

Governments mobilize revenues in three ways: by levying taxes, by generating nontax revenues, and by borrowing from local or international capital markets. Most of the off-market resources are raised through taxes; nontax revenues are less than 5 percent of GDP in most countries.[10]

A country's capacity to raise tax revenue depends not only on tangible economic factors but also on a variety of noneconomic factors such as political will, administrative efficiency, and a culture of tax compliance, and as such it is almost impossible to prescribe a priori what proportion of GDP should be raised as taxes in any particular country. There are several different techniques and measures to evaluate a country's tax system. Tanzi and Zee note that one can estimate a hypothetical tax to GDP ratio by isolating several independent variables such as per capita income, share of agricultural output, openness of the economy, and ratio of money supply to GDP and comparing tax performance to that of similar countries.[11]

Resource Mobilization through Taxation

Taxation is the main policy instrument for transferring resources to the public sector. It can also assist in creating an atmosphere within which the private sector operates in conformity with national objectives. It has been argued by multilateral institutions, among others, that the tax system should be used only to raise finances that are sufficient for meeting the minimum necessary level of public expenditure, for example to preserve territorial integrity, to maintain law and order, to provide various public goods and to regulate undesirable activities. In terms of efficiency, taxes provide the best means of financing most public expenditures. However, taxes impose on society three types of cost: a direct cost or revenue foregone as taxpayers reduce their disposable income by paying the amount due; an indirect allocative effect, or excess burden, which is the welfare cost associated with the economic distortions induced by taxes as they alter relative prices of goods, services, and assets; and an administrative or compliance cost, since tax forms, tax control, payment procedures, and tax inspection are costly.

Not all tax systems impose the same distortions. For a given amount of tax revenue, the final burden of taxation depends on the features of the tax system, namely the composition of tax revenues (income versus consumption), the size of the tax base (affected by tax evasion and tax fraud), tax rates, and other administrative factors. Available evidence for developing countries indicates that corporate and personal income taxes have a negative impact on economic activity, whereas taxes on imports and exports have a significant negative effect on investment. On the other hand, nonneutralities in the taxation of savings and investment severely distort capital markets. These distortions become even worse when tax evasion is widespread and the informal sector is large. Given the disincentive effects of taxes, efficiency-oriented tax reforms should be characterized by reliance on a dominantly consumption-oriented set of broadly-based taxes, moderate tax rates on labor and capital incomes, and simple taxation of profits and returns to financial capital—with few incentive schemes and as neutral as possible.

Many aspects in a tax system design may affect inequality and poverty. Traditionally it has been thought that taxing income is inherently more progressive than taxing consumption, since the personal income tax generally uses graduated tax rates and a standard personal exemption, while rate differentiation in consumption taxes according to income or wealth of individuals proves more difficult or even unfeasible.

Countries with different economic and demographic characteristics will have different appetites for different tax instruments. In determining the relative tax mix, it is useful to have estimates of revenue potential for each tax instrument. Because the design considerations for each instrument greatly affect revenue estimates, calculations are required for different assumptions about the design and scope of a particular tax instrument (such as assumptions as to rates, base, and coverage of a particular tax). For example, revenue estimates for an individual income tax will depend on the percentage of population subject to the tax (the choice of the tax threshold or zero-rate band), the income subject to tax and the allowable deductions, and the rate structure.

It is also necessary to have estimates of compliance and enforcement costs for each tax instrument based on different scenarios (as to rates, base, and coverage). Substantial variations in these costs may influence the roles that a particular tax instrument plays in the tax system. For example, the collection costs and auditing costs for an individual income tax per unit of tax revenue collected may be much higher than the collection and auditing costs for a value-added tax (VAT). In addition, it is important to estimate the level of tax evasion for different tax instruments and the cost and probability of reducing evasion to acceptable levels.

Tax incidence studies of developing countries tend to reaffirm this impression: almost all income tax systems are found to be progressive, while only a minor part of overall tax systems share this feature. This finding should not be surprising, since developing countries have a tax structure dominated by indirect taxes, with a limited number of capital and wealth taxes. Progressiveness is further limited by the use of payroll taxes. When only wage earners pay taxes in countries with large informal economies, rich taxpayers do not comply with the income tax, payroll taxes become a "tax on honesty" paid by the lower and middle-income class. Broadly based tax systems, with fewer deductions and exemptions (apart from a personal exemption not larger than per capita income), relatively low tax rates (albeit moderately progressive in the case of the personal income tax), and compatible with administrative capabilities, are likely to provide a stable, reasonably efficient and more pro-poor alternative of financing public expenditures.

However, governments have traditionally used tax resources to finance some of their other development or political agendas.[12] Multilateral organizations typically favor a broad-based sales tax such as VAT, a relatively low level of import duties for protective purposes only, and simplified personal income and corporate profit taxes. A sales tax on consumption of domestic and imported products helps reduce consumption and, if combined with an excise duty on luxury goods, can also reduce conspicuous consumption. While direct taxes are both equitable and elastic, they can reduce incentives to work and, possibly, to save and invest. However, empirical evidence is not conclusive regarding their impact on either labor supply or savings. The net effect of a tax change on total savings depends on the relative marginal propensities to save of different groups, on the one hand, and an increase in public investment or reduction in fiscal deficit on the other. Obviously if the reduction in private savings exceeds the increase in public savings, aggregate savings will fall. The VAT has been introduced in most developing and transitional countries. Usually the tax rate is uniform, with unprocessed food and exports generally exempted. The tax does not usually distinguish between domestic production and imports. The VAT is considered neutral as the tax burden falls equally on different products and as such avoids the cascading effects of conventional sales or turnover taxes.

High personal income and corporate tax rates can result in adverse incentives to work, save, and invest.[13] Accordingly, it is often suggested that income tax rates be reduced to improve compliance and lessen the burden of tax administration. In most developing countries, average income and corporate tax rates have progressively fallen, taxable income categories have been narrowed, and the minimum threshold of income to be taxed has been increased. Obviously if the maximum marginal tax rates have to be reduced and the total tax revenue has to be defended, then the middle rates will have to be increased. Alternatively, imposing direct taxes may compensate for the loss of revenue.

While investors, indigenous or foreign, rely on their judgment of the fundamentals of an economy rather than on the incentives offered, most developing countries have been providing fiscal incentives, including reduction in the corporate income tax rates, tax holidays, accelerated depreciation allowances, deductions of social security contributions, and deductions on gross earnings for income tax purposes. While these may be redundant, a country that does not offer fiscal incentives may lose FDI to countries that do. Clearly, these tax incentives should be harmonized rather than left to compete with each other.

Land and property taxes are levied on private land ownership in many countries. While land taxes often include agricultural land, property taxes are mainly an urban phenomenon. In addition, the authority to set the rate and collect these taxes is sometimes delegated to local government units in order to provide them with their own revenue collection mechanism.

Governments in developing countries and economies in transition that wish to undertake fiscal reforms should also take into account concomitant tax administration reform, since weak tax administration will make it difficult to achieve the objectives of overall fiscal reform. Tax administration reform should encompass the redefinition of fiscal relationships, and the adaptation, as appropriate, of the organizational structure of tax methods and administration procedures. The organizational structure should be such as to enable the tax administration to achieve the highest possible degree of voluntary taxpayer compliance, and to administer the tax laws efficiently, effectively, and fairly, with the highest degree of integrity.

Tax policy and tax administration are intrinsically linked. In this interrelationship, however, tax policy formulation is generally seen to precede tax administration. Only when a tax structure is legislated does tax administration come to play its role in the implementation of the tax law. In developing countries and economies in transition, however, the direction of the link may not be quite so apparent. Indeed, in most developing countries tax administration *is* tax policy. This would imply that, however fine the design of the tax structure might be in a representative developing country, it is the manner of interpretation and implementation of the law that counts. These elements reflect the need for adequate capacity of the tax administration in place to implement the law.

In many developing countries, tax laws themselves may be extremely well designed and detailed. But unless the accompanying tax administration is able to handle those laws in terms of having the appropriate staff to interpret and implement them, the field-level reality of the actual incidence of the tax system may be quite different from the original objectives. The taxes may be passed on to those on whom they are not meant to fall, and the distribution of the burden may turn out to be indiscriminate. Economists will have a field day carrying out exercises regarding the true incidence and efficiency costs of various taxes, lawyers will find it easy to litigate tax matters because of the difficulties in interpreting complex tax laws, and accountants, ploughing through myriad pages of the tax code will successfully advise clients in careful tax planning such that their tax burden is minimized.

Increasing public revenues is the key to achieving noninflationary growth and ensuring enough resources to finance essential public expenditures, including poverty-eradication programs. Within the constraints imposed by the structure of the economy, the domestic tax system and nontax revenues should be designed to raise enough revenue to finance public expenditures, result in sustainable fiscal balances, and reduce the need to rely on increasing public borrowing or money creation.

Ongoing transformations and evolving national development strategies in the context of globalization of the international economy suggest that many developing countries and economies in transition may have to adapt their tax policy, administration, and legislation including the international dimension of national tax systems to the changing domestic and external economic, fiscal, and financial environment. Globalization, liberalization, international trade agreements, and efforts to attract foreign capital have persuaded countries to lower rates and tariffs, often privileging the mobile factor—financial capital—at the expense of labor and underlining the need to establish or strengthen a progressive tax system.

Past experience also points to the need to strengthen or put in place a tax system that is fair and equitable, that minimizes disincentives for economic efficiency, that is simple (easy to understand and administer), that eliminates evasion and avoidance, that is flexible enough to secure equitable tax revenue from income attributable to innovative financial instruments, and that allows for gradually widening the tax base and integrating the informal sector in the mainstream of the economy. The selection of taxes and duties needs to ensure that they are administratively feasible and result in realistic revenue collection. The system should protect national revenues from tax havens and other shelters and prevent location competition from becoming a race to the bottom.

A transparent budget process and linking of revenues to delivery enhance accountability and legitimize revenue collection. Successful outcomes of public programs in education and health are a case in point.

An efficient, transparent tax administration system, free of corruption, can expand revenue collection. While mobilization of domestic resources is in the long-run essential for sustained development, for a large number of developing countries and economies in transition, in particular least developed countries and other countries that have difficulties attracting financial resources, there will be a need for substantial external resources to make major strides in poverty eradication.

Taxes play an important role in any poverty reduction strategy. The most important function is to raise revenue to fund government expenditure programs. Whether taxes can aid in redistributing income or providing targeted relief is a difficult question, the answer to which depends on country-specific factors. However, until personal income taxes play a greater role in developing countries, redistribution via taxation will be very difficult. Even then, income tax competition from other countries and limitations of tax administration will limit the ability to use the tax system to redistribute income and wealth. Addressing poverty concerns through the design of specific tax instruments may be more promising. Although any specific proposal needs to be considered in the context of the entire tax system, reducing the number of individuals subject to income taxation and the lower rating of certain basic foodstuffs and fuel merits serious consideration.

Public Debt

The proper use of public debt can contribute to economic growth and poverty reduction and smooth consumption in response to shocks. However, if inefficiently allocated, the cost of borrowed external resources can contribute to macroeconomic management problems in the form of high and unsustainable levels of external debt servicing obligations. External debt management has close links with the management of fiscal budget, foreign exchange reserves, and the overall balance of payments.

The external debt burden of many low-income developing countries increased substantially since the 1970s, due to exogenous factors such as adverse terms of trade, shocks, and weather; a lack of sustained macroeconomic adjustment and structural reforms; nonconcessional lending and refinancing policies of creditors; inadequate debt management; and political factors such as civil wars and social strife. The institutional arrangements for debt management necessarily differ from country to country but their activities should revolve around formulation of debt management policies and strategies, providing macroeconomic projections and analysis to support policy-making, and undertaking operations to implement terms of loan agreements and maintaining loan records (i.e., monitoring and maintaining information on disbursements and debt service payments).

For many countries, even full use of traditional mechanisms of rescheduling and debt reduction—together with continued provision of concessional financing and pursuit of sound economic policies—may not be sufficient to attain sustainable external debt levels within a reasonable period of time and without additional external support. In 1996, the IMF and World Bank addressed this problem through the HIPC Initiative designed to provide exceptional assistance to eligible countries following sound economic policies. HIPC would help them reduce their external debt burden to sustainable levels, that is, to levels that would comfortably enable them to service their debt through export earnings, aid, and capital inflows. This assistance reduces the net present value of the future claims on the indebted country, provides an incentive for investment, and broadens domestic support for policy reforms. The HIPC Initiative is a comprehensive, integrated, and coordinated approach to debt reduction that requires the participation of all bilateral, multilateral, and commercial creditors. The HIPC Initiative seeks a country's continued effort toward macroeconomic adjustment and structural and social policy reforms, and provides additional financing for social programs.

Issuing government bonds to the private sector either directly or through the banking system is a second alternative to printing money. While avoiding the immediate inflationary impact of money financing, this type of financing could put pressure on real interest rates and reduce the credit that would otherwise be available to the private sector. The impact on private sector activity and real output will depend on the private saving and investment response to higher real interest rates. A growing body of evidence supports the notion of an ambiguous relationship between private saving and real interest rates. Although real interest rates affect the way economic agents spread their consumption and saving over time, this effect may be offset due to substitution, income, and wealth effects, as well as to financial market constraints preventing consumers from responding to interest rate fluctuations across time. Most case studies provide little evidence that real interest rates favorably affect private saving. The effect of higher interest rates on private investment depends to a large extent on the existing degree of financial liberalization.

When there is financial deepening and interest rates are market determined, a rise in domestic public debt increases the risk of default and reduces public sector confidence in fiscal sustainability, putting pressure on real interest rates. The cost of capital for private users increases, thus contributing to reduced profitability of private investment. On the other hand, higher interest rates contribute to further deteriorating the fiscal balance, in some cases creating explosive debt dynamics. The government has to face the direct consequence of servicing the domestic debt by making payments of both interest and amortization. For an unchanged level of the primary balance, a rise in interest payments associated with higher domestic debt or a rise in interest rates will increase the size of the fiscal deficit, creating additional constraints to the potential growth of economic activities.

In countries where interest rates are controlled, excessive internal borrowing reduces the credit available in the banking system, often leading to higher interest rates in the informal market. When interest rates are regulated and the public sector is given preferential access to credit, the crowding-out effect of private investment is exacerbated.

FACTORS AFFECTING FINANCIAL RESOURCES MOBILIZATION

While taxation remains one of the major instruments in promoting financial resources mobilization efforts of governments, certain interrelated factors connected with external economic and financial environment such as adverse developments in prices of exports, sharp fluctuations in key exchange rates, or instability in the international financial system can constrain such efforts adversely. In general, the degree of economic security in a country is crucial to its success in raising resources to finance its development.[14] The political and economic environment variables affecting savings and investment decisions include government leadership, the risk of external conflict, corruption, the rule of law, racial and ethnic tension, political terrorism, civil war, the quality of the bureaucracy, the risk of repudiation of contracts, the risk of expropriation by government, political rights, and civil liberties. Insofar as taxation is concerned, the factors affecting effective resource mobilization are described in the following paragraphs.

Widening the Tax Base

Developing countries and economies in transition should endeavor to attain optimum revenue realization potential by widening of the tax base, which has both legislative and administrative implications. Despite best efforts, very few countries have been able to define precisely the concept of income.[15] As a consequence, due to the inadequate and noncomprehensive concept of income, large quantities of taxable receipts do not become eligible to tax and escape the tax net altogether. On the other hand, a vague and ambiguous basis of charge creates situations where legislative provisions become prone to multiple interpretations leading to tax avoidance. Hence legislative amendments become necessary, time and again, to plug the loopholes and to make legislative intent clear by broadening the concept of income. It may also become necessary to make the legislative amendments retrospective, thereby unsettling completed assessments to recoup the loss of revenue in years past. The absence of indexation may also result in collecting taxes that were due many years earlier in a depreciated currency at a fraction of its true worth. Tax administrators must be constantly vigilant to unearth devious schemes of clever taxpayers to avoid payment and watch for adverse judicial decisions that may require legislative amendments to clarify intent.

Enforcing Tax Compliance

Tax evasion and tax avoidance at both the national and international levels have serious implications for fiscal policy. They violate the principle of fiscal equity and undermine the concept of voluntary compliance with tax laws. They can greatly diminish the value of statutory incentives and thereby affect allocative behavior to thwart redistribution programs, create artificial biases in macroeconomic indicators, and increase the tax burden when tax rates must be increased to offset the revenue losses incurred—and thereby impose an unfair burden on taxpayers who cannot shift their tax liabilities. The greater the extent of tax evasion and avoidance, the more difficult it is to finance government expenditure without inflation, or in other words, to increase tax revenue adequately. The result can be an excess of expenditure over taxation that is positively correlated with the tax burden. Tax payment has, in fact, come to be regarded as unfair, since public expenditure has been increasingly perceived as failing to yield commensurate benefits either to taxpayers personally or to their communities.

Managing Tax Competition

Many countries are trying to lure foreign consumers to do their shopping in their territory by offering low rates of sales tax and excise on easily transportable and expensive commodities. By exporting part of their tax burden, they reduce other countries' tax revenues while increasing their own. For most such countries, the elasticity of tax revenue with respect to changes in their tax rates may be particularly high because of the possibility of cross-border shopping, which has increased due to more open borders, better information, more international advertising, lower transportation costs, greater mobility of persons, mail order and internet shopping, technological and policy developments, and advances in and greater use of credit cards to pay for cross-border shopping. The cross-border shopping caused by tax rate differentials is growing in importance.

Many multinational enterprises undertake integrated production activities in different countries to take advantage of differential tax rates and reduce their aggregate group tax liability by locating their operations in countries where the statutory tax rates are low or where generous tax concessions or incentives are offered. The benefits accruing to countries from attracting more investment and more profits will inevitably induce other countries to follow the same course. This results in harmful tax competition among countries that prompts many governments to legislate lower tax rates or to provide more generous tax concessions or incentives than other countries to attract more foreign investment.

Where capital is mobile and the country is small, the revenue effect of lower tax rates or tax concessions can be low or even negligible if it is able to attract foreign investment away from other countries. Moreover, multinational enterprises can, through transfer pricing mechanisms, arrange their affairs so as to pay the least aggregate amount of tax for the group companies, by shifting profits artificially to subsidiaries located in low-tax jurisdictions and away from jurisdictions where the tax rates are high. The manipulation of transfer prices has become a significant world problem leading to the erosion of tax bases. Apart from manipulation of factor costs as part of transfer pricing mechanisms, assignment of trademark costs, headquarters expenses, research and development expenses, and loans to different group companies create possibilities for manipulations intended to reduce aggregate tax burden of the enterprise. Tax considerations are likely to weigh heavily in multinational enterprises' investment location decisions.

Increased personal mobility, technological advances, and increased facilities to save and invest abroad allow many people to derive substantial incomes from investments, business, or professional activities carried out in countries with lax tax systems. Many such individuals underreport foreign income with the firm belief that the local tax administration has neither access nor ability to discover suppressed income. Unfortunately, exchange of information among tax authorities in different countries is limited and incapable of preventing nonreporting of concealed income and detecting tax evasion. The absence of bilateral tax treaties requiring cooperation in exchange of information, or conflicting objectives of tax administrations in different countries limit access to vital information that can be used to uncover tax evasion. The recent proliferation of tax havens—countries imposing low or even no taxes—encourages individuals and enterprises to channel their incomes earned in other countries, often with provision of total immunity regarding banking transaction information, thus facilitating tax evasion and tax avoidance. The countries from which this income or capital originates lose revenues and control over their tax bases. Many hedge, investment, or mutual funds also take up residence in tax haven jurisdictions, raising doubts about whether or not investors make proper declarations of their income from these funds to their own tax authorities. It is becoming increasingly evident that many tax evaders, smugglers, drug-traffickers, and money-launderers use services provided in tax havens. The total deposits reported by some of these tax havens far exceed their GDP and are disproportionately large compared to their economies and the number of their inhabitants.

In addition, the advent of new and innovative financial instruments such as derivatives and their subcomponents have created complex problems for tax administrators and further possibilities for tax competition. It is becoming increasingly difficult to trace the income generated by these financial instruments, the location or the source thereof, and the identity of the taxpayer who has earned such income. As a result, tax administrators the world over have experienced considerable difficulties in identifying such income, allocating it to specific countries, and taxing these incomes. Few attempts have been made to clarify the legal position on taxation of income attributable to new financial instruments. Tax policies often lag far behind technical developments. As financial markets become increasingly integrated and complex and as capital movements intensify, the ability of national tax administrations to deal with these issues comprehensively is unlikely to keep pace.

Coordinating Trade Liberalization and Resource Mobilization

Empirical evidence supports the hypothesis that when tariffs and export taxes are important sources of revenue for developing countries and economies in transition, and when these countries have narrow tax bases and high tax rates, trade liberalization will come about when governments diversify their revenue sources through efficiency-enhancing, revenue-increasing tax reform. In a global economy, many developing and transitional countries have adopted tariff reforms and dismantled trade barriers, lowered import duties, and opened their economies to international competition.

Trade liberalization should lead to economic efficiency, international competitiveness, and an expansion of trade, especially in imperfectly competitive markets. But freer trade can also result in loss of considerable revenue as tariffs and other trade-related taxes are cut. For developing countries and economies in transition, with significant fiscal imbalances, any loss of revenue would be an important consideration, primarily because taxes on international trade are a large source of revenue for them. In fact, tariffs (designated as trade taxes) constitute a major source of revenue for most fiscally stretched countries.

Hence, for countries embarking on tariff structure reforms, the main concern should be how to recover from other revenue sources the losses from lowering tariffs. In a small economy, a small radical contraction of tariffs combined with equal but opposite changes in consumption taxes, leaving consumer prices unchanged, does increase both welfare and public revenues. In other words, by simply offsetting tariff reductions point-for-point, with increases in destination-based consumption taxes, leaving consumer prices unchanged does not lead to loss of revenue. For a small open economy, coordinated reforms of this kind are certain to increase both welfare and public (tax plus tariff) revenues if the underlying tariff reform improves production efficiency. This result clearly shows the importance attached to the development of domestic sales taxes, notably VAT, as an accompaniment of tariff reform.

Implementing such a strategy may not always be easy because it is not always possible to precisely offset complex tariff reforms by adjusting an indirect tax structure consisting only of a simple sales tax and a few excises. However, such simple indirect taxation structures may indeed be preferable to the more complex structures that exact offsetting would require.

In short, it is clear that globalization has increased the scope for tax competition since it enables countries to export part of their tax burden to other countries. Tax competition creates difficulties for countries by eventually leading to lower tax revenues, by changing the structure of tax systems in directions not desired by policymakers, and by reducing the progressivity of the tax systems, making them less equitable. No empirical evidence as yet shows the effect of globalization and tax competition on total tax revenue to be significant, but the impact on tax structure has been more evident.

ALTERNATIVE FINANCIAL INSTRUMENTS

Global instruments for raising revenue, including various taxes and fees, offer a major new potential source for development finance. Most proposals of this type involve very small taxes or fees on very large global transactions yielding large revenues while imposing a relatively light burden on any individual. In 1972, James Tobin proposed a tax on currency exchange transactions to reduce speculation in the exchange markets, a goal that is even more important today than when he first proposed it. The revenue-raising potential of the idea is enormous. With an estimated $1.5 trillion in foreign exchange trades every business day in 1998, yearly trading volume is well over $350 trillion. A tax of just one percent would yield $3.5 trillion per year, more than fifty times the total of Official Development Asssistance (ODA). Even assuming a major reduction in market volume caused by the tax, the potential yield would remain substantial.

The Tobin tax has several major advantages in implementation, since most foreign exchange transactions are carried out by a small number of money center financial institutions. If their computers could be programmed to deduct the new tax and forward it to a collecting agency, the cost of collection would be virtually zero. And the process of oversight would be fairly simple: a team of a dozen experts, endowed with the proper authority, probably could do the job.

Another major proposal calls for a global environmental tax, such as a tax on carbon emissions or the carbon content of fuels. This tax would be more complicated to administer, since it would have to be levied on tens of thousands of fuel producers. But there is a very compelling case for such a tax as an environmental policy instrument, quite apart from its revenue-raising potential. As a revenue device, like the Tobin tax, it could generate very large sums with a relatively small percentage tax, given the very large volume of carbon-based fuels involved. A higher tax, which would substantially reduce the use of carbon-based fuels, might raise an even larger revenue stream, at least in the short run.

Many other proposals have been made for global revenue-raising, including fees or various uses of the global commons—that is, use of the oceans and the atmosphere, parking of satellites in earth orbit, and commercial use of the airwaves. Taxes on international air and sea travel and on Internet traffic, fines for environmental pollution like dumping in the oceans, and even an international lottery have been proposed as further approaches to global revenue-raising.

Global tax advocates must overcome serious public suspicion that such taxes would be imposed and spent unaccountably. There is a need to ensure democratic oversight and control over the tax mechanism and how the resulting revenues will be spent. Some reformers have a technocratic conception of the tax and would prefer a more-or-less automatic flow of funds. But if the concept is to succeed, it must have the confidence and support of ordinary citizens. For this, there must be more democratic and more responsible decision-making bodies at the global level. The first global taxes will probably not be as ambitious as the Tobin or carbon tax proposals, with their billions of dollars of income, for they are vulnerable to opposition from exceptionally powerful vested interests. Instead, more modest proposals are likely to set the early precedents. The European Union is moving forward with an air fuels tax, an idea that might be extended to global application. But planning must go forward for the larger taxes, and political backing for them must now be assembled. No solution to the crisis of development finance is more promising than this one.

CONCLUSION

The following recommendations are suggested for mobilizing financial resources through taxation. Developing and transitional countries should:

- Adopt progressive and equitable national taxation systems that are consistent with the country's social and economic framework and that generate adequate revenues while minimizing disincentives.
- Ensure that the incidence of taxation falls equitably on labor and owners of financial capital and other assets; extend the tax base to cover electronic commerce and innovative financial instruments, but exclude the subsistence sector; and expand indirect taxes and make them more equitable by targeting the growing service sector and socially undesirable activities, as well as focusing on luxury consumption.
- Undertake appropriate administrative and legislative measures to combat tax evasion, prevent tax avoidance, and reduce the efficacy of tax shelters and tax havens that undermine national tax revenues.

- Devise innovative measures such as presumptive taxation to target hard-to-tax groups and aim to effect progressive transition of the informal economy sector through reform of labor legislation, the legal and regulatory framework, rationalization of allowances, incentives, and reasonable exemptions.
- Simplify tax laws and improve the efficiency and effectiveness of tax administration; enhance enforcement by strengthening institutional, technical, and technological capacities, including the development of a transparent and accountable system free from corruption; and provide better taxpayer services to facilitate compliance.
- Enhance multilateral cooperation among national tax authorities to promote conclusion of tax treaties, with the goal of eliminating double taxation and promoting equitable distribution of taxation among competing jurisdictions and improving international income allocation.
- Supplement tax revenues by exploring sources of nontax revenues, with due consideration given to equity concerns, including institution user fees or improving the targeting of subsidies for publicly financed goods and services.

Most of the international declarations and action programs of recent years emphasize the need to mobilize domestic resources for social and environmental purposes. But when faced with calls to increase funding for sustainable development, governments usually reply that they lack financial resources. A serious analysis of national budgets shows, however, that sufficient money would be available if existing public and private resources were reallocated. The world economy is more productive and prosperous than ever and should easily be able to afford the needed new spending. Both the expenditure and revenue side of government budgets offer many possibilities for reallocation. Controls on corruption also offer huge possibilities for savings.

On the revenue side, new resources could be obtained through an ecology-based, more socially responsible, and egalitarian tax policy. Such a policy would raise taxes on corporate profits, assets, inheritance, and high incomes; it would also eliminate tax loopholes and other forms of tax avoidance. The current tax system in many countries discriminates against labor as a production factor while favoring the exploitation of natural resources. Consequently, the tax system must be reorganized on an ecological basis so that the consumption and use of resources are subject to higher taxes. In doing so, care must be taken to ensure that such a reform does not lead to inequitable redistribution. Blueprints for a comprehensive ecological tax reform were drawn up years ago but have yet to be put into effect. These plans involve an energy or CO_2 tax and taxes on nonrenewable resources. Although harmonized taxes on the global level would be the best solution, regional and even national initiatives may inspire wider reforms.

NOTES

1. K. Chu, H. Davoodi, and S. Gupta, *Income Distribution and Tax and Government Social Spending Policies in Developing Countries,* IMF WP/00/62 (Washington, D.C.: IMF, 2000).

2. G. Mackenzie, *Estimating the Base of the Value-added Tax (VAT) in Developing Countries: The Problem of Exemptions,* IMF WP/91/21 (Washington, D.C.: IMF, 1991).

3. Musgrave, *Public Finance in Theory and Practice* (New York: McGraw-Hill, 1989).

4. J. Stiglitz, *Economics of the Public Sector* (New York: Norton, 2000).

5. P. Shome, *Taxation in Latin America: Structural Trends and Impact of Administration,* IMF WP/99/19 (Washington, D.C.: IMF, 1999).

6. P. Shome (ed.), *Tax Policy Handbook* (Washington, D.C.: IMF, 1995).

7. J. Slemrod and J. Bakija, *Does Growing Inequality Reduce Tax Progressivity? Should It?* Working Paper 7576 (Cambridge, U.K.: National Bureau of Economic Research, 2000).

8. J. Slemrod, *Optimal Taxation and Optimal Tax System* (Cambridge: National Bureau of Economic Research, Working Paper 3038, 1989).

9. J. Slemrod (ed.), *Tax Policy in the Real World* (Cambridge, U.K.: Cambridge University Press, 1998).

10. Alan A. Tait, *Value-added Tax: Administrative and Policy Issues.* Occasional paper no. 88 (Washington, D.C.: IMF, WDC, 1991).

11. V. Tanzi and H. Zee, *Tax Policy for Emerging Markets: Developing Countries,* IMF,WP/00/35 (Washington, D.C.: IMF, 2000).

12. V. Thuronyi, *Tax Law Design and Drafting* (The Hague and Boston: Kluwer Law International, 2000).

13. Thuronyi, *Tax Reform for 1989 and Beyond.* Tax Notes (U.S.) February 20, 1989, 42:981–96.

14. Helene Poirson, "Economic Security, Private Investment, and Growth in Developing Countries," IMF Working Paper WP/98/4 (January 1998): 17–19.

15. M. Govinda Rao, "Tax Reform in India: Achievements and Challenges" and Ilho Yoo, "Experience with Tax Reform in the Republic of Korea," *Asia-Pacific Development Journal* 7, no. 2, December 2000.

8

Building Social Capital Through Civic Engagement

Khalid Malik and Swarnim Waglé

CIVIC ENGAGEMENT has an essential role to play in successful development.[1] Although in moral philosophy it is often advanced as an end in itself, civic engagement is also an important means of fostering social capital and effective development. Development policies are likely to yield better long-term benefits if they build in components of civic engagement. This chapter reviews the concept of civic engagement, identifies its critical attributes, and examines policy implications.[2]

THE LINK BETWEEN SOCIAL CAPITAL AND CIVIC ENGAGEMENT

Despite growing appreciation of the concept, the literature on social capital is diffuse. Though arguably different in character, it is best understood when presented as an analogy to human and physical capital and as a factor that influences productivity. As Putnam puts it, social networks have value, and like physical capital (machines) and human capital (education), social contacts influence productivity of groups and individuals.[3] If human capital is embodied in individuals, social capital is embodied in relationships. Woolcock is more succinct when he limits the understanding of social capital to "norms and networks that facilitate collective action," cautioning that any definition of social capital should differentiate between its "sources" and "consequences."[4] In this context, social capital would, for example, exclude "trust" from its definition since it is an outcome, not a source, of social relations that foster repeated interactions. Social capital is linked to the idea of civic virtue, which is most powerful when embedded in a dense network of reciprocal social relations.

The concept of social capital is derived from the concept of civic engagement. Lyda J. Hanifan, the superintendent of schools in West Virginia in 1916, first used it to highlight the importance of community involvement in the success of public schools.[5] The theme was independently picked up by social scientists in subsequent decades, including by James Coleman in the late 1980s.

Social capital's scholarly credibility reached new heights with the 1993 publication of Putnam's twenty-year experimental study, *Civic Traditions in Modern Italy,* which sought to establish links between successes in regional governance and stocks of social capital in different Italian provinces.[6] In the early 1970s, twenty regional governments, identical in form, were implanted in provinces with very different characteristics. Some failed; others succeeded. Putnam attributed this difference in quality of performance not to party politics and ideology, not to affluence and population movements, but to traditions of civic engagement—voter turnout, newspaper readership, and membership in choral societies, literary circles, soccer clubs, and other social organizations. Putnam places this finding in the context of an observation made by Alexis de Tocqueville in the 1830s about civic engagement and the successful working of democracy in the United States: "Americans of all ages, all stations in life, and all types of disposition . . . are forever forming associations."

Putnam also argues that when networks of civic engagement are dense, reciprocity and trust are fostered, thereby "lubricating social life."[7] Coordination and communication among agents amplify information about the trustworthiness, or general reputation, of other individuals, reducing incentives for opportunism and malfeasance. The association between social networks and economic growth has been extensively explored in the economics literature. Fukuyama elaborates on the virtue of trust in spurring economic growth by drawing a distinction between "low trust" and "high trust" societies.[8] He identifies their respective abilities to generate social capital as keys to mitigating the adverse consequences of the discipline that market economies impose. The success of some East Asian economies in making great material advances within a generation has been partially attributed to the positive externalities of network capitalism.

Social capital and civic engagement, of course, have downsides. Establishing and maintaining relations may require a level of investment that may not be cost effective. Adler and Kwon cite a study that argues while social capital may generate informational benefits, they may be costly to maintain.[9] The same forces of solidarity that "help members bind can turn into ties that blind," as overembedded relationships stop the flow of new information and ideas into the group and create noneconomic obligations that hinder entrepreneurship. Dreze and Sen, for example, attribute high dropout rates for girl from schools in India to family obligations and pressures to fulfill community expectations.[10] Indeed, it has to be recognized that religious cults, terrorist organizations, gangs, and drug cartels are groups with strong internal ties among members that nonetheless impose severe damage on society.

DEFINING CIVIC ENGAGEMENT

In this domain of social capital, civic engagement is a key subset. If civic engagement is understood as a process that organizes citizens or their entrusted representatives to influence, share, and control public affairs, then we see this contributing to social capital through interactions between people and processes they engage in for a positive public outcome. More generally, civic engagement contributes to social capital and to development efforts through the channels of voice, representation, and accountability. This link between civic engagement and development can be organized in a variety of ways, both formal and informal. The latter refers to processes that may complement the formal processes of electing officials or making development plans in a consultative manner.

Discussions here use the terms civic engagement and participation interchangeably for convenience, with both terms concurring broadly with the definition that participation is a process through which stakeholders influence and share control over development initiatives, and the decisions and resources that affect them.[11] However, it is still worth noting that civic engagement is a more specific term than participation, with an emphasis on civic objectives and concerns. The UNDP *Human Development Report 1993* sees participation in similar terms, describing it "as a process, not an event, that closely involves people in the economic, social, cultural and political processes that affect their lives."[12] The report places the issue within a wide developmental, and in some ways even philosophical, paradigm—seeing it as both a means and an end. Because the paradigm of human development stresses investment in human capabilities and the subsequent functional use of those capabilities to allow people to lead the kind of life they choose, participation is viewed as facilitating the use of human capabilities, hence serving as a means for socioeconomic development. In this context, by allowing people to realize their full potential and enhance personal fulfillment, participation is also seen as an end in itself.[13]

David C. Korten frames civic engagement as an issue of governance, stating, "if sovereignty resides ultimately in the citizenry, their engagement is about the right to define the public good, to determine the policies by which they will seek that good, and to reform or replace those institutions that no longer serve."[14] This is a useful definitional reference for the purposes of this chapter, because our attempt here is also to talk about activities among entities at the higher echelons and departments within the central government whose work is usually difficult for common citizens to access and influence, both procedurally, because of centralization or bureaucratic restrictions, and substantially, because of technical content. This perspective on governance in a sense draws upon the notion that members of groups and society at large enter into social compacts that present mutual or reciprocal obligations, and that civic engagement is an active process of exercising these obligations. In this sense, exercise of this obligation implies the essential right of all citizens to voice to their concerns and enforce accountability.

At a more technical level, the scope of the term civic engagement is best understood on a continuum spanning information-sharing to empowerment. Following Edgerton et al., this continuum can begin with a) a one-way *flow of information* to the public in the form of, say, media broadcasts or dissemination of decisions, progressing on to, b) bilateral or multilateral *consultation* between and among coordinators of the process and the public in the form of participatory assessments, interviews and field visits, c) *collaboration* encompassing joint work and shared decision-making between the coordinators and the stakeholders, and d) *empowerment,* where decision-making powers and resources are transferred to civic organizations in the form of, for example, forestry or irrigation user groups.[15] It might also be useful to highlight Hirschman's concept of "exit."[16] He contrasts the issue of voice, or the capacity to influence policy and debate within an institution, with a group's capacity to get what it wants by choosing a specific institution or switching to another through exit. This concept reminds us that people choose to express dissatisfaction with an institution or process by ignoring or moving away from it rather than necessarily working from within. More broadly, it might be useful to recognize the existence of a complex interplay between different forms of civic engagement, and the role and function of state institutions—rather than civic groups being only on the receiving end of the process, for instance as communities or groups that need to be involved in projects or programs in order to make development more effective.

THE CONUNDRUM OF POLICY IMPLICATIONS

Can state institutions assume or introduce specific roles and policies that support or hinder advancement of civic engagement? If public policy is an instrument, and productive civic engagement as a form of social capital is a target, can a workable link between the two be established? If not, why? If yes, how? What kind of capacities do we require to create productive social capital, which can then be leveraged for developmental transformation?

Social capital, including more specifically civic engagement, can be thought of as a missing block in many development parcels, but it is not a solution to all ills. And while its influence should be recognized, it ought not be exaggerated. It does, however, point us toward a direction that is useful in development—it helps us focus on how and under what terms we associate with each other. Woolcock highlights the following points.[17] First, if the low stock of "bridging capital" makes it difficult for information and resources to flow among groups, larger socio-economic-political forces that divide societies, such as discriminatory practices along gender, caste, and ethnic lines, will stand in the way of growth. Second, if social capital is part of an effective risk-management strategy in crises, its absence implies a difficult time for countries during times of volatility. Third, institutions affect how communities manage risks and opportunities. In countries where corrupt bureaucracy and lack of rule of law are the norm, it will be difficult to showcase well-maintained schools and roads, for example. It is rare for a country to be characterized simultaneously by strong social capital and weak systems of government responsiveness to citizen concerns.

Can we then find a role for public policy to nurture, or create, or at least stop the destruction of the positive aspects of social capital? Social relations are neither culturally determined in a permanent way, nor are they always shaped by responses of rational agents. Institutions and history play a large role in shaping social relations. Public policy can shape institutions that support social relations that in turn sustain high levels of productive social capital. The *World Development Report 2000/2001* cites an example where the Brazilian state devised a health program that increased vaccination and reduced infant mortality, and in the process created social capital by building trust between government workers and poor people.[18]

An arena where the state can step in to influence social norms is in instances of exclusionary practices linked with race, gender, and ethnicity. Some forms of exclusion can simply be redressed by improving the outreach of public services such as rural primary schools and hospitals to areas of neglect. Stronger manifestations of discrimination ought to be dealt with legally through state institutions or special policies such as affirmative action. The broader agenda of social capital, however, risks being belittled by practitioners because, as Edwards points out, attributes such as trust and tolerance are hard to engineer, and development organizations tend to focus on things measurable in the short run.[19] This focus can be useful, but it assists "forms" not "norms" of social capital. Helping countries build social capital is complex, however, as assistance dedicated to "building other people's civil societies by investing in their social capital" encourages the idea of picking winners, which spreads mistrust among groups, and even backlash as indigenous groups become associated with foreign interests.

In sum, as Narayan and Woolcock put it, a new consensus is emerging about the importance of social relations in development: they provide opportunities for mobilizing growth-enhancing resources; they don't exist in a vacuum; and the nature and extent of interactions between communities and institutions hold the key to understanding development prospects in a given society.[20] Edwards paraphrases Ramon Daubon in likening social capital to the Indian Ocean, "everyone knows where it is, no-one cares where it begins or where it ends, but we know we have to cross it to get from India to Africa."[21]

GOING BEYOND CIVIC ENGAGEMENT AS AN INSTRUMENT OF DEVELOPMENT

At a broader level, though, the virtues of social capital can only be exploited fully by internalizing civic interaction in mainstream political and development processes. Narayan and Woolcock call for social capital to be seen as a component of such orthodox development projects as dams, irrigation systems, local schools, and health clinics. As Esman and Uphoff posit, "where poor communities have direct input into the design, implementation, management and evaluation of projects, return on investments and sustainability of the project is enhanced."[22]

The idea of civic engagement at the grass-roots level has been tested and has generally been seen to generate benefits that contribute to better planning, implementation, and sustainability of projects. Civic engagement has costs and constraints, of course, but it is to the credit of the successes at the micro level that questions are now being asked about the desirability of scaling civic engagement up to the macro level. But equally, there is a growing question as to the development value of micro-level interventions, however successful or well meaning they might be, along with a corresponding search for improved understanding about the necessary factors and conditions that can more fundamentally ensure broader progress in the issues raised. A concrete example is microfinance: however successful or well-designed individual schemes might be, the larger development outcomes of increased access to credit by the poor can only be tested by examining the functioning of capital markets, and how they might be adjusted to allow for such access.

Civic Engagement at the Micro Level

The term civic engagement has been used frequently since the early 1960s in the narrower sense of people's engagement in small projects. Only in recent years has civic engagement received much academic attention as an important development theme. Following the gradual replacement of the coercive socialist order by democratic regimes in many countries around the world, together with the heightened quest for new ways to achieve a sustained rise in standards of living for the world's poor, participation has been rediscovered as an instrument that can be used both to consolidate democratic systems of governance and to strengthen global development. The fundamental premise is that the people have the urge as well as the right to be part of events and processes that shape their lives.

Much of this analysis is drawn from what we have learned from participation in projects. What has become increasingly clear is that where participation works, it does so because boundaries are pushed and horizons extended. These boundaries include the framework of the project itself, the structural norms that confine people within the prevailing set of social relations, and the limitations that individuals impose on themselves concerning their competencies and potential. The assessments of failed projects often reveal that they lacked perceived relevance for local people or we placed in a social and political environment that was resistant to change. The remedies may range from modifications to the existing project to a complete reassessment of what changes are most wanted and what is required to bring them about. Issues of project ownership become central as does identification of structural constraints to change. Tackling these structural constraints and fostering ownership frequently require changes and broader involvement in a policy level and subsequent reformulation of activities. While lessons have been drawn from projects, the implications of these changes are a demand for more participation in policy: "It is an impossible task

. . . to isolate the project as a distinct phenomenon and examine participation only in that context. Clearly the concept of participation knows
no boundaries and its dynamic process cannot be contained within a
projects framework."[23]

Benefits, Costs, and Constraints

A compelling body of empirical evidence makes a strong case for people's participation at the micro level.[24] Most foreign-aid–financed programs in the developing world today make participation an essential
component of project design and implementation. Theoretically, the
channels through which participation contributes to the effectiveness
and sustainability of development outcomes are information-driven efficiency, ownership, transparency and accountability, and constructive
partnerships. It is very difficult to quantify success in these broad terms,
and this is probably one of the reasons it is difficult to make a strong
case for civic engagement, even when the gains seem obvious. While
attempts to quantify success can be made, the best indicators are likely
to continue to be qualitative—whether people perceive the processes to
be successful or not.

Involving the beneficiaries in its design can lead to a more accurate
perception of needs based on direct exchange of information.[25] When
the people are not consulted, policymakers work on assumptions that
are subject to problems of information asymmetries, such as moral hazard and adverse selection, as discussed extensively in the economics literature. Participation can be expected to alleviate this problem to some
extent by allowing a more accurate flow of information that translates
into better decisions. Informed decisions are more efficient in terms of
resources consumed and outcomes generated than those that are not.
Often, there may not have been demand for the project, or it might not
have been a priority. With people's participation, not only can the most
important needs be identified, but by having people play a role in the
entire project cycle—formulation, adoption, implementation, and monitoring—ownership can be ensured, and with it project sustainability.[26]

In a study of 121 diverse rural water supply projects in forty-nine
countries in the developing world, the World Bank provided evidence of
a strong correlation between project success and high levels of benefi-
ciary participation. It claimed that of the forty-nine projects with low
levels of participation, only eight percent were successful, while of the
forty-two projects with high levels of participation, sixty-four percent
were successes.[27] When project coordinators are subject to civic scrutiny

of their decisions and actions, it forces them to be more accountable and responsive to the needs of beneficiaries. By getting rid of the communication vacuum between the two groups, bureaucratic obstructions can be overcome, which can make government more answerable.

If public policy is about deciding the most efficient allocation of scarce public resources, policy decisions often take the form of analyzing trade-offs between options. Participation of the people, especially differing groups with divergent interests, can allow an exchange of each other's positions and interests and kick-start a deliberative process of mutual understanding of the trade-offs involved in the collective decision. Not only can the groups then enter into constructive alliances, but they are also likely to be less combative and disruptive to the processes and programs on which they subsequently decide.

Beyond the instrumental roles in ensuring better decisions and sounder implementation, participation is also seen as a good in itself that deepens democracy. By giving citizens an opportunity to access and shape governance and the exercise of power, participation complements the systems of electoral competition that may fail to meet citizen needs directly.[28] Along these lines, participation has also been viewed as a process that politically educates citizens in the art of governance, and in the pursuit of rights and civic roles.[29]

The virtues of participation are, however, not unanimously appreciated. Concerns often raised about participatory processes are costs in terms of money, time, and management (high transaction costs); risks of elite capture; the possibility of instability; and legitimate representation. In addition, Brinkerhoff and Goldsmith suggest that participatory processes may also result in policy stalemates and unrealistic expectations on the part of those involved.[30]

Civic engagement as a process needs to be managed, and it requires resources. In developing countries, where many equally deserving ends compete for scarce resources, opportunity costs in terms of money and bureaucratic resources diverted to manage a participatory process may be significant. While all development and all politics is about, and for, the people, any argument to avoid their engagement in these processes on the pretext of inconvenience can confuse ends with means. While participatory processes impose real costs in time, money, and management, a balanced tally indicating clearly the benefits and costs of the process may justify a better case for civic engagement.

Scholars further talk about the danger of elite capture when development and political processes become more open and participatory. The fear is that as more opportunities become available for citizen

participation, local elites may become more dominant and reap a disproportionate share of the possible benefits that emanate from benign
processes aimed at bringing "governance closer to the governed."[31]
When opportunities for participation in development and political
processes are extended to the village level, the local elite—who are better off financially as well as in power relations—may be the first ones
to capture control of the local administrative and political bodies. Roodt
adds that local elites monopolize power and are hostile to widespread
participation of common people, which they attempt to prevent from
occurring by using their power positions.[32] For every optimist who sees
participation as a genuine tool for transformation, it seems there is a
less-optimistic person who views it as a mere legitimizing tool for top-
down implementation.

A related fear expressed by scholars such as Huntington—and even
John Stuart Mill, in an earlier context of whether democracy is well-
suited for all countries—is that a society without strong institutions to
set and enforce rules may easily create environments where greater participation, without the institutional safeguards, leads to anarchy.[33] In
this spirit one hears arguments such as Agrawal's that "a high level of
participation could be antithetical to democracy, for it may endanger
freedom and rights, impede governability and destroy pluralism." This
has, of course, been countered by arguments that in the absence of
broad-based citizen participation, electoral democracies may instead run
the risk of becoming hostage to the manipulations of the powerful
minority.

On balance, however, there is a growing recognition of the conditional virtues of civic engagement. As Oakley et al. note, "whereas up
to ten years ago a review of project-based literature would probably
highlight technological effectiveness, good planning and management,
and resource efficiency as the key ingredients of project success, today
participation figures prominently; some would say that it is the single
most important ingredient."[34]

THE LEAP FROM THE MICRO LEVEL TO THE MACRO LEVEL

If we recognize that the experiment of civic engagement at the micro
level has been, on balance, a positive experience it might be reasonable
to expect similar outcomes at the macro level. Is it realistic to expect to
reap the micro level benefits of enhanced efficiency through better
information flow, improved program effectiveness through solicitation

of local knowledge, greater accountability, stronger ownership and partnerships, and empowerment of stakeholders? If yes, what are the channels? Is there a higher-order case for civic engagement as an essential part of democracy and development sustainability, and as a key channel for strengthening the "glue which binds and holds society" together, especially in circumstances of development transformation?[35]

Expected Benefits

Brinkerhoff and Goldsmith suggest that the outcomes of civic engagement at the macro level can be expected to be very similar to those at the grassroots. They, among others, posit that inclusive participatory processes can create:

- better socio-macroeconomic policy content based on better information,
- social consensus on policy priorities because of civic involvement in the discourse,
- a positive signaling effect to international donors and investors because of national consensus,
- equitable policies and distribution of benefits to the vulnerable, such as the poor,
- accountable and responsive government, and
- better implementation of policy and programs.

While these are a direct extension of anticipated benefits at the macro level, based on the micro-level evidence, there also exists a set of related reasons that strengthen the case for civic engagement at higher levels. Rodrik presents empirical evidence on the association between participatory political regimes and lower levels of aggregate economic instability, suggesting that this may be because participatory political regimes moderate social conflict and better induce compromise among citizen groups.[36] While no convincing econometric evidence exists on the link between democracies and long-term economic growth, evidence on the positive link between democracies and volatility (annual standard deviations in GDP growth rates) is statistically significant.

Because economic volatility triggers high welfare losses in a world with incomplete insurance markets and inadequate levels of intertemporal trade, Rodrik accords this finding much importance. It suggests that participatory processes induce cooperation and generate stability. First, as individuals meet and discuss, they "understand each other's view points, develop empathy, recognize the value of moderation, internalize the common interest, and de-emphasize self interest." Participatory regimes induce cooperation not by "changing the constraints we face, but by changing the type of people we are," or by altering preferences of agents. Second, democracies with constitutional provisions that prevent the majority from suppressing the minority, or the winners from marginalizing the losers, induce cooperation among groups ex-ante who are aware of the costs of noncooperation. Third, cooperation among groups is ensured by the possibility of repeated interactions.[37] As long as this probability is strong and past actions influence future behaviors, groups who have a sufficiently long-term time horizon have an incentive to cooperate rather than renege on negotiations for short-term gains.

Similarly, building on an observation by Sen that "there are no famines in democracies," the World Bank highlights the importance of the free press in preventing famines in India—the world's largest democracy. In participatory political regimes, where informed citizens can exact accountability from politicians on the speed of relief programs, responsiveness to disasters is swift, preventing major calamities.[38] Given shock, in the form of drought or flood, higher newspaper circulation leads to greater public food distribution or relief spending. Freedom of the press can be thought of as a reasonably good proxy for the freedom and the scope of the activities of civic organizations.

Civic engagement can strengthen state capacities in two additional ways. First, when citizens can express and press for demands legally, states acquire some of the credibility to govern well. This is partly because wide-ranging and open discussion of policy goals tends to avoid the risk of a small elite or minority influencing the course of government. Second, where public services are inefficient because of weak state capabilities and incentive problems, the user groups and citizen associations can inform public officials of their needs and press for improvements. In Kenya, for example, better information flows from the supposed beneficiaries led to better decisions, resulting in the kind of efficiency that alleviates budgetary pressures on central governments—a crucial point in resource-starved nations.[39]

Costs and Constraints

The costs and constraints briefly discussed above for microactivities apply to the following section as well. It is important to note, however, that when an argument in favor of civic engagement is presented as supporting state legitimacy, there may be inherent difficulties in attaining this goal. As Mathur describes, central governments and the bureaucrats usually are very reluctant to give up powers as they consider their decisionmaking authority an exclusive preserve.[40] Government institutions and their staff are quite suspicious and feel threatened by people who organize themselves for participation, hence the often lackluster or even hostile reception of participatory initiatives by government officials. As Ghai adds, "many participatory initiatives have to contend with hostility, harassment and attempts at suppression. Certainly few attract resources of the type and amount reserved for more conventional development projects."[41] This, he contends, is because the dominant groups mistakenly tend to equate participatory movements with subversion or revolutionary doctrine. It is in this context that Agrawal views participation as a thoroughly political process. He argues that, among the many factors related to the success of participation, two key issues are the management of political relationships at the central level to extract commitment from powerful actors, and the creation of institutional mechanisms at the local level.

THE DISTINCTIVE CASE OF MACRO-LEVEL POLICYMAKING

While cases may be made for both advocating and downplaying the roles of civic engagement in policy processes, civic engagement is certainly not a solution to all things wrong with policymaking or program implementation. There is now broad acceptance that participation is a necessary if not solely sufficient ingredient for attaining successful policy outcomes.

Some areas of macroeconomic policymaking, however, are slightly different. Neoclassical economists point out the technical nature of macro policies, for example, noting that monetary policies about interest rates or decisions on currency devaluation should not be issues subject to civic influence. Similarly, it may be unreasonable to expect informed public debates to take place on issues such as optimal credit targets or the sustainability of fiscal deficits. But participation can play a role in public education about the consequences of these technical decisions, and, perhaps even more importantly, about the role macro policies can play in development. On issues such as the inevitability of short-term pains to reap medium-term benefits in inflation-reducing policies, for example, the public ought to be informed and convinced about the rationale for short-term austerity. Even on this, however, there is disagreement over such issues as how short-term austerity is to be achieved and whether or not expenditures on health or education are protected. On questions of public sector reform, or privatization, there are economic and political choices to be made, and bringing groups with varying priorities to a common forum to hear and understand each other and deliberate on tradeoffs can be helpful.

Since macro policies are public goods which, by definition, are characterized by people's understatement of their willingness to pay for them, there may be situations when outcomes of certain participatory mechanisms ought to be overruled, for example, when externalities are involved. Along these lines, it has been argued that participation, when used as a management tool, as in a farmer's ownership of irrigation systems, may also give rise to problems of moral hazard through incentives for excessive risk-taking. When macroeconomic decision-making on resource allocation is subject to popular influence, there is a fear that participatory processes might generate an outcome that is not only populist but also laden with conflicting demands of different segments of the society (for example, simultaneous calls for imposition and removal of import tariffs, specific subsidies, low taxes, and greater expenditures).

Broad-based consultative exercises can result in lengthy lists of demands. It becomes a challenge then to square the wish-list of people with the budgetary realities. After the agenda is defined, reality presented, and trade-offs regarding revenue and expenditure examined through a process of consultation, the elected government officials ultimately have to decide how to proceed. While scope for participation in macro policies may well be limited, it is by no means a given. Citizen groups can be engaged in debates over trade-offs among priorities, such as, between low inflation and growth-generating high public expenditures.

A recurring concern about participation pertains to an apparent contradiction. While participatory processes are usually credited as instruments that lend legitimacy and credibility to policies, valid questions may be asked about stakeholder identification and representation. Who exactly does a particular civic group represent and to whom is it accountable? Furthermore, by creating ad-hoc participatory processes in addition to established political-legal processes, a question that can emerge is whether the former subverts the latter, and if it does, whether that is desirable. Since participation does not have a constitutional feel to it, practitioners suggest that governments should be drawing on established institutional resources, not bypassing them, in order to reap the kinds of benefits that civic engagement could be expected to generate.

One area in which participation of people, especially the poor, has been found to be valuable in formulating national strategies is in poverty reduction, where policies have relied extensively on information fed through Participatory Poverty Assessments, which employ flexible visual and verbal techniques of inquiry, as opposed to predetermined statistical questions asked in household surveys. Robb argues that these participatory approaches have resulted in a broader definition of poverty and better-informed public policies that are more responsive to the needs of the poor. She draws on a range of African examples to conclude that broad policy dialogue on poverty typically widens the constituency for reform and strengthens a country's sense of policy ownership.

Weighing the competing claims and arguments about the virtues and the vices of participatory processes, it is clear that, at a theoretical level, while participation can be expected to yield benefits, the channels through which this may happen are specific and conditional on an array of circumstances. The challenge for policy entrepreneurs is to identify the right channels and circumstances for employing processes of civic engagement.

PRSPs: A CASE OF MACRO-LEVEL CIVIC ENGAGEMENT

Between 1999 and 2001, around fifty countries prepared interim or full Poverty Reduction Strategy Papers (PRSPs), which are now the primary source of 1171 lending for most poor countries. Although triggered by the Group of Seven (G-7) initiative to relieve the debts of the Highly Indebted and Poor (HIPC) countries, and by the World Bank and IMF requirement that countries must articulate how they have sought to channel resources to fight poverty after debt relief, the PRSPs have now developed into an elaborate development policy vehicle of their own. According to the World Bank, there is a renewed emphasis on six principles: country driven process, results-orientation, comprehensive coverage of issues, prioritizing of issues for improved implementation, a strong base in partnerships, and a long-term perspective. A feature most worth noting in the PRSPs is that they are supposed to be prepared in a participatory manner. While in the interim PRSPs participation is not mandated—the only requirement is a plan indicating how participation will be cultivated—at the full PRSP stage countries are required to follow a participatory process.

Over the past two years of PRSP preparations, there have been numerous assessments by leading NGOs and agencies external to the World Bank and the IMF. Some of the recurring findings on civic engagement that emerge are as follows:

- there is considerable divergence in the conceptual understanding of civic engagement,
- the breadth and depth of civic engagement is insufficient, with the real poor, ethnic minorities and the poor outside urban areas not generally consulted,
- civic engagement has enriched and widened the description and analysis of poverty, but has not greatly influenced the technical areas of macroeconomic choices and public expenditures,
- the participatory processes have spun off many positive externalities, such as new legal developments and creation of civil society alliances, and
- correlates of an open regime, such as freedom to speak and to form sociopolitical organizations, seem conducive for the flourishing of civic engagement processes, although little direct link is observed between a political regime per se and the quality of a civic engagement process.

CONCLUSION

Following the publication of the UNDP *Human Development Reports*, and the increased attention of large development institutions such as the World Bank to human development sectors such as education and health over the past decade, the development debate has refocused on the basics of the ends and means of development.[42] What are we seeking to achieve? For whom? And how? People informed by both personal value judgments and empirical results make the case for specific policy measures. This chapter has attempted to introduce one such notion of social capital. If we recognize this to be a desirable input, output, and outcome of development, then the question that policy professionals need to ask is: Can it be created or nurtured? This chapter explored the theme of civic engagement as one possible policy response, and we discussed its many dimensions, appreciating its perceived successes at the micro level and positing whether the fundamental aspects of civic engagement could be extended to the macro level. Effective civic engagement derives from an understanding of dimensions of participation and empowerment set within a context of social and political relations— dimensions that extend from nominal involvement of citizens to their empowerment and shifts in power relations.

Increasingly, what we do in development is becoming as important as how we do it. The theme of development as transformation emphasizes the process as much as the product, and as various disciplines—from philosophy to sociology, from urban planning to economics—converge to shape the multidimensional field of development, concepts and issues that were hitherto ignored as irrelevant to the basic pursuit of enhancing national incomes have emerged as important ingredients to meaningful and sustainable development.

NOTES

1. J. Stiglitz, "Towards a New Paradigm for Development: Strategies, Policies, and Processes," Prebisch Lecture, UNCTAD, October 1998; and K. Malik, "Technical Cooperation, Capacities, and Development," UNDP (draft, 2001).

2. This is a revised version of a paper by Khalid Malik and Swarnim Waglé, in *Capacity for Development: New Solutions to Old Problems* (New York: UNDP, 2002). The opinions expressed here are personal and should not be attributed to the institutions with which the authors are affiliated.

3. R. Putnam, *Bowling Alone: The Collapse and Revival of American Community* (New York: Simon and Schuster, 2000).

4. M. Woolcock, "The Place of Social Capital in Understanding Social and Economic Outcomes," *Canadian Journal of Policy Research* 2, no. 1 (2000): 11–17.

5. L. J. Hanifan, "The Rural School Community Center," *Annals of the American Academy of Political and Social Science*, 67 (1916): 130–138.

6. R. Putnam, *Making Democracy Work: Civic Traditions in Modem Italy* (Princeton, N.J.: Princeton University Press, 1993).

7. R. Putnam, "The Prosperous Community: Social Capital and Public Life," *The American Prospect* 4, no. 13 (1993): 35–42.

8. F. Fukuyama, *Trust: The Social Virtues and the Creation of Prosperity* (New York: Free Press, 1995).

9. P. Adler and S. Kwon, "Social Capital: The Good, The Bad and the Ugly," paper presented at the Academy of Management Meeting (Chicago, 1999).

10. J. Dreze and A. K. Sen, *Economic Development and Social Opportunity* (Oxford, U.K.: Oxford University Press, 1995).

11. World Bank, *The World Bank Participation Sourcebook* (Washington, D.C.: World Bank, 1996).

12. United Nations Development Programme, *Human Development Report 1993* (New York: UNDP, 1993).

13. A. K. Sen, *Poverty and Famines: An Essay on Entitlement and Deprivation* (Oxford, U.K.: Clarendon Press, 1981).

14. D. C. Korten, "Third Generation NGO Strategies: A Key to People Centered Development," *World Development*, Supplement, vol. 15 (1988): 145–159.

15. J. Edgerton, K. McClean, C. Robb, P. Shah, and S. Tikare, "Participatory Processes in the Poverty Reducation Strategy," Draft Working Paper (Washington, D.C.: World Bank, 2000): 30.

16. A. O. Hirschman, *Exit Voice and Loyalty: Responses to Decline in Firms, Organizations, and State* (Cambridge, Mass.: Harvard University Press, 1972).

17. M. Woolcock, "The Place of Social Capital in Understanding Social and Economic Outcomes," *Canadian Journal of Policy Research* 2, no. 1 (2000): 11–17.

18. World Bank, *World Development Report 2000/2001* (New York: Oxford University Press, 2000).

19. M. Edwards, "Enthusiasts, Tacticians and Skeptics: The World Bank, Civil Society and Social Capital," *The Kettering Review* 18, no. 1 (2000): 39–51.

20. D. Narayan and M. Woolcock, "Social Capital: Implications for Development Theory, Research and Policy," *The World Bank Research Observer,* August 2000.

21. M. Edwards, "Enthusiasts, Tacticians and Skeptics: The World Bank, Civil Society and Social Capital," *The Kettering Review* 18, no. 1 (2000): 39–51.

22. M. Esman and N. Uphoff, *Local Organizations: Intermediaries in Rural Development* (Ithaca, N.Y.: Cornell University Press, 1984).

23. P. Oakley, et al., *Projects with People: The Practice of Participation in Rural Development* (Geneva: International Labour Organization, 1991): 24.

24. N. Uphoff, J. Cohen, and A. Goldsmith, *Feasibility and Application of Rural Development Participation: A State of the Art Paper* (Ithaca, NY: Cornell University Press, 1979).

25. C. Robb, "How Can the Poor Have a Voice in Government Policy?" *Finance and Development* 37, no. 4 (December 2000): 22–25.

26. World Bank, *The World Bank Participation Sourcebook* (Washington, D.C.: World Bank, 1996).

27. World Bank, *World Development Report 1997* (New York: Oxford University Press, 1997).

28. A. Agrawal, *Decentralization in Nepal: A Comparative Analysis* (Oakland, Calif.: Institute for Contemporary Studies Press, 1999).

29. P. Freire, *The Pedagogy of the Oppressed* (New York: Herder and Herder, 1970).

30. D. Brinkerhoff and A. Goldsmith, "Participation in Macroeconomic Policy: Experience and Implications for Poverty Reduction Strategies" (Washington, D.C.: World Bank, 2000).

31. A. Agrawal, *Decentralization in Nepal: A Comparative Analysis* (Oakland, Calif.: ICS Press, 1999).

32. M. J. Roodt, "Participatory Development—A Jargon Concept?" in J. K. Coetzee and J. Graaf (eds.) *Reconstruction, Development and People* (Johannesburg: Thomson International Publishing, 1996).

33. S. Huntington, *Political Order in Changing Societies* (New Haven, Conn.: Yale University Press, 1968).

34. P. Oakley, et al., *Projects with People: The Practice of Participation in Rural Development* (Geneva: International Labor Organization, 1991).

35. J. Stiglitz, "Toward a New Paradigm for Development: Strategies, Policies and Processes," Raul Prebisch Lecture, Geneva: United Nations Conference on Trade and Development, 1998.

36. D. Rodrik, "Participatory Politics, Social Cooperation, and Economic Stability," *American Economic Review* 90, no. 2 (May 2000): 140–144.

37. D. Rodrik, "Participatory Politics, Social Cooperation, and Economic Stability."

38. World Bank, World *Development Report 2000/2001* (Washington, D.C.: World Bank, 2000).

39. P. Smoke, "Local Government Fiscal Reform in Developing Countries: Lessons from Kenya," *World Development* 26, no. 6 (1993): 901–923.

40. H. M. Mathur, "Participatory Development—Some Areas of Current Concern," *Sociological Bulletin* 46, no. 1 (March 1997): 53–59.

41. D. Ghai, "Participatory Development: Some Experiences from Grassroots Experiences," Discussion Paper No. 5 (Geneva: UNRISD, 1988).

42. Over 25 percent of World Bank lending has gone to the social sector in recent years, with the agency becoming the world's largest source of funds for education, health, and HIV/AIDS programs.

9

Creating and Applying Knowledge, Innovation, and Technology

Jennifer Sisk

KNOWLEDGE, INNOVATION, AND TECHNOLOGY are key resources that must be marshaled if the goals of the United Nations Millennium Declaration and Secretary General's Road Map for implementation are to be realized.[1] Although they make many explicit references to those tools, knowledge, innovation, and technology are applicable in many other ways to the development challenges described in the Millennium Declaration and Road Map.

INFORMATION AND COMMUNICATION TECHNOLOGIES

In the Millennium Declaration, the General Assembly resolved to ensure that the benefits of new technologies, especially information and communication technologies (ICTs), are available to all.[2] The Road Map describes ICTs as potent instruments for accelerating broad-based growth and sustainable development and for reducing poverty.[3] It cites the need to promote universal and affordable access to ICTs; create ICTs for development, support human resources development and institutional capacity building, and build partnerships within government and with the private sector.[4] Moreover, it suggested "bridging the digital divide" as the reporting theme for 2004. ICTs can facilitate almost every area of the Declaration, improving the quality, reach, and timeliness of many development solutions and generally enhancing information and knowledge flows, collaboration, and capacity building.

163

Transforming Government and Governance

Because government is a central player in realizing each of the Millennium Declaration's goals, developing its capabilities and effectiveness is crucial. The Declaration and Road Map make repeated references to good governance and democracy in order to improve capacity for public-service delivery, reform public administration, integrate planning, increase citizen participation in decision-making, advance decentralization, and combat corruption. Foremost among the innovative tools for realizing improved capabilities mentioned by the Declaration are ICTs and e-government. Used in support of good governance, e-government has tremendous transformative potential. It can significantly change the way government approaches its mandate, solves development problems, and interacts with citizens and with business. It can give rise to a new paradigm of governance: one that places citizens at its center, responds to their needs and expectations, and is transparent, accountable, and participatory.

Both rewards and challenges are associated with e-governance initiatives. One of the benefits of applying ICTs in government is particularly important—increased transparency.[5] E-government allows for greater transparency of government decision-making and can reduce corruption. Transparency can also engender greater trust in government and citizens' willingness to participate in governance. E-government also provides additional channels for interaction by opening governments to public scrutiny and accountability and allowing citizens to assess their performance.[6] Those aspects of transparency can, in turn, help improve the effectiveness with which governments deliver basic social services, help policymakers and citizens to make more informed and judicious decisions, implement decentralization, and empower civil society.[7] The Road Map also emphasizes the need for better access to state information, and for greater freedom for the media to receive and impart information.

Economic Development and Poverty Alleviation

The Road Map calls for capacity building in technology, upgrading and diversifying export capabilities (including food production), and improving nutrition to alleviate poverty. Technology can increase productivity and accelerate economic development and poverty alleviation. By fueling a knowledge-intensive economy and enhancing the value of ideas, intellectual capital, and the ability to innovate, globalization offers developing countries opportunities to upgrade and reshape traditional industries by establishing links with a wider set of knowledge sources and developing a local knowledge base.[8] Technology, innovation, and knowledge drive productivity and competitiveness by improving products and production processes, increasing efficiency, and stimulating innovation. Ultimately, increased productivity and technological development can lead to the growth of entirely new sectors from small and medium-sized enterprises to large industries, improvements in traditional sectors, better employment opportunities, and improvements in the quality of life.

Sector Applications

Health care and the challenges of infectious and other diseases are major concerns in the Millennium Declaration and Road Map. Technology and knowledge are particularly critical inputs to sector development. The Road Map calls for greater access to affordable medicine and drugs while supporting the process of innovation. It particularly welcomed national efforts to promote innovation and the development of domestic pharmaceutical industries to ensure medicine for all, increased research and development on advanced medicines for diseases that primarily affect developing countries, enhanced immunization and vaccination programs, general strengthening of health-care systems, access to technologies related to HIV/AIDS, and the dissemination of knowledge and research. A wide range of technologies and innovative approaches are available to meet those goals and to manage ICTs.

The Millennium Declaration also refers to environmentally sound technologies, especially pollution abatement, and calls for consideration of the impacts of the revolutions in technology, biology, and communication. Moreover, the Road Map states that all should share equally in the benefits of genetic resources and should carefully assess biosafety issues, particularly with regard to genetically modified living organisms. In the field of disaster management, the Road Map refers to the increased application of science and technology designed to reduce the impact of natural disasters and related technological and environmental phenomena, as well as technology transfer and training. Knowledge, information, and technology (KIT) practices (for example, geographic information systems for environmental management) can aid in water management, the prevention of land degradation, and other environmental protection issues.

In addition to ICTs, other KITS can help governments achieve Millennium Declaration cross-sector goals, including biotechnology and basic scientific research. For example, scientific knowledge underlies the understanding of mineral, land, forest, and marine resources and their sustainable use, and is critical in identifying development issues, such as epidemiological knowledge of the patterns and causes of human and animal disease and hydrological knowledge of the patterns and causes of pollution.[9] In biotechnology, the emerging sciences of genomics and modern genetics indicate that a scientific paradigm shift is taking place with profound implications for developed and developing countries alike. Biotechnology solutions in health care, in the environment (such as genetic engineering of crops for improved pest resistance), and industry (such as the use of enzyme technology for improving the quality of textiles) can add value for economic development.[10] Finally, innovation is not limited to technical issues but should be encouraged in a social context as well. Innovation should apply to creative policy solutions across all dimensions of society.

KIT and Development

An examination of the broader relationship between development and knowledge, innovation and technology supports the Millennium Declaration's emphasis on those tools, and presents the more complex links between them. The relationships between development and KIT are complex and mutually reinforcing. As the UN's *2001 Human Development Report* notes, technology is not a reward of development but is a tool, much like education, for development. Nor is it a dichotomous choice between either technology or development. Indeed, many policymakers and development experts agree that building science and technology capacity helps developing countries create the social capital necessary for development, particularly in a globalizing world.

Both the benefits of KIT and the risks associated with exclusion have even greater implications for developing countries today than in the past. The confluence of several factors—the information revolution, the exponential pace of development in other scientific and technological fields, globalization, pressures from such forces as epidemic diseases, the depletion of natural resources, the demography of young populations, or continued access gaps in mature technologies—face developing countries in the future. Therefore the concerns of the Millennium Declaration and Road Map about KIT access, transfer, and capacity building are of special importance.

Ultimately knowledge, innovation, and technology are not luxuries for developing countries. Even the least developed countries should develop a basic level of KIT capacity, not necessarily to place them at the forefront of technology innovation but to better position them for development and competitiveness. Although it is not a panacea, the development of technology, knowledge, and innovation—appropriately applied—can have a transformative effect, and governments should seek to unlock its potential.

KNOWLEDGE, INNOVATION, AND TECHNOLOGY SYSTEMS

Realizing the full potential of KIT for development cannot be achieved solely on an initiative-by-initiative basis. Nor is it a matter of merely importing new technologies, knowledge, and innovative practices from abroad. Equally important as the technologies themselves are the processes and relationships surrounding KIT. Governments should address the effective elevation, enhancement, and harnessing of KIT in the context of a society's ability to produce, acquire, adapt, diffuse, and appropriate KIT, whether existing, new, or emerging and whether indigenous or exogenous. The internal dynamics—including dependencies and complementarities—of those components are complex. For example, fostering medical research and development to address some of the most prevalent diseases affecting the poor will be less effective if not accompanied by concurrent efforts to strengthen national health systems and channels of health service delivery.[11] One cannot address the issue of environmentally sound technologies in isolation from economic policy and trade-related technology transfer. Moreover, innovation policy will have less impact if local learning processes are not in place. Therefore, capacity building and KIT development must address the systemic links between those components.

UN agencies, regional organizations, national governments, academics, and practitioners have examined the issue of developing a Knowledge, Innovation and Technology System (KITS). However, there is no one size fits all model; nor can a standard blueprint readily be adopted. Each country may have different priorities, needs, and capacities that will determine the look and feel of its own KITS. However, some common features of KITS development can be identified, including infrastructure, processes, and sector applications.

Infrastructure

Underlying the KIT infrastructure are institutions and actors such as government science and technology councils, public and private research institutes, academia, professional associations, firms and industries,

NGOs, and local communities. KITS also requires physical infrastructure, such as communication systems, rural health-care clinics, transportation and electricity; policy instruments and legal and regulatory frameworks, including intellectual property rights, standards, contract laws, privacy protection, and relevant trade policies. The infrastructure includes global policy-making organizations such as the World Intellectual Property Organization (WIPO), the WTO and other standard-setting bodies. It also includes risk management capability, such as biosafety issues and monitoring; research and development by both the public and private sectors; and human capacity development through primary education (general and science and math skills), tertiary education, specialized capacity, vocational training, and technological literacy programs.

Processes

KIT is not only about static products and goods but also about the associated processes. At the highest level is the overall process of catching up, getting ahead, and leapfrogging with regard to KIT development. At the next level are the processes of KIT acquisition, generation, adaptation, diffusion, and appropriation. All of these processes including learning cycles that generally come with high transaction costs, require learning by doing, and involve putting new KITS into productive use.

Sector Applications

A KITS requires strategic development of sector applications, policy, and capacity (such as biotechnology, ICT, energy, and health care), and synergies between and across sectors. KIT should take into account development in other sectors and help integrate them to create complementarities. KITS are not inherently good or bad; they reflect social, cultural, political, and economic structures of the countries that create and apply them and embody the values of that society. Understanding those interactions is critical to ensuring that KIT is relevant and successful in meeting human needs and the MDGs.

CURRENT LANDSCAPE OF KITS IN DEVELOPING COUNTRIES

The Special Adviser to the Secretary-General on the MDGs has stated that inequalities of scientific output and technological innovation exceed global income inequalities.[12] Despite specialized pockets of excellence that can be seen in some developing countries, most fare poorly on global ratings of innovative and technological capacity.

Assessments of where countries stand in terms of scientific, technological, and innovative capacity traditionally rate them according to a set of indicators. Those indicators generally include the number of patents; enrollment in primary, secondary, and tertiary education; gender enrollment; number of scientists and engineers; high-technology exports; number of computers, Internet hosts, and telephone lines; public and private research and development; FDI; or diffusion of agricultural and manufacturing technologies. By many of these benchmarks, developing countries are lagging significantly behind. For example, twenty-two nations in the world (all developed countries) account for 90 to 95 percent of all public and private research and development spending.[13] About 15 percent of the world's population provides nearly all the world's technology innovations, while perhaps half the world's population is able to adopt those technologies, and the remaining third of the world's population is technologically disconnected.[14] Only thirty-seven countries can be considered technological leaders or potential leaders, a handful of which are developing countries. Twenty-six developing countries make up the dynamic adopters, while the remaining ninety-five developing countries fall into the marginalized or other category (for which sufficient data was not available—itself a meaningful indicator).[15]

While these statistics paint a gloomy picture, many of them do not capture the local or informal knowledge and innovation that exists within developing countries among individuals and communities. Neither do they capture the qualitative aspects of a developing country's KITS. However, those and other statistics indicated the challenges facing developing countries. Given this overall landscape, the question remains how to proceed toward overcoming obstacles and making progress in putting a KITS in place. The one certain answer to this question is that government and the public sector will be instrumental in achieving these goals.

NATIONAL KNOWLEDGE, INNOVATION, AND TECHNOLOGY SYSTEMS: ROLE OF THE PUBLIC SECTOR

Governments have traditionally had a hand in the development of science and technology capabilities by strengthening underlying knowledge bases and providing the physical and policy infrastructures on which technological progress depends. They must also play an active part in developing and strengthening KIT. The precise role of the public sector depends on several factors including the level of development, existing capacities (for example, where there is a limited private sector the degree of government action will be higher), location factors (geography, regional priorities, and niches), development priorities (such as pressing public goods and strategic competitiveness), and whether the state is a direct provider of public goods (KIT or development related) or contracts this function out to the private sector.

An essential function of government is correcting market failures, and the degree to which they exist in a developing country will determine the level of government activism in KIT development. Market failures pose a significant challenge to developing countries' ability to use KITS to meet basic human needs and achieve many of the Millennium Declaration's goals. Indeed, developing countries are often beset with market imperfections.[16] Barriers to the application of technology to public goods result in serious underprovision. For example, underinvestment in fighting infectious diseases arises because the private sector does not see commercial gain in research and development for treatments for which the poor cannot pay. The size of a developing country's market may not be large enough to warrant investment in specific KIT aspects that depend on a critical mass of ideas and technology.[17] Finally, KIT—or commercial products—from developed countries do not always transfer well to poorer developing countries with qualitatively different markets.[18] Therefore a viable KITS may rely on government to overcome market barriers through supply and to create and respond to demand. On the other hand, where markets function well, KITS can operate without government intervention. An effective private sector and civil society free from excessive control is also crucial to KIT development.

The public sector should not be cast in an interventionist or non-interventionist role. Without an approach that acknowledges the imperfections of both the market and the state, a balanced and realistic view of KITS development cannot be reached.[19] The state should rather be seen as playing a facilitating role, intervening where necessary—especially where public goals are not being met by the private sector—and otherwise creating an enabling environment conducive to KIT generation and use across all levels of society and in support of human development.

Consistent with this role, the public sector can carry out two overarching functions in the development of a KITS: 1) formulating a strategic framework and policies for implementation; and 2) value-added activities.[20]

Strategic Framework and Policy

The primary roles of government in supporting the development of KITs are policy development and implementation, which can take several forms, including national strategies, enabling environments, and sector strategies and measures. Within each of those, there is a need for more sophisticated policy frameworks that respond to the complex processes discussed in the previous section.

Government can have a major impact by establishing an overall strategy and action plan related to a country's KITS. It can provide the impetus for KIT development by formulating a vision and serving as a leader. It can play a key role in setting priorities and goals and developing a broad conceptual framework based on a systems approach. To that end, government can initiate a participatory process that brings together multiple stakeholders and results in a holistic and people-centered KIT strategy.[21] As part of that process, it can also help raise awareness to ensure public interest and understanding of the relationships between KIT and development. In the process, government can also define the possibilities for using KIT in the public sector, for instance through e-government. The objective of the strategy and action plan should be to think and act in a way that suits local demands and conditions, resisting any impulses to introduce technology anywhere and everywhere or simply to imitate policies from other countries.

In the implementation stage, government can also lead in taking stock of existing technological and institutional capacity at the national and community levels and within the private sector through ICT and regular e-readiness assessments. Governments must also consider the proper timing and sequencing of policies and the design of appropriate incentive structures and institutions so that both credible precommitments and feasible implementation and enforcement devices are in place.[22] Moreover, while KITS can take more than a generation to put into place, the implementation plan should consider immediate targeted interventions that can make a difference in the short term. Ultimately, government leadership should not be a top down exercise. Community activities and small-scale initiatives throughout the nation should complement strategies and policies developed by the central government.

A second key aspect of policy development is creating an enabling environment that will allow not only government but also other key actors—civil society, academia, and the private sector—to benefit from and contribute to the development of a national KITS. Such an enabling environment would include a transparent legal and regulatory system; trade policy; conditions for attracting FDI; balanced intellectual property

rights that combine incentives and better protection of developing country assets with fair use and recognition of the interests of the poor;
telecommunications policy; security and privacy policy; commercial
policy; and environmental, biosafety, and health regulations.[23]

Beyond a national strategy, government should develop and
strengthen sector technology strategies and policies consistent with the
KIT framework and national goals. For example, in the case of ICT,
sector policies can build upon and complement KIT by focusing specifically on e-literacy, ICT private sector development and entrepreneurship, connectivity, and the applications of ICTs to development, among
others. Moreover, the KIT framework should integrate scientific and
technological policy and understanding into nontechnical sectors such
as the environment, where it can help address reciprocal contingencies.
It should emphasize the importance of the basic rule of law and good
governance for effective technology transfer through FDI or the integration of KIT into poverty reduction strategies and economic policy.
All of this requires cross-disciplinary thinking and an integrated
approach to problem-solving.

Value-Added Activities

In addition to setting overall strategy and policy and identifying general
action plans, a second mandate of government is to provide strategic
investments and value-added activities in support of KITS that ensure
effective delivery of public goods and meet the needs of the poor. Some
examples of value-added activities by government include:

Research and development. Innovation and knowledge have strong
public goods properties, which hinder the attainment of optimum levels
of investment in technology by the private sector.[24] Because it is difficult for private firms to capture all the benefits of such investments,
total research and development spending, if left only to private sources,
result in underinvestment and the loss of potential social benefits, especially in such areas as the environment, health care, and other public
services. Therefore, many people consider government-sponsored
research and development a public good.[25] Research and development
involves fundamental research from which many scientific and technological innovations arise by chance or through deliberate design. It also
involves adaptation of external or internal knowledge and technologies
to local conditions. Ultimately, government-sponsored research and
technology development can be instrumental in ensuring that KIT meets
the needs of the poor.[26]

Several challenges are associated with public research and development, in addition to resource barriers. One is to better link inputs from the grass-roots level and traditional knowledge to research and development. Another is to better connect the outputs of research and development to actual products and services (commercial or social, for example, new medicines), through linkages with research labs, industry, and small and medium-sized enterprises. Another challenge is to promote competition and avoid crowding out the private sector. To that end, government can also encourage private sector research and development and technology development, especially if it focuses on the needs of the poor, through a variety of incentives such as loans, research grants, subsidies, and matching funds.

Partnerships. Many benefits result from establishing partnerships between government and the private sector. Public-private partnerships can help overcome capacity gaps through transfer of capital, ideas, methodologies, and experience, and by pooling resources, generating economies of scale, and increasing market access. Furthermore, partnerships can distribute risks and avoid duplication of effort. However, many conditions determine whether or not a partnership will succeed, including ensuring equity in the relationship and in the distribution of benefits and determining how products will be developed commercially. Governments can encourage partnerships by establishing networking infrastructure, designing a regulatory framework to ensure that the rights and obligations of partners are respected, providing a forum for the exchange of information, funding research and development projects, and promoting basic absorptive capacity.[27]

Knowledge brokering. Governments are one of the largest producers and consumers of information and knowledge. Given their policy-making role and interest in promoting knowledge for development, governments can act as knowledge brokers to support KIT.[28] Government information and knowledge is useful in achieving many development goals and can be crucial in overcoming coordination failures across sectors. Although much government information exists in the public domain, it is often dispersed, unorganized, and inaccessible.[29] Therefore, the challenge lies in extracting, codifying, and deploying information and knowledge in a meaningful way. That can be done through a variety of devices, such as one-stop-shop portals, databases, Web sites, networks, and traditional technologies (such as print, radio, and television), and through local intermediaries. To be effective, however, government must address issues of trust, privacy, timeliness, quality, relevance, and the increasing complexity in providing data, information, and explicit or tacit knowledge.

Promoting diversity and pluralism of knowledge and information. Government is an important source of information and knowledge, but it is not the only one. Therefore governments must promote knowledge diversity and pluralism by recognizing different knowledge systems in society, including traditional and local knowledge and innovation systems based on people's experience and insight. Government, through its extension workers and local offices, can actively tap and promote those resources. It can also promote other forms of knowledge by encouraging debate within society and soliciting input from citizens on public policy issues. Government may have to purchase proprietary knowledge or engage in creative partnerships that make private knowledge more readily available to society. Government can also facilitate the development of the national content industry, including broadcast, film, publishing, software, and information services. The active role of public universities and libraries in making diverse sources of knowledge available and designing education policy are also crucial sources of intellectual and creative capacity.

Promoting the capacity to disseminate and use knowledge and information. Without the capacity and mechanisms for society to absorb information and knowledge, their full impact will not be felt. Absorptive capacity depends on many of the factors discussed earlier, including learning cycles, basic levels of education, and technological literacy. Governments have to address critical cultural issues involving the social appropriation of new knowledge, including traditional practices, gender dynamics, and factors of control. Within government, the sharing and use of new knowledge may require incentives and rewards, as well as the portrayal of those activities as a means of enhancing power and relevance.

E-government and enabling policy. Sharing government information and knowledge requires e-government strategies.[30] E-government strategies consist of enabling and regulatory policies. Information policy—laws on access to information, privacy and security, regulation of media and freedom of speech, and intellectual property rights—are of particular importance. Furthermore, e-government policies can facilitate access to information infrastructure by promoting connectivity and networking. Finally, they can address critical organizational, cultural, and knowledge management issues within government and generally highlight the importance of technology for development.

CONCLUSION

This chapter presented a relatively complex but still incomplete picture of the relationships between the Millennium Declaration, a systems approach to KIT, and the role of the public sector in development. Some specific policy recommendations flow from the discussion in this chapter.

First, governments should put in place a KIT framework that is highly contextualized, responsive to local needs, and linked to human development. Policymakers in developing countries should focus on long-term capacity building, while also acting incrementally and strategically in the medium term to focus on key MDGs. For some, that may mean emphasizing more advanced high-technology innovation, and for others focusing primarily on developing human capacity and learning.

Second, since government is only one player in KIT, it must work actively to create an enabling environment for academia, civil society, the private sector, and local communities to develop and benefit from KIT. Moreover, it should concentrate on value-added activities when market failures inhibit the delivery of KIT public goods and services.

Third, as government embarks on KIT for development, it should start with its own operations and examine how they can benefit from knowledge, innovation, and technology. Governments should pursue e-government strategies, policies, and activities together with other interventions.

Fourth, because global policies influence national KITS, developing countries should build partnerships that collectively influence international policies on KIT and that address market failures and build capacity.

Finally, governments must share information, knowledge, and experiences with KIT, particularly among developing countries. Governments should explore how to build effective KITS and ways of overcoming bottlenecks in doing it. They need to develop better indicators and benchmarks for analysis and evaluation of what works, what does not, and why.

Developing an effective KIT system requires policymakers and public officials to have a basic understanding of KIT and of the related issues that affect the ability of KIT to contribute to development.

NOTES

1. Technology should be read to include scientific research and discovery; technological applications or the physical objects of human design; techniques, practices, methodologies, and know-how to use technological artifacts; mature and traditional technologies, whether new or emerging, basic or advanced. Knowledge and innovation include bodies of knowledge and intellectual capital, both tacit and codifiable, and the ideas produced by society. See Jan Berting, "Technological Impacts on Human Rights: Models of Development, Science and Technology, and Human Rights," in *The Impact of Technology on Human Rights: Global Case Studies,* Weeramantry, C. G. ed. (Tokyo: UNU Press, 1993).

2. United Nations, *Millennium Declaration,* G.A Res. 55/2, 8 September 2000.

3. United Nations, "Road Map Towards the Implementation of the United Nations Millennium Declaration," A/56/326.

4. See A/56/326, para. 61.

5. Other benefits include improved efficiencies and cost savings; more effective service delivery (reach, relevance, and timeliness); decentralization; mechanisms for coordination; complementary channels for participation; income generation; and other economic, social, and governance benefits.

6. Shahid Akthar, et al., "Transparency, Accountability and Good Governance—Role of New Information and Communication Technologies and the Mass Media," *International Journal on Media Management* 2, no. 3–4 (2000): 124–132; and Michiel Backus, E-Governance and Developing Countries: Introduction and Examples, The Hague, The Netherlands, International Institute for Communication and Development (IICD), 2001.

7. Vikas Nath, "E-Governance and an Intolerable Civil Society, communication to GKD listserv, 12 February 2002.

8. Mongi Hamdi, correspondence, April 2002.

9. John A. Daly, "Building Science and Technology Capacity in Developing Countries," *Sustainable Development International* (February 2002): 1. Available at http://www.sustdev.org/industry.news/022002/Sdi-web.pdf.

10. Calestous Juma and Victor Konde, "Technical Change and Sustainable Development: Developing Country Perspectives," American Association for the Advancement of Science Annual Meeting and Science Innovation Exposition, February 2002.

11. Katell Goulven and Inge Kaul, "Global Public Goods: Making the Concept Operational" (New York: UNDP, 2002: 8). Available at www.undp.org/worddocs/concept-operational.doc.

12. Jeffrey Sachs, "Helping the World's Poorest" (Cambridge, Mass.: Center for International Development, Harvard University (14 August 1999): 3. Available at http://www.cid.harvard.edu/cidinthenews/articles/sf9108.html.

13. In developed countries, biotechnology may be focused on creating more attractive foods, while in developing countries the need is to create hardier crops resistant to drought and pests. Furthermore, there is considerable

need for research and development for tropical foodstuffs where tropical countries face poor nutrition and cannot pay for food imports. See Sachs, "Helping the World's Poorest," 6–7.

14. Jeffrey Sachs, "A New Map of the World," *The Economist* (June 24, 2000): 81–83.

15. United Nations Development Program, *2001 Human Development Report: Making New Technologies Work for Development* (New York: Oxford University Press, 2001).

16. See Anthony Bartzokas and Morris Teubal, "A Framework for Policy-Oriented Innovation Studies in Industrializing Countries," UNU/INTECH, September 2001; Anthony Bartzokas and Morris Teubal, "The Political Economy of Technology Policy in Developing Countries: Introduction to a special issue of the *Journal of the Economics of Innovation and New Technology*, June 2000. Available at http://www.intech.unu.edu/publications/conference-workshopreports/sussex/instruction.pdf, and Bartzokas, correspondence.

17. Jeffrey Sachs, "A New Map of the New World," 3.

18. Jeffrey Sachs, "A New Map of the New World," 4.

19. Anthony Bartzokas, correspondence.

20. They will be discussed broadly and should not be seen as the total or comprehensive account of government intervention with regard to the many features of KITS discussed above. Rather, this presents a sample of activities that may be undertaken by government.

21. UNDP, *2001 Human Development Report,* 80.

22. J. Aherns, "Governance and the Implementation of Technology Policy in Less Developed Countries," UNU-INTECH Workshop on the Political Economy of Technology in Developing Countries, United Kingdom (October 1999): 15–16.

23. Jeffrey Sachs, "A New Map of the World," 8.

24. Mongi Hamdi, correspondence.

25. Caroline Wagner, et al., "Science and Technology Collaboration: Building Capacity in Developing Countries?" (Stanford, Calif.: RAND Corporation, 2001): 4.

26. Jeffrey Sachs, "Helping the World's Poorest," 2.

27. United Nations Conference on Trade and Development, "Working Groups on Science and Technology: Partnerships and Networking for National Capacity Building," Commission for Science and Technology for Development, E/CN.16/1999/2 (Geneva, UNCTAD, 1999): 9.

28. It is useful to distinguish between data, information and knowledge. Data and information are relatively self-contained and easier to transfer, whereas knowledge tends to reside in the individual, is based on experience, and is much more difficult to transmit. Tacit knowledge is more important in the long run, but how to turn tacit knowledge into explicit or codifiable knowledge without stripping it of its context is more challenging. Context is key to development and to many of the MDGs because it reflects gender, race and culture, and influences how people value, share, use, create or interpret knowledge, and how they convert information into knowledge. See Maya Van Der Velden, "Knowledge Facts, Knowledge Fiction: The Role of ICTs in Knowledge

Management for Development," *Journal of International Development* 14 (2002): 25–37; and PANOS, "Perspective Paper: Information, Knowledge and Development," October 1998. Those distinctions and requirements should not be lost on policymakers and government officials.

29. Inge Kaul, "Public Goods in the 21st Century" (New York: UNDP, 2002): 8. Available at http://www.undp.org/ods/worddocs/publicgoods.doc.

30. For more information on e-government strategies see the Government of Italy and United Nations Department of Economic and Social Affairs (UNDESA) Action Plan for E-Government, as well as discussions on national ICT strategies, see Second Italian Conference on E-government, "Overview of E-Governance Agenda" (2001). Available at http://www.globalforum.it/htm/frame/inglese/sessioni_ing.htm.

Part III

Governments as Partners

10

Strengthening Local Governance Capacity for Participation

John-Mary Kauzya

GOVERNMENTS AND INTERNATIONAL ORGANIZATIONS promote local governance in many developing countries because it provides a structural arrangement through which people and communities can participate in the fight against poverty. To succeed, however, they must strengthen the capacities of stakeholders and citizens.[1] This chapter discusses the issues and challenges related to capacity building for local governance, with a focus on developing countries in Africa.

While the quest for good governance has being going on in Africa for quite some time, a common understanding of what constitutes good governance is elusive.[2] In order to discuss good governance or local governance we need to understand the concepts. The word governance has its origin in Greek and refers to steering. Steering a ship, for example, is not only a matter of keeping the ship afloat and in motion; those steering must know the direction in which they want to move and ensure that the ship is on course. Above all, for everyone in the ship and those waiting for its arrival, a captain can claim good seamanship only when the ship gets to where it is expected. Governance, as steering, involves institutions, systems, structures, processes, procedures, practices, relationships, and leadership. Good governance is the exercise of political and administrative authority with the participation of the governed.[3]

ELEMENTS OF GOOD GOVERNANCE

Universal agreement on what constitutes good governance is hard to come by. However, governance design workshops in Uganda, Rwanda,

181

and Liberia identified basic elements of good governance.[4] These elements include constitutionalism; the rule of law; an effective system of justice that is just, fair, and accessible to all, including the poor; security of persons and property; electoral and participatory democracy; respect for human rights; and basic freedoms of the press, expression, worship, and conscience. Other characteristics of good governance include transparency, accountability, ethics, and integrity in public and private conduct; equity (both intra- and intergenerational); an informed citizenry (through an effective free media, education, and access to information); and effective and efficient delivery of public services by the public or private sectors or civil society organizations. Good governance seeks at least a minimum decent standard of living for all.

Local Governance

If we confine ourselves to this chapter's working understanding of governance, then local governance refers to the exercise of authority at the community level. We need to bear in mind, however, that what determines whether governance is local or not is the extent to which the local population is involved in steering, that is, in determining direction, according to their local needs, problems, and priorities.[5] In this sense, governance ceases to be only the responsibility of government. It encompasses relationships among different actors in the public and private sectors as well as civil society at local, national, and international levels. These actors play different roles—sometimes conflicting, and sometimes mutually reinforcing and complementary—focusing on satisfying the interests of the local community.

While it may be true that "local governments act more in accordance with the needs and priorities of local communities than would higher authorities," local governance requires that in carrying out their tasks even higher authorities focus on the needs and priorities of local communities and work in partnership with them.[6]

Local governance refers not only to local government, but to a situation where whatever a governance organization (an international NGO, a central government institution, a local government agency, or a private sector enterprise) does is planned, implemented, maintained, evaluated, and controlled with the needs, priorities, interests, participation, and well-being of the local population as the central guiding consideration. This distinction is important because not all local governments work in the interests of local populations. Some local governments can become dictatorial and exploit citizens to serve the interests of local leaders.

Vertical and Horizontal Decentralization for Effective Local Governance

Effective local governance requires some decentralization of two types: vertical decentralization or the transfer of authority, functions, responsibilities, and resources from the central government to local governments; and horizontal decentralization or the empowerment of local communities to determine plan, manage, and implement their policies.[7]

While vertical decentralization requires shifts in central government policies, laws, and organizational structures, horizontal decentralization may take place without necessarily making legal or organizational adjustments. It does require mobilizing and organizing local communities to participate fully in planning and implementing socioeconomic activities and in strengthening their capacities to participate in decision-making.

Conceiving of these two types of decentralization is useful in situations in which the transfer of power from the central government to local communities, for whatever reason, is a slow, long-term process. In such cases, it may be possible to start with programs that empower local communities through community organizations or NGOs.

LOCAL GOVERNANCE CAPACITY BUILDING

In addressing issues related to capacity building for local governance, the tendency is to focus on local government organizations and civil servants. However, using our definition of local governance this would be inadequate because it leaves many organizations that can participate in governance out of capacity building efforts. The appropriate way to approach capacity building for local governance is first to conduct stakeholders' and key players' identification and analysis. This enables us to know who stakeholders are and to understand what capacity they possess or lack. We propose a stakeholders' analysis model that departs from the simple question, "Who are the stakeholders and key players in local governance?" Figure 10.1 offers a framework for analysis of local governance actors.

When it comes to local governance, there are many stakeholders and players in the public sector, the private sector, civil society, among donors and development partners, and at local community, national, regional, and international levels. We cannot measure the capacity or lack of it for local governance only in the community in question. The appropriate predisposition for capacity building for local governance is

Figure 10.1 Model for Analyzing Local Governance Stakeholders

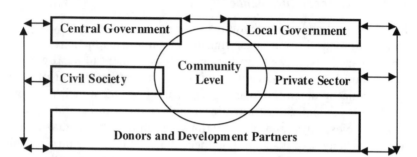

to assess each player's capacity in relationship to its roles. For example, in many countries central government authorities hesitate to embark on decentralized governance policies because they believe there is inadequate capacity at the local level. Yet, these same central governments sometimes do not possess adequate capacity to analyze, formulate, and effectively manage decentralized governance policies. Also some international assistance organizations and donor governments tend to blame local governments for inadequate capacities to implement local development projects, even though the same aid givers often do not have a clear understanding of local culture and society or the ability to work effectively in local communities. In reality, almost all organizations involved in decentralized governance in developing countries have problems of capacity. The differences are in the extent and degree to which capacity is lacking.

In a globalizing world, challenges and requirements of capacity building for local governance should always be analyzed and diagnosed, taking into account the full range of stakeholders at community, local, national, regional, and international levels. Such an analysis should be conducted participatively to allow the stakeholders and actors involved in local governance to share a common understanding of one another's strengths and weakness. The author used the framework in Figure 10.2 to conduct governance capacity assessments in Uganda, Rwanda, Liberia, and Tanzania.

LOCAL GOVERNANCE CAPACITY BUILDING
FOR PARTICIPATION (FOUR Ps + C)

Participation is not only a matter of structural arrangements, but also of will and capacity. Most advocates of local governance as a vehicle for promoting development argue that decentralization encourages local

Figure 10.2 Local Governance Stakeholders and Actors Analysis Framework

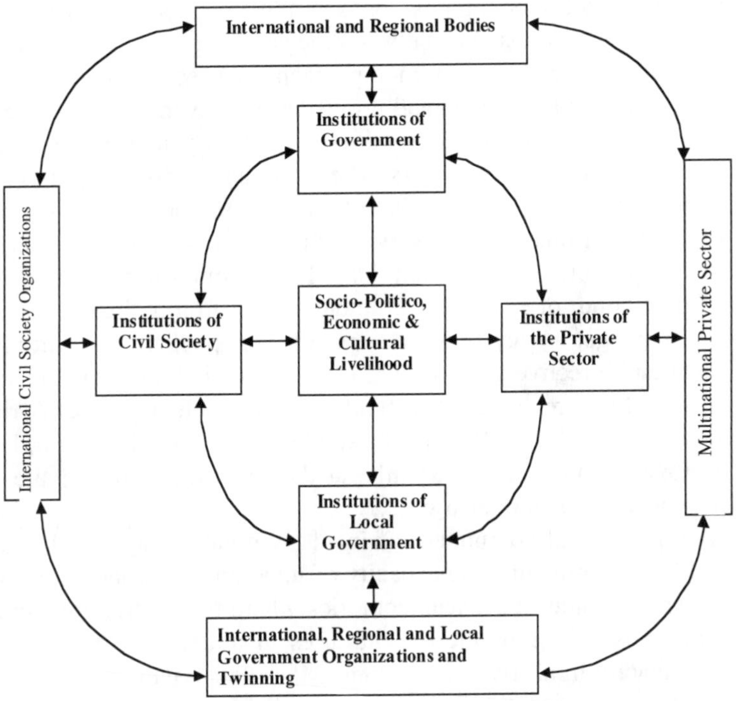

participation. However, in poor countries, we must better understand the extent and nature of the participation itself.

Participation can be examined using the 4 Ps + C concept. Complete participation involves priority setting, planning, producing, paying (financing), and consumption. Consumption leads to livelihoods, but when it is not supported by participation in setting priorities, planning, production, and paying, then it is not sustainable. The biggest problem for developing countries is that because of their very low incomes, people expect to participate in consumption without participating in paying. This makes consumption unsustainable because there is no support for production.[8] On the other hand, those in positions of authority often concentrate on promoting participation in planning, producing, or paying, but not participation in consumption. The consequence is that the poor do not see any change in their livelihoods even when they have participated.[9] Improving their potential for consumption is often more attractive than any other incentive for mobilizing people to participate in a local program or activity.

Local governance, when well practiced, more easily encourages political participation (for example, making decisions and having a say in who takes up leadership positions), production, and delivery by narrowing the physical distance between the service producers, deliverers, and consumers, and by convincing the private sector and NGOs to engage in service production and provision. However, when it comes to participation in financing the production and provision of these services, the poor are often at a loss. The challenge for developing countries, given their low incomes, is to find ways of encouraging the poor to participate in financing the services they need. Most poor people are quick to agitate for participation, but when it comes to financing, they want some donor or central government agency to foot the bill. Central governments get money from taxes paid by the people. No matter how efficient and effective a tax system is, if it is taxing a poor population, it will yield low revenues. The fundamental problem in most African societies is that they suffer from a double weakness. The central and local governments are weak while, at the same time, the private and civil society sectors are also weak.

A fundamental component of local governance capacity building should be strengthening the capacity of local communities to generate sustainable income. In African countries where the central government controls most of the public expenditures, it undermines local governance capacity in all five dimensions. Many local, national, and international financing institutions hesitate to disburse funds to local communities either because local organizations cannot provide guarantees for the funds or because the central government does not accept such disbursements, or both. This jeopardizes the capacities of local communities to manage programs, projects, and funds even when they have participated in the formulation of such programs.

A local governance policy that is conceived with capacity building in mind should include provisions for financing that would put funds at the disposal of local organizations so that they can use them to cater to the needs of local communities and provide opportunities for them to generate revenues and strengthen their financial management capacity.[10]

Holistic Local Governance Capacity Building

One of the mistakes often committed in local governance capacity building is to equate capacity building to training. Capacity-building activities usually include workshops, seminars, and long or short courses. Such activities constitute just a small portion of a holistic approach to capacity building, which assesses capacity of the policy environment, institutions, individuals, and teams before determining whether there are adequate facilities, funds, and logistics. Figure 10.3 provides an overview of a holistic approach to local capacity building.

The important point to note here is that trying to build capacity in one area without doing so in the others often wastes time and resources because, in the final analysis, the ultimate results are not achievable. For example no matter how much computer training and skills building is done to strengthen the capacity of a secretary, if the same secretary does not have computer hardware and software to do the work, the resources and the time spent on training will have been wasted. As another example, if governments do not design a decentralization policy

Figure 10.3 Framework for Holistic Capacity Building

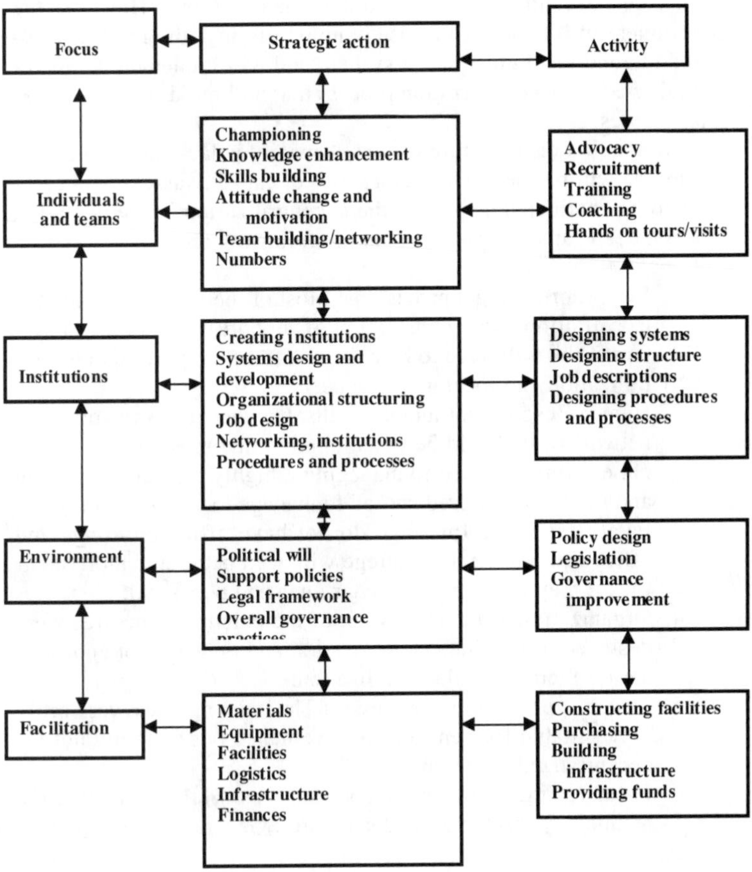

effectively in terms of goals, policies, or institutional arrangements, no matter how many funds they provide for its implementation, very little will be achieved.

LOCAL GOVERNANCE CAPACITY ASSESSMENT

A crucial element in local capacity building is the assessment of capacities in all local governance organizations. In Rwanda, for example, the government based its strategy for implementing decentralization on a comprehensive capacity assessment. The policy implementation strategy document states:[11]

> A country like Rwanda, which has been governed by highly centralized and dictatorial systems inevitably, has a lot of capacity shortages to manage a decentralized and local governance system. However, the government of National Unity is committed to installing a decentralized and good local governance system, and will implement an incremental, gradual decentralization process that will build the capacity as it progresses.
>
> Although a clear picture of what capacity is lacking and in what magnitude will be specified after a series of capacity assessment exercises to be conducted as part of the decentralization implementation process, deep capacity gaps exist in the following areas:
>
> 1. Inappropriate legal provisions: Most of the laws, including the Constitution, were constructed to support the centralized system. They will have to be reformed to be supportive to decentralization and local governance.
> 2. Human Resources: (number, skills, knowledge, motivation, and networks). It should be borne in mind that most of the personnel existing are used to managing a highly centralized system and therefore not predisposed to manage local governance.
> 3. Facilities: Some Imirenge do not have office buildings and office equipment; the Akarege will need better and more facilities if they are to attract better qualified personnel.
> 4. Organization structures: Most of the existing structures were designed to facilitate centralization and they are not appropriate for facilitating decentralization.
> 5. Systems, procedures, processes: The existing ones were probably suitable for centralized governance but certainly not for decentralized governance.
> 6. Data, records, information systems as well as information technology (both hard and software): Generally, this is a weak

area in the administrative system of Rwanda, but it is acute in local government structures which have not been using information technology.

7. Funds: Government revenue is very low and local revenues are even lower. As a post-colonial state with a centralized system of administration, Rwanda's population is not adequately sensitized about tax payment. This is a considerable handicap for decentralization.

8. Networks: (e.g., local government associations). It is understandable that these could not have developed under a highly centralized governance system.

Any capacity building endeavor should identify solid and clear objectives. To use the management jargon, these should be objectives that are S.M.A.R.T. (Specific, Measurable, Attainable, Realistic, and Time-bound). Most developing countries, especially those in Africa, have put in place decentralization measures and policies but not all of them have the same objectives. As an example, below are the objectives pursued by the decentralization policy in Rwanda:[12]

1. To enable and reactivate local people to participate in initiating, making, implementing, and monitoring decisions and plans that concern them taking into consideration their local needs, priorities, capacities and resources by transferring power, authority and resources from central to local government and lower levels.

2. To strengthen accountability and transparency in Rwanda by making local leaders directly accountable to the communities they serve and by establishing a clear linkage between the taxes people pay and the services that are financed by these taxes.

3. To enhance the sensitivity and responsiveness of Public Administration to the local environment by placing the planning, financing, management, and control of service provision at the point where services are provided, and by enabling local leadership to develop organization structures and capacities that take into consideration the local environment and needs.

4. To develop sustainable economic planning and management capacity at local levels that will serve as the driving motor for planning, mobilization, and implementation of social, political, and economic development.

5. To enhance effectiveness and efficiency in the planning, monitoring, and delivery of services by reducing the burden from central government officials who are distanced from the point where needs are felt and services delivered.

The Government of Rwanda makes decentralization a high priority policy to use as an instrument of people's empowerment, a platform for sustainable democratization; a structure for mobilization of economic development; and a weapon for people's reconciliation, social integration, and well-being. The government sees it as a means of promoting a culture of political, economic, civic, and managerial and administrative good governance. The nature and extent of the objectives pursued will determine the extent of capacity building for implementation.

In the case of Rwanda the recently concluded assessment of the decentralization policy implementation emphasizes the point. While at the beginning civil society organizations and the private sector were not involved in the policy analysis, the implementation process, given the objectives, clearly centers on empowering local communities and involving these two sectors.[13]

The case of Rwanda shows that once the objectives comprehensively target all local governance actors, the implementation process is more likely to involve a wide spectrum of stakeholders. Therefore, the very first element of building local governance capacity is to ensure that the objectives for decentralization or for supporting local governance are clear and give room to the involvement of all stakeholders.

Political, Social, and Bureaucratic Will

Most decentralization policies and programs falter during implementation because governments introduce them with political hesitation, bureaucratic resentment, and suspicion or incomprehension from the general society. Political will and support for decentralized governance is a crucial component of capacity for local governance. Political systems and politicians who are not predisposed to entrench democratic participation in local leadership do not support the kind of local governance that would empower local communities. Their tendency is to adopt lukewarm decentralization policies with unclear objectives or to implement policies for deconcentration, which only serve to make central government agents the principle actors at the local level.

Support for local governance capacity building must also come from central government bureaucracies. Because central government bureaucrats usually believe that decentralization will diminish their power, they tend to oppose or quietly sabotage decentralization policies. Yet they are the very ones who are supposed to plan for decentralization and coordinate its implementation. If they are to play an effective role in implementation and coordination, their fears about decentralization must be overcome.

There is also a tendency to believe that local communities will accept decentralization policies automatically. This is not always true. If local communities are to be involved in implementing decentralized governance, they need to understand the objectives and benefits of decentralization policy. In countries accustomed to highly centralized governance, people are used to receiving services from central governments and so they tend to perceive of decentralization as a way for them to abandon their service provision roles and neglect the people.

Because insufficient political, administrative, and social support will kill local governance capacity building, initial activities should seek to create awareness and mobilize support from political leaders, government agencies, and the local community. Sustained publicity and communication is a crucial element of capacity building. People tend to take time to assimilate policies and new ways of doing things. In assessing the decentralization implementation in Rwanda, the government discovered that

> the new legal and regulatory framework is not yet well known at the district levels. It is rare to find an official gazette at the district levels, despite that it is a valuable source of information and reference. For example, during training in December 2001, the District Executive Secretaries showed that they did not share the understanding of their responsibilities not because they interpreted differently what is written in the laws, but because many of them had not read the laws. The consequence is that, in many cases people act according to what they think is right and not in according with what is defined by the regulations.[14]

Effective local governance requires strong central and local government institutions that bring together all stakeholders. For example, it is not adequate to create and strengthen local governments' councils if a national legislature does not support them at higher levels and put in place national legal frameworks that guide and facilitate their work. Both central and local governments must be strengthened to work together for local governance development.

CONCLUSION

In this chapter, we have proposed a concept of local governance that is people-centered, focusing on the participation, interests, and well-being of the local community. Strengthening capacities for effective local governance needs to be holistic, encompassing horizontal capacity building to empower local communities, NGOs, civil society organizations, and the private sector, as well as contain vertical capacity building to strengthen central and local government institutions. Capacity building for effective and responsive local governance should include strengthening capacities of all local actors and organizations. The central pillar of good local governance must be local participation in planning, priority setting, production, paying (financing), and consumption if people's livelihoods are to be sustained.

NOTES

1. G. Hyden (ed.), *African Perspectives on Governance* (Trenton, New Jersey: Africa World Press, 1999); G. Hyden and M. Bratton, *Governance and Politics in Africa* (Boulder, Colo.: Lynne Rienner Publishers, 1992).

2. See United Nations Conference on Governance in Africa, "Governance: The Africa Experience, Working Paper 1 (Addis Ababa: Economic Commission for Africa, 1998).

3. The author developed this understanding of good governance during workshops with stakeholders to design programs to strengthen good governance in Uganda, Rwanda, Tanzania, and Liberia. It incorporates the definition of governance by the UNDP. See UNDP, "Governance for Sustainable Development" (January 1997) p. 3: "Governance can be seen as the exercise of economic, political and administrative authority to manage a country's affairs at all levels." See also UNDP, "Reconceptualizing Governance," Discussion Paper 2, 1997.

4. See www.unpan.org for official documents of programs to strengthen good governance in Rwanda, Liberia, and Uganda.

5. See John-Mary Kauzya, "Local Governance, Health and Nutrition for All: Problem Magnitude and Challenges with Examples from Uganda and Rwanda," paper presented during the Global Forum on local Governance and Social Services for All (Stockholm, Sweden, May 2–5, 2000). An interesting discussion can be found in the report of the Forum: "Responding to Citizens' Needs: Local Governance and Social Services" (UNDESA and UNDP, 2001).

6. For a literature survey on local governance, see Jeni Klugman, "Decentralization: A Survey of Literature from a Human Development Perspective," Occasional Paper (New York: Human Development Report Office, 1994).

7. Most decentralization policies, programs, and activities in African countries are conceived on the two planes, and the cases of Uganda, Rwanda, and South Africa illustrate this. See Apolo Nsibambi (ed.), *Decentralization and Civil Society in Uganda: The Quest for Good Governance* (Kampala: Fontana Publishers, 1998), and *Decentralization Policy,* Government of Rwanda, Ministry of Local Government and Social Affairs.

8. The causes of weak participation in Africa are not only a consequence of poverty. The entire issue of participative capacity must be assessed to include knowledge, skills, institutional arrangements, awareness, opportunity, and related factors.

9. For example, the Mbombela Local Municipality Integrated Development Plan states that the objectives of participation in the IDP include obtaining inputs, ensuring acceptable levels of representation, ensuring mutual consensus, ensuring focus on resource mobilization, and promotion of good governance. There is no objective concerning shifts and increases in consumption of the poor.

10. The Community Development Fund built into the Decentralization Policy of Rwanda has such an objective. It provides that 10 percent of the annual revenue of government be put in the fund for community development. The arrangement is also interesting because it minimizes the funds' administrative cost so that as little as possible of the disbursed money gets to the local level without being reduced by administrative costs.

11. Government of Rwanda, Ministry of Local Government and Social Affairs: *Decentralization Implementation Strategy,* 2000.

12. Government of Rwanda, Decentralization Implementation Strategy.

13. See "Rwanda Decentralization Assessment," Strategies 200 SARL, Under Contract of United States Agency for International Development, July 2002.

14. Rwanda Decentralization Assessment.

11

Decentralizing Governance: Participation and Partnership in Service Delivery to the Poor

Robertson Work

HUMAN DEVELOPMENT AND GOOD GOVERNANCE are indivisible. The UNDP defines human development as "pro-people, pro-jobs, and pro-nature. It gives the highest priority to poverty reduction, productive employment, social integration, and environmental regeneration."[1] Human development not only generates economic growth, it also distributes its benefits equitably, regenerates the environment rather than destroys it, and empowers people rather than marginalizes them.

Governance is the system of values, policies, and institutions by which a society manages its economic, political, and social affairs through interactions within and among the state, civil society, and the private sector. The core characteristics of good governance include participation, rule of law, transparency, responsiveness, consensus orientation, equity, effectiveness and efficiency, accountability, and strategic vision. These core characteristics are interrelated, mutually reinforcing, and cannot stand alone. For example, accessible information means more transparency, broader participation, and more effective decision-making. Broad participation contributes both to the exchange of information needed for effective decision-making and to the legitimacy of those decisions.

Through broad-based, consensus-building processes, societies need to develop their own visions of good governance and aim to define the core features most important to them and the best balance for them between the state, the market, and society. The challenge for all societies is to create a system of governance that promotes, supports, and sustains human development to realize the highest potential and well-being of all, thus eliminating poverty and all other forms of exclusion.

DECENTRALIZED GOVERNANCE

As part of the overall governance system of any society, decentralized governance offers important opportunities for enhanced human development. However, if improperly planned or poorly implemented, decentralized governance can also be a challenge that frustrates local efforts to enhance human development.

Organizationally, decentralized governance refers to the restructuring of authority so that there is a system of coresponsibility between institutions of governance at the central, regional, and local levels according to the principle of subsidiarity, thus increasing the overall quality and effectiveness of the system of governance, while increasing the authority and capacities of subnational levels. Conceptually, decentralization relates to the role of, and the relationship between, central and subnational institutions, whether they are public, private, or civic. Improved governance will require not only strengthened central and local governments but also the involvement of other actors from civil society organizations and the private sector in partnerships with government at all levels. Building capacity in all three domains of governance—state, civil society, and the private sector—is critical for sustaining human development.

Four major forms of public sector decentralization arrangements are often included in the discussions on decentralization:[2]

1. *Administrative decentralization* aims at transferring decision-making authority, resources, and responsibilities for the delivery of a select number of public services from the central government to other lower levels of government, agencies, field offices, or central government line agencies. This transfer implies two basic types with different accountability implications for resource mobilization and management and for service delivery.
2. *Political decentralization* normally refers to situations where political power and authority have been decentralized to subnational levels. The most obvious manifestation of this type of decentralization are elected and empowered subnational forms of government ranging from village councils to state level bodies. Devolution is considered a form of political decentralization, involving a full transfer of responsibility, decision-making, resources, and revenue generation to a local level of public authority that is autonomous and fully independent from the devolving authority.

3. *Fiscal decentralization* cuts across all forms of decentralization, some level of resource reallocation is made to allow local government to function properly. Decentralizing responsibilities, authority, and accountability without assignment of adequate levels of resources to the decentralized units does not work.
4. *Divestment or market decentralization* is a form of transfer of government responsibilities and authority that is done in favor of nonpublic entities where planning and administrative responsibility or other public functions are transferred from government to voluntary, private, or nongovernmental institutions with clear benefits to and involvement of the public.

UNDP uses the term decentralized governance to describe a situation of power sharing between the central and local government that is based on the principle of subsidiarity and that transcends government to also include the private sector and civil society. UNDP seeks to promote such a governance arrangement that significantly enhances service delivery to the local population equitably and cost-effectively while observing the tenets of good governance and striving to reach sustainable human development.

The Management Development and Governance Division of the Bureau for Development Policy (MDGD/BDP) of the UNDP sponsored a series of case studies that examined the impact of participation on local governance in nine developing countries. National research institutions in Brazil, Honduras, India, Jordan, Pakistan, the Philippines, Poland, Uganda, and South Africa conducted the research, with the assistance of the Massachusetts Institute of Technology. The conceptual framework for the research and an outline of the final report were developed during April and May of 1997, in consultation with the researchers.

The primary question of the research was: "Under what conditions, with regard to what aspects and through which mechanisms, processes or procedures does decentralization successfully contribute to key elements of good governance and the achievement of sustainable human development goals, particularly poverty eradication, equity building in gender, and environmental improvement?"

The research focused on local cases of relative success in each country. Good performance was defined as those instances in which decentralization activities have:

- Enhanced inclusiveness in decision-making processes,
- Improved the quality of services delivered by local governments (in terms of quantity, quality, or cost),

- Increased local revenue generation,
- Resulted in greater equity in the distribution of services,
- Raised public satisfaction with local governments, etc.

While none of these types of results guarantees longer-term poverty alleviation and other broader sustainable human development goals, they can begin to move the system in the right direction and raise the probability that the longer-term goals will be attained eventually. It is important to keep in mind that the context in which the various decentralization successes have developed is quite different. First, systems differ in the number of levels of government that exist and the constitutionally and legislatively mandated relationships they have among each other. Second, local authorities differ in their degree of political decentralization and grass-roots legitimacy. Third, local authorities differ in their degree of autonomy in revenue raising and expenditure decision-making. Fourth, local authority systems differ in the typical degree of fiscal capacity relative to service responsibilities. Fifth, the decentralization experience of most of the countries studied is recent.

These contextual realities point to the complexity of the relationship between decentralized governance and sustainable human development. The results of the research and the findings discussed in this overview should be interpreted with these realities in mind.[3] The salient thematic findings that collectively emerge from these case studies reflect the complexity of the relationship between sustainable human development and decentralized governance. These findings relate to the interrelated themes of:

- Enhancing the broader enabling environment for decentralization,
- Developing innovative institutional structures to support decentralization,
- Broadening and deepening community and neighborhood participation,
- Creating formal multiactor partnerships to support or manage various aspects of decentralization,
- Providing initiative from different levels to begin the reform process and move it forward, and
- Developing adequate technical assistance and support mechanisms—procedures, sources of finance, capacity building—to operationalize and sustain reforms.

Table 11.1 relates the various developmental objectives intended by, or resulting from, the decentralized governance activities undertaken in each of the cases. Table 11.2 describes the cases in relation to good governance principles.

Enabling Environment for Decentralization and Good Local Governance

The enabling environment was a key factor in improving performance at the local level. In all of the cases, the improved performance occurred in at least partial response to efforts by some level of government to change the environment under which local governments and community groups worked.

The variety of experience is substantial. In some cases, changes to the enabling environment were pivotal, while in other cases they were really just background activities that played no direct critical role in good performance. In most cases the enabling environment substantially emerged from broad policies and pronouncements at the central level.

The cases show a direct correlation between the extent of devolution and the margin for action at the local level. Devolution translates to greater empowerment than deconcentration, as was evident in the contrast between the more devolved governance systems in the Philippines and Uganda and the deconcentrated system in Jordan. Devolution to the municipal level is the most effective, provided the community is significantly involved in the planning and implementation process.

The legal, constitutional basis is indispensable in providing the framework for the devolution of political power, fiscal powers, administrative authority, and leverage for social mobilization of people and stakeholders to participate in the governance processes. This is confirmed by the Philippines study that found that the Local Government Code provided a window of opportunity for local officials to provide leadership in accelerating participatory processes and program activities, as well as in the Brazil, Honduras, Poland, and South Africa cases.

The amendment to the constitution to empower the Panchayat Raj institutions and related legislation has played three critical roles in decentralization in India:

- Providing a mandate for legal restructuring to maximize democratic participation of all segments of society. This mandate is essential for peaceful change to occur in society. It provides

**Table 11.1 Objectives of Case Studies as They Relate to Sustainable Human
Development Objectives**

Country	Sector	Objective	Implementing Agency	Partners
Brazil	Municipal health	Enhanced access to basic health services	Local councils through municipal health councils	Ministry of health and local health services suppliers
Honduras	Municipal planning	Improved overall municipal planning	Local council and in particular the mayor	The central government
India	Local Panchayats	Improved service delivery	Local Panchayats	Community-based organizations and the private sector
Jordan	Education	More effective management of education at the local level	District education directors and school principals	Ministry of Education
Pakistan	Squatter settlements normalization	Reduction in illegal squatting and improved conditions in squatter settlements	Specialized agency for squatter settlements	The central government and the private sector
Philippines	Village health services	Enhanced access to local health services and reduced maternity risks	Local government	Community-based civil society organizations
Poland	Private partnerships	Enhanced municipal services to attract investments and create jobs	Local government	The private sector and the central government
Uganda	Privatization of market services	Privatization of market services	Local government	The private sector and a vendors association
Uganda	Local tax collections	Local tax collections	Local government	The private sector
South Africa	Participatory budget preparation	Participatory budget preparation	Local government	Community-based organizations

Source: UNDP 1999

Table 11.2 Relation of Case Studies to Good Governance Principles

Case	Participation	Partnership	Transparency	Equity
Brazil municipal health	Open community level forums with management	Some public, limited private. Good community-based organization	Public reporting of expenditures	Improved delivery of affordable public services
Honduras municipal planning	Open participation of civil society at the municipal level	Partnership potential with all sectors	Public reporting and accountability is strong	Increased equity through local participation
India local Panchayats	Active public leadership in participative approach	Opportunity for partnerships is open	Public reporting and accountability is provided for	Equity only occurs where Panchayat leadership is exercised
Jordan education	The Local Parental Council and the committees of Educational Development	Limited collaboration between public education and that offered by NGOs and private institutions	Funding centrally controlled and allocated with limited expenditure authority at the local level	Generally felt that remote and less fortunate areas are not prioritized
Pakistan squatter settlements normalization	Squatter settlement participation in planning, improving, and managing their own services	Government in partnership with NGO Training Institute, and squatter community-based organization	Community plans and implements many of its own improvements	Leasing of public land to qualified squatter communities who chose to participate
Philippines village health services	Local village health committees–planning, education, and implementation	Local government units; partnerships with local health committees.	Committees focus on leveraging wise use of available resources	Primary health care in the hands of local people
Poland private partnerships	Municipalities negotiate agreements, represented by their mayors	Municipalities horizontal cooperation with central government vertical cooperation	Public reporting and accountability for use of funds	Same quality of service goes to all municipality members and the households in them
Poland municipal associations	Local participation in planning new services	Tax incentives, public investment, and spatial planning in partnership with private enterprise	Public accounting for revenues and expenditures	Increased tax revenues from new business applied to social service and housing for the poor

(continues)

Table 11.2 Cont.

Case	Participation	Partnership	Transparency	Equity
Uganda privatization of market services	Market vendors association subcommittees open to 18,000 vendors	Partnership with government contracted management firm	Increased revenues reapplied to municipal services	Market services, improved for the millions who use the market
South Africa participatory budget preparation	Community-based stakeholder participation	No partnership involved	Open participation in budget preparation	Aimed at thorough system of local tax collection

the basis for collaboration, partnerships, and negotiation of differences.

- Providing a framework for fiscal resource allocation and generation that benefits equitably all segments of society. This framework must deal with the fiscal means for authority and responsibility to be exercised.
- Providing guidelines for the cultural transition and that educate all segments of society. People at all levels must understand both how participatory processes work and why they are essential to society's health.

However, such legal frameworks, although necessary, are not sufficient by themselves. For example, the critical role that local leadership plays is illustrated in the case of Brazil. A broader national decentralization initiative embodied in constitutional and legal reform was initiated at the central level; however, a proactive role for the local government of Belo Horizonte allowed it to register notable success in implementing the decentralization of basic health services through the Brazilian Unified Health System. By advocating for and supporting popular participation, engaging various types of partners including civil society and the private sector, and enhancing its capacity to develop its own plan while integrating them with national objectives and goals, Belo Horizonte expanded access to its basic health coverage and succeeded in securing an increasing stream of resources from the health system and from users. While the legislative environment played an enabling role, it was proactive leadership at the local level that made the difference.

The case of Poland, on the other hand, focuses on enabling activities undertaken by municipalities to promote economic development such as the removal of administrative barriers to help develop local entrepreneurs in Bilgoraj, provision of infrastructure to support tourism and industry in Ilawa, and the formulation of a spatial plan to attract investors to Tarnovo.

Service Delivery and Institutional Structures

Many of the cases involved the creation of new institutional mechanisms to support successful decentralization activities. In some cases, such as Brazil and South Africa, these mechanisms were essentially initiated at the national level. In other cases, such as Honduras and India, they emerged primarily from lower tiers. In some cases, the mechanisms were highly formal, in other cases, primarily consultative. In all cases, these mechanisms broadened the decision-making or managerial base, sometimes through community participation, and at other times through even broader partnership coalitions.

Decentralization, through the institution of innovative institutional structures, contributes to service delivery improvement, as measured by: extended coverage (Brazil and the Philippines), cost effectiveness (Pakistan), increased payment rates for utilities (South Africa), or by subjective measures such as community perceptions. In the Philippines, for example, the Balilihan Countryside Action Program used puroks (neighborhood associations) extensively in addressing sectoral concerns. In Irosin, citizens have participated in the Integrated Area Development Program (IIADP) through their membership in the municipality's eighteen special local bodies and through representation in the Municipal Development Council and the Municipal Agrarian Reform Council. These local bodies have allowed national government representatives, municipal officials, and citizens to work together in planning and implementing antipoverty programs within the IIADP context. Both the Philippine cases reported show marked improvement in health, nutrition, agricultural productivity, and land reform as a result of people's participation in program design and implementation.

Centralized bureaucratic procedures are unlikely to succeed in the delivery of local services at the neighborhood and settlement levels. In Pakistan, for example, the Sindh Katchi Abadis Authority (SKAA) attempted to reverse its bad performance by terminating its partnership with ineffective local government councils and taking direct responsibility for the regularization and improvement of squatter settlements.

The agency simplified its complex procedures for processing lease applications by setting up lease camps in target squatter settlements to serve as outreach posts for project beneficiaries, with authority delegated to mobile or camp team leaders to review and grant leases through a "one-window" operation.

Quality and quantity of services depend on interaction between stakeholders, especially local government and civil society. A holistic people-centered approach leads to greater effectiveness. In addition to the Philippine and Brazilian cases described above, the South Africa experience provides another illustration of a people-centered approach to development initiatives at the local level. Broad-based involvement in local government activities has been facilitated through the creation by Ivory Park of a steering committee that has engaged officials, residents, and interest groups in the determination of service needs. As a result, Ivory Park succeeded in convincing its residents to pay for municipal services that eventually led to the development of the township.

Participation

All of the coordinating institutional mechanisms discussed in the section above tried to broaden stakeholder participation. In each case, there were specific attempts to involve local businesses, communities, and neighborhood groups in the process of local planning, decision-making and implementation.

The degree to which participatory decision-making was institutionalized, or formalized, varied from one case to the other. Moreover, distinction is made between direct participation and representative participation. In this regard the situations in India, the Philippines, and Uganda appear comparable to formally constituted local community governance units with elected members and delimited mandates. In Jordan the village councils are appointed by the governor. In both Brazil and Honduras local neighborhood associations apparently have no legal or constitutional basis, but they provide and are regularly utilized as informal mechanisms for involving local communities in some form of participation in the municipal decision-making processes. In Pakistan and Poland, local communities seem to be consulted on an ad hoc basis on specific issues.

Participation is efficient when practiced through institutionalized channels or through clearly legitimate, though informal, mechanisms such as neighborhood associations. In Brazil, for example, the government created decentralized health councils to implement the restructuring of the health sector. The Municipal Health Council of Belo Horizonte plays an important role in providing voice for health users and in advocating for health service reforms, including the organization of a popular movement for improvement of basic health care services for the lowest income groups. In Honduras, all communities in the municipality of Sinuapa have organized neighborhood associations that engage in dialogue with CODEM, the coordinating municipal-level body. Consultations between the associations and CODEM provide a basis for allocating municipal resources and providing services by central state bodies in education, health care, and environment.

Effective Commitment to Participation and Organized Movement

In India, the rural local government, Jamunia Tank Gram Panchayat, focuses on community-level participation, involving local residents in a wide variety of activities from which they were formerly excluded or only marginally involved, for example, site selection, identification of target beneficiaries, and actual building of low-cost latrines. Residents also provide labor and financial contributions for construction of a village drainage system and for adult literacy classes. This community participation developed a sense of unity among those involved, strengthened their capacity for and skills in negotiating with higher level authorities, and increased their confidence in managing local affairs.

While local participation is a nascent concept in Poland, it is emerging as an increasingly important factor in improved local development. Tarnovo formed citizen committees, which have played an important role in financing and implementing municipal infrastructure projects. Local residents have provided substantial financial contributions to a host of investment projects, including gas lines (41 percent), development of the telephone network (77 percent), and water supply systems (48 percent). The municipal budget and subsidies from the central government covered the balance of the investment requirements. In Bilgoraj, about ten voluntary local committees are involved in the development of infrastructure, including water supply and sewerage systems, street lighting, and road construction.

Partnerships

Many of the institutional and participatory reforms discussed above involved some degree of broadening of the set of actors involved in service planning, financing, or delivery. Partnership can be an on-off affair confined to a specific issue or situation, or it can be a regular practice.

It can also be a matter of policy to foster partnerships with all stakeholders across the board in all matters in all sectors.

Partnerships between and among different levels of government, the
private sector, civil society, and other stakeholders can contribute to
successful decentralization. Jordan's educational system reforms in
Ma'n and Irbid involved a three-way dynamic interaction of institutional actors at central and local levels. The Ministry of Education
played a vital role in implementing a more decentralized process of
decision-making and capacity building through delegation of authority,
upgrading of the performance of the ministry staff, curricula modernization, and interactions with the local community. Local Parent Councils
and Committees of Educational Development have had substantial roles
in organizing citizens' participation in planning, implementing, and eval-
uating the educational process. Moreover, the involvement of the private
sector, NGOs, and other civic and religious organizations has also been
crucial in the successful decentralization of the education sector.

Partnerships between public authorities and the local business communities have been the cornerstone of the successful municipalities in
Poland. In addition to improving the business operating environment,
the Polish cities have all privatized or contracted out various types of
public facilities, and in some instances partnerships were developed
with higher levels of government, both in the delivery of services and in
the promotion of local businesses.

Clear delineation of complementary roles and responsibilities con-
tributes to effective partnerships. Perhaps the best example among the
current cases is Uganda. When the Jinja Central Market was previously
under the control of the Jinja municipality, it was plagued by inefficient
revenue collection, high recurrent expenditures, unsanitary conditions,
and poor security. The relationship between vendors and local authorities was often acrimonious. With the passage of a decentralization act in
1993, the Jinja Central Division (a subcounty—Local Council Level 3
or LC3) took over the administration of the Jinja Central Market. The
LC3 then decided to transfer the responsibility for revenue collection
from local authorities to GOKAS, a private entity. The present arrangement emphasizes comanagement of the market by a broader coalition of
stakeholders, including the municipality, the LC3, GOKAS, and the
vendors, with the delineation of responsibilities clearly specified from
the outset. The municipality sets service delivery standards, while the
LC3 is responsible for ensuring that revenues are collected and that

selected services, such as garbage removal, are provided. GOKAS manages the collection of dues and provides and maintains key services, including water, electricity, and sanitation. Finally, the vendors are responsible for security on the market premises and settlement of inter-vendor disputes. These changes in market management have contributed to higher revenue collection without rate increases, a reduction in recurrent expenditures, and improved hygiene and security.

Initiative and Leadership

Most of the cases examined were successful because of the initiative taken by some person or group willing to do things differently. The enabling environment discussed earlier is clearly important, but unless some strategically placed actor is willing to take the initiative to implement new possibilities creatively, there is no guarantee that new laws and regulations will be implemented. Such initiative may come from the center, but in many of the cases examined here it comes from a local actor such as a mayor or an NGO.

Participation is a social and political activity that requires awareness, organization, and mobilization for it to become an effective, reliable, and predictable mechanism of decision-making and action. Individuals in key positions and voluntary organizations often play a crucial role in activating, initiating, or mobilizing public participation in issue-specific activities, interest-based initiatives, or institutional mechanisms of governance. In the studies, this phenomenon is variously referred to as change agents, catalysts, windows of opportunity, or leadership.

The critical role of leadership in creating opportunities for people's participation and partnership with stakeholders that can help transform communities is evident in several of the studies. The Honduras study highlighted the leadership of the mayor in Sinuapa, who was a consensus-builder among key players within the communities and mediator with departmental, national, or international assistance bodies on which the local government depends for resources and technical support.

In India, a relatively informal coalition of local actors, led by a dynamic local NGO, put pressure on the Department of Public Health and Engineering to improve the performance of local projects. In the Philippines, all three success cases involved strong leadership by an individual in a key position, whether public sector or civil society. NGOs and community groups have taken the critical initiative to bring about the successful reforms in the provision of primary health care services.

Leadership has also been cited as important in most of the other cases under review. In Brazil, community leaders worked together to ensure that the new health committee system would work properly in Belo Horizonte. Additionally, local councilors played a critical role in pursuing issues of equity and universality and in ensuring that these were addressed in forums where there was strong competition for scarce resources by the stakeholders represented. The reform-minded minister of education in Jordan pushed forward with some decentralization efforts that were radical in the context of that country. In Pakistan, there was a change in leadership of SKAA. The new director general was heavily influenced by Orangi pilot project, an internationally known shelter innovation in Karachi, and he was further motivated by the cessation of funds from the provincial government. Enlightened and energetic local leadership is perceived as extremely important in all of the successful municipalities in Poland.

Thus some catalyst—in the form of strong leadership, NGO initiative, a crisis that threatens the viability of the local institution—is often a critical factor in stimulating successful reform. It is important to keep in mind, however, that decentralization policymakers and practitioners should be concerned less with the catalysts themselves and more with the replicable actions that the catalysts took to bring about productive change.

Making Reforms Operational: Routine Procedures, Finance, and Capacity Building

Most of the cases involved innovations in routine operating procedures that brought in new actors, increased transparency, and created incentives for better performance, in some cases simplifying complex bureaucratic procedures. In the Brazil, Jordan, and Philippines cases, standards for sector-specific services were developed and new ways of delivery were tested. Procedural innovations were also made in the multisector approaches undertaken in Honduras and India. The SKAA in Pakistan completely changed the way to approach its core business of upgrading squatter settlements, allowing bureaucrats more flexibility in meeting their responsibilities. The Polish municipalities changed their procedures and mechanisms for developing infrastructure and in interacting with the private sector, and the South African local government developed new mechanisms and incentives to improve revenue collection. The Uganda case focused on the innovative partnership arrangement for managing the Jinja market, but the procedures that were developed to implement and sustain this arrangement were equally important.

Mobilizing adequate resources for the local communities to pursue their goals effectively is a major challenge in decentralization, particularly since the requisite fiscal powers are seldom devolved on a significant scale. The majority of the cases also involved financing innovations that either brought new resources from higher levels or cost sharing among various partners. The Philippines presents the clearest evidence of the transfer of a significant level of resources to local levels (40 percent of internal revenues) and the devolution of some fiscal powers. Moreover, the primary health care innovations in the Philippines have been financed from various sources, including the municipality's share of the internal revenue, appropriations from sectoral departments, contributions from neighborhood members, and revenues from income-generating projects. Service-specific decentralization in Brazil and Jordan brought both new resources and cost sharing among partners. In Honduras and India, local resource mobilization was enhanced and additional resources from higher levels of government were tapped. The SKAA was forced to raise revenue from its activities and to become financially independent when the resources provided by the central government were cut. The Polish cases all involved substantial local cost recovery and mobilization of capital from the private sector. In South Africa, local communities dramatically increased contributions to finance local service delivery. Finally, in Uganda, the partnership approach to managing the Jinja market led to substantial increases in market fee yields.

In all of the cases examined, there has been some type of technical assistance, training or capacity building. In Brazil, educational programs were developed to stimulate community interest and participation in the health service reforms. Similar efforts were also required in the Honduras and India cases to more fully involve residents unaccustomed to or disinterested in working closely with the local governments. In Ivory Park in South Africa, the local authority made substantial efforts to inform and communicate with citizens, and there were also educational campaigns financed by the central government.

LESSONS LEARNED

The cases provide many lessons that governments can use in designing and implementing decentralization, partnering, and participation policies.

1. The broader enabling environment for decentralization, including government policies and attitudes about local governments,

is typically important for reform, but the degree of significance varies.

All of the cases under review here were involved for at least some time in decentralization and local governance efforts considerably broader than the specific innovations studied in the cases. A strong national enabling framework, however, clearly does not guarantee successful decentralization. Many other elements need to be developed to facilitate success in decentralization, for example, effective participation, equitable partnerships, capacities at the local and central levels, innovative leadership, and sufficient resources.

2. Carefully crafted new institutional structures that go beyond the common "business as usual" approach and alleviate the resistance of existing institutions to change can play an important role in supporting decentralization.

The form of institutional innovation to support decentralization can vary with local circumstances, but there is evidence that innovative local government in partnership with local communities can be more effective in delivering services than central bureaucracies. Additional lessons specific to service delivery include the following.

First, there are contradictions in attempts to involve the formal private sector in service delivery to people living in poverty, as the Brazil study clearly articulated. The principal contradiction facing the Brazilian health system is in financing the higher cost of professional care needed by the very young and the aging. When there is a lack of funds from central governmental sources, negotiations are marked by controversies and political confrontations in attempts to change the distribution of funds. This, coupled with the fact that private medical professionals resist the hardship involved in working in rural areas and poor communities for lower compensation, engages the health system in a no-win battle to provide the level of professional services needed by the poor.

Second, in the area of local economic development, the Poland study confirmed the lesson learned elsewhere that infrastructure development and land use planning are more important factors in attracting investment than are tax incentives. Third, the Uganda study observed the lesson that the success of a decentralization and privatization strategy is contingent on democratic organizational structures and processes; clear distribution of duties, obligations, and rights under a legitimate framework; and complementary and compatible interests, roles, rights, and obligations. Fourth, the participation of people and partnership with all stakeholders facilitates a holistic approach to development management in which it is no longer adequate to deal with narrow sectoral concerns in isolation from other closely interrelated factors. Finally, a holistic people-centered approach to service delivery leads to greater effectiveness in the achievement of well-being values.

3. Enhanced community and neighborhood participation, if appropriately structured and implemented, are often critical in improving successful local government activities.

Effective mechanisms for community participation must be credible and must include marginalized groups in a meaningful way. Innovative local leaders and civil society organizations have a vital role in stimulating participation around issues, interests, causes, and visions that engage people in civic life. There is no automatic recipe, but it is clear that appropriately conceived participatory mechanisms can more fully connect people to their local governments and make local officials more accountable to local residents.

Five additional lessons can be articulated with regard to participation. First, decentralized decision-making facilitates community involvement in the planning and execution of service upgrading schemes and in emphasizing cost-effectiveness by specifying affordable standards of service provision (Pakistan). Second, public management with the participation of society helps foster an atmosphere of mutual trust and a culture of cooperation. This leads to greater awareness and responsiveness, legitimacy, and improved services (Brazil).

Third, apathy to civil society and paternalism combined with bureaucratic resistance together form a major obstacle to decentralization and citizen participation (Honduras). Fourth, the possible negative effects of administrative and professional shortcomings in a municipal administration can be reduced when civil society participates in advising and monitoring the performance of a municipal corporation (Honduras). Fifth, the Honduras, India, and Philippine studies suggest the following lessons learned about the role of leadership:

- The promotion of citizen participation must include influencing the mayor to adopt participatory management practices and facilitating greater civil society involvement in municipal management.

- The role played by local leadership is critical for effective grassroots change.
- In the initiation of programs that involve the people, a change agent with whom the people can identify must be able to organize the people and enable them to plan and implement their own programs.

4. Appropriately designed partnerships among different interested parties can lead to major improvements in the way local governments do business.

The actors to be included and the degree of formality in the relationship may vary with circumstances, but it is clear that each partner must know their responsibilities and be held accountable to perform if the partnership is to work well. In addition, vertical coordination is needed to deal with the conflicts that can develop when there are several levels of relative autonomy within the same national system. Performance weakness at the state level in organizing and coordinating a network of regionalized, hierarchic, innovative health services may put at risk any improvements achieved by the municipality. There is an inherent dilemma in segmentating the health system into public and private systems. The providers of public services face critical financial barriers in acquiring the qualitative services that are generally only available to and affordable by private enterprise. Another issue is the differential in remuneration between public and private personnel (Brazil). An external development organization (an NGO in the Honduras case) with sufficient economic resources may usurp the leadership role of the local civil society and mayor by forming temporary alliances to develop its own plans and organize citizens to achieve its objectives. This may result in improved services, but it is not sustainable because of the excessive dependence on an element outside the community.

5. Decentralization is normally thought of as a central government undertaking, but motivated actors from various levels of government and society can play a crucial role in initiating and energizing decentralization and local government reforms.

Although the impetus for decentralization and good local government performance can come from the center, this is not always the case. Local governments took largely independent major initiative in Honduras, India, and Uganda. Individuals were credited with substantial responsibility for driving success in a few cases, such as the mayors in Honduras and one of the Philippines cases. NGOs took the lead on reforms in two of the Philippines cases and were integral in the Pakistan case. Leaders at various levels—local government and community, public sector, and private sector—if aware of opportunities, properly motivated, and adequately informed can play an important role in stimulating important decentralization reforms. Indeed, the political will on the part of a local leader, mayor, or corporation director to create opportunities for participation and partnership is a critical factor in determining the actual extent and quality of participation. The role of mayors and other local leaders in several of the studies—Brazil, Honduras, India, Pakistan, Philippines, and Poland—demonstrates this.

6. Decentralization reform programs need to integrate key components of local governance and service delivery systems rather than focus on single dimensions.

Improving technical capacity cannot guarantee better decentralized governance if political consultation mechanisms are not also developed to determine the preferences of the people. Simply developing new political mechanisms does not necessarily lead to greater accountability if local governments do not have the technical capacity to deliver what the local people want. Neither improved local government technical skills nor innovative ways of consulting communities will result in good performance if the financial resources required to deliver services are not available. In the Brazil, Honduras, and Philippines cases, for example, some attention was given to improving skills, improving governance, and raising adequate resources.

7. Certain vital support components are required to make operational and then sustain decentralization reforms.

No matter what the motivation level and the suitability of institutional arrangements, certain support functions and reforms are needed to decentralize and strengthen local governments. Basic operating procedures consistent with the reform objectives are required. This often involves simplifying and consolidating status quo bureaucratic procedures, improving their transparency, allowing greater flexibility, and developing incentives for good performance. Although access to funds is no guarantee of good performance, mobilizing adequate revenue sources is another key concern. This often involves some sort of partnership among levels of government, NGOs, and private firms; a degree of local contribution seems to connect people to local activities. Finally, it is necessary to provide appropriate technical assistance, training, capacity building, and information. In situations where democracy is evolving and people do not expect much from local governments, higher levels of government, and NGOs may have to educate local people about their rights and responsibilities as local government constituents.

8. Successful decentralization is a process of gradually and strategically building capacity and trust, not just a goal or output.

Local governance institutions need to be nurtured to maturity as quickly as possible, but they need time to be able to develop their capacities and a tradition of democratic and effective governance practice. Imposing standards of effectiveness and efficiency that are not fully mastered by central government institutions after decades of training and practice on fledgling local institutions is not only unrealistic, it also undercuts the latter's confidence and motivation. In all of the cases considered here, the success did not come about immediately, and those driving the reforms did not try to do everything at once.

In Brazil and Honduras, for example, the multiactor committees needed time to develop and become operational, and all of the actors had to learn to think about service delivery and their respective roles in a different way. In the Pakistan case, substantial failures led to increasingly more radical and more effective experimentation with new ways of doing business. In the Philippines case, the reforms began with a focus on one sector and gradually incorporated other sectors. Thus, decentralization reforms are best started in a limited and strategic way. If success with less complex tasks can be demonstrated early on and well marketed, reformers can use the foundation of good performance, however modest, to build on. Developing the capacities of a governance system to function as a whole requires that a development perspective and systems approach to capacity development be taken. Learning by doing is the basic mode of capacity acquisition, complemented by creating demand-driven opportunities to accelerate learning. Finally, the whole system of governance must function on people-centered values and principles through community-led strategies, creating enabling environments at every level for optimal performance and progress on the ground.

9. Decentralization can help to achieve sustainable human development goals, but this is a long-term process.

   Many of the decentralization innovations seem to lead to improved service delivery, but the extent to which this genuinely increases the incomes of the poor and better integrates them into society is a longer-term concern. Even in the short term, however, the cases examined have made some demonstrable progress in the right direction. Providing the poor with better access to basic services may not guarantee that their incomes will increase in the near term, but it does improve the quality of their daily existence and increases their chances to lead lives that are more productive. In addition, some of the process and political reforms undertaken in these cases have at least begun to incorporate marginal members of society more fully into the way public decisions are made. This type of empowerment can lay the foundation for more engaged citizens gradually to take greater control over their own lives. Ultimately, however, ensuring adequate local economic growth is needed to ensure that human development goals can be achieved.

10. All of the actors involved in decentralization—from communities to local governments to central governments to international donors—must make an effort to learn from experiences to date.

    The cases provide some lessons that can be used to improve future performance. Central governments need to understand the importance of setting a national climate conducive to good governance and supporting lower levels of government and civil society as they move forward with reform. Local governments need to realize that they can independently take some important actions to improve governance and local government performance—they do not have to stand idly by until the center moves forward. NGOs and citizens should see that they need not wait for the public sector to act—there may be steps they can take to pressure the government to move forward with reforms. At the same time they need to be careful not to substitute communities but rather work with them. Donors need to accept that decentralization is a long-term process requiring a great deal of national consensus building. At the community level, intensive outside promotion of decentralization may sometimes be counterproductive if those who resist the process become middle agents, provide misinformation to a passive civil society, substitute the community, and benefit from the process (Honduras). All actors should recognize that they must work together in creative and mutually supportive ways to make local governments more effective.

CONCLUSION

The case studies covered in this synthesis vary widely in the range of issues that they covered and the particular aspects on which they focused. The contextual realities are also widely different, covering areas such as deconcentration with limited popular participation to devolution with wider and more effective participation. The studies support the initial hypothesis posited in the research framework regarding a positive relationship between effective service delivery at the local level and decentralized governance.

Decentralized governance can contribute to sustainable human development. The evidence is primarily for first round effects, such as participation by previously excluded groups and the extension of basic services to them. Such results suggest at least modest improvements in the quality of life for people at the local level. More time and experience is required to understand whether and how such results eventually affect aspects of poverty alleviation related to sustainable development, such as income generation.

Effectiveness of service delivery at the local level is highly enhanced and can be sustained only if certain conditions are met by the decentralized system of governance. The range of parameters includes institutional structures, resources, skills, and capacities at both central and local levels; participation; and partnerships as well as local leadership. Centralized bureaucratic procedures are unlikely to succeed in delivering local services at the neighborhood or settlement level. Centralization precludes recognition of local needs and preferences, stifles local participation, and slows response to changing situations. Cost effectiveness is impaired and cost recovery possibilities are diminished because beneficiaries are not owners and stakeholders in the process. Bureaucratic approaches to service delivery that rule out community involvement are unable to tap the considerable human and financial resources of the beneficiaries and maintain the dependent status of the recipients. Deconcentration is an important first step in policy formation.

Decentralization can help create an enabling environment for a holistic people-centered approach to development management. In all of the cases, decentralization was critical in broadening local participation in many aspects of local development—planning, design, implementation, monitoring, and evaluation. Many of the cases show how involving the community in these activities can help improve local government performance. Some of the cases also provide evidence that local people were more satisfied with the decentralized decision-making processes than with the systems they replaced, suggesting a degree of empowerment and improved governance.

Partnerships between government and local development actors help facilitate positive initiatives for development because different stakeholders complement one another to obtain better results. The more diverse the partnering, the more comprehensive the outcome and impact. Additionally, central governments that provide a mandate for legal restructuring to maximize democratic participation from all segments of the society also provide the basis for peaceful change to occur in society as well as the basis for participation, partnerships, and transparency in decision-making that promotes negotiation of differences.

Providing mechanisms for citizen participation through legal frameworks is essential but not always sufficient. The leadership style of the mayor or other local leaders and their readiness to open up opportunities for promoting citizen participation is also critical. When civil society has not evolved its capacities enough to leverage the opportunity to participate, dynamic leadership helps in securing popular participation.

With regard to sustainability, the studies present clear evidence of the positive relationships between people's participation and the likelihood that improvements will be sustained. Sustainability in financial terms can be achieved by focusing simultaneously on issues of cost-effectiveness and cost-recovery.

Decentralization does not always result in a more participatory approach to development management. It does not always foster greater partnership with other stakeholders, nor always lead to more effective service delivery and hence to improved quality of life for people at the grassroots. However, the right combination of all these elements is more likely to meet the needs of people at the local level and improve the quality of their lives. Thus where there is clear devolution of decision-making powers, combined with sharing commensurate resources and other enabling environment policies, decentralization is most likely to make a positive difference at the local level.

This probability in turn will be increased if these features of decentralized governance are combined with strong capacity building measures at the central and local levels, effective coordination mechanisms, clear accountability to all stakeholders, dynamic local leadership that mobilizes effective participation, and equitable partnerships with all key stakeholders. Under these circumstances, the probabilities are strong that service delivery quality and quantity will improve and there will be measurable improvements in people's quality of life.

NOTES

1. United Nations Development Programme, *Human Development Report 1996* (New York: UNDP, 1996).

2. G. Shabbir Cheema and Dennis A. Rondinelli (eds.), *Decentralization and Development* (Beverly Hills, CA: Sage Publications, 1983).

3. Ten national research institutes conducted these studies: The Jordan Institute of Public Administration, Amman, Jordan (Team Leader: Dr. Zuhairal-Kayed; Team Members: Dr. Mohammed Ta'Amneh, Dr. Awni Halseh, and Mr. Mutaz Assaf); the Social Policy Development Centre, Karachi, Pakistan (Dr. Aisha Ghaus-Pasha); Makerere Institute of Social Research, Kampala, Uganda (Dr. Harriet Birungi, Betty Kwagala, Nansozi Muwanga, Tobias Onweng and Eirik Jarl Trondsen); Local Government Centre, University of the Philippines, Quezon City, The Philippines (Dr. Proserpina Domingo Tapales); Center for Policy Studies, Johannesburg, South Africa (Steven Friedman, Richard Humphries, Paul Thulare, and Tebogo Mafakoana); Governance School of Minas Gerais, Belo Horizonte, Brazil (Merces Somarriba, Edite Novais da Mata Machado, Telma Maria Concalves Menicucci); Society for Participatory Research in Asia, New Delhi, India (Mr. Chandan Datta); the European Institute for Regional and Local Development, University of Warsaw (Prof. Grzegorz Gorzelak, Bohdan Jalawiecki, Wojciech Dziemaianowicz, Wojciech Roszkowski, and Tomasz Zarcycki); the Centre for Social and Economic Research, Warsaw, Poland (Richard Woodward); and Centro de Documentacion de Honduras (CEDOH), Tegucigalpa, Honduras (Leticia Salomon and Dr. Oscar Avila). The synthesis of the case studies benefited from inputs from Prof. Paul Smoke, Dr. Jan Loubser, and Mr. George Walters. Further synthesis and editing was done by Mr. Mounir Tabet and Ms. Elena Marcelino. Dr. Shabbir Cheema and Ms. Kendra Collins provided substantive support for the research program overall.

12

Partnering for Development: Government–Private Sector Cooperation in Service Provision

Dennis A. Rondinelli

THE PRIVATE SECTOR is playing increasingly important roles in producing goods and providing services that were once considered public and therefore exclusively the responsibility of governments.[1] Public-private partnerships (PPPs) and other forms of cooperation between the private sector and local and national governments are used frequently around the world to develop and expand energy and utility networks and services; extend telecommunications and transportation systems; construct and operate water, sewer, and waste treatment facilities; and provide health, education, and other services.[2] In many developing countries, governments are also using PPPs to finance and manage toll expressways, airports, shipping ports, and railroads and to reduce environmental pollution, build low-cost housing, and develop ecotourism.[3]

Governments and the private sector are cooperating to provide services and infrastructure through a variety of mechanisms including contracts and concessions, build-operate-and-transfer arrangements, public-private joint ventures, and informal and voluntary cooperation.[4] Governments are also deregulating many industries and allowing the private sector to compete with public agencies and state enterprises. They are "corporatizing" state-owned enterprises (SOEs) that are not privatized, requiring them to compete with private firms and cover their costs and manage their operations more efficiently. They are allowing or encouraging businesses, community groups, cooperatives, private voluntary associations, small enterprises, and other NGOs to offer social services. Some countries use PPPs as an intermediate phase in the process of privatizing SOEs or as an alternative to full-scale privatization.

WHY ARE GOVERNMENTS AND
THE PRIVATE SECTOR COOPERATING?

Interest in PPPs and other forms of government-private sector cooperation has emerged in countries around the world for a variety of reasons.
Neither national nor local governments in most countries have sufficient
budgetary resources to extend services and infrastructure or to subsidize
inefficient state enterprises or agencies. The UNDP points out that in
developing countries "the current and projected revenue base of most
municipalities is inadequate to finance capital improvements and associated operating costs . . . [and] many municipalities have large debt
obligations, leaving little room for major new loans."[5]

Public dissatisfaction with the quality and coverage of government-
provided services and the slowness with which national and local governments extend infrastructure often pressure them to seek more private
sector participation. Prior to the reform and introduction of private sector
participation in the telecommunications sector in Jordan, for example, the
country had a telephone service penetration rate of only about seven lines
per 100 population, and about 72 percent of those lines were concentrated
in Amman. More than 120,000 people were on the waiting list to obtain
service, and the waiting time for a telephone line was nearly nine years.[6]
The state-owned telephone monopoly could not meet growing demand for
telecommunications services from businesses seeking to become competitive in regional and global markets or provide data communications, cellular mobile, and satellite-based services that were in great demand.
Before Thailand began inviting private firms to help expand its telecommunications systems, the Telephone Organization of Thailand, a state-
owned enterprise, had a waiting list of close to one million and a near ten-
year wait time for responding to customer demand.[7]

Experience suggests that many goods and services for which people
can pay—transportation, telecommunications, electric power, piped
water, or housing—can be delivered more efficiently by involving the
private sector.[8] Involving the private sector often brings stronger managerial capacity, access to new technology, and specialized skills that
governments cannot afford to develop on their own.

Economic globalization is also creating strong pressures on private
firms to respond more flexibly to rapidly changing world markets and to
gain access to modern transportation and telecommunications systems
that facilitate international trade and investment. They can fill a void
in countries where governments are slow to respond to demands for
the technologically sophisticated infrastructure and services on which

improvements in economic competitiveness depend.[9] Moreover, international assistance organizations such as the World Bank and the International Finance Corporation often require, as a precondition for infrastructure loans to developing countries, that governments mobilize private investment and improve public service delivery. Privatization of SOEs is usually a basic component of economic reform programs, and PPPs can help privatize commercially viable services.

WHAT ARE THE POTENTIAL ADVANTAGES OF PUBLIC-PRIVATE COOPERATION?

Forming public-private partnerships to assume functions that were formerly public sector responsibilities has potential benefits for both citizens and governments. PPPs can increase competition and efficiency in service provision, expand coverage, and reduce delivery costs. As the British government points out, PPPs allow optimal overall risk allocation between the public and private sectors, facilitating risk distribution to the organizations that can most effectively manage it.[10] Involvement of the private sector ensures that projects and programs are subject to commercial discipline and sound financial due diligence. Moreover, the private sector can often more efficiently manage the entire supply chain needed to provide and distribute goods and services than can government agencies. Public-private partnerships can introduce new ideas for designing programs and projects and provide greater synergy between design and operation of facilities. Through public-private partnerships, governments can avoid expensive overspecification and design of public assets and focus on the life-of-project costs of initiating new activities or building new facilities.

By outsourcing or working in partnership with the private sector, governments can benefit from the strong incentives for private firms to keep costs down. Often, private firms can avoid the bureaucratic problems that plague national and municipal governments, and they can experiment with new technology and procedures. PPPs allow government to extend services without increasing the number of public employees and without making large capital investments in facilities and equipment. Private firms can often obtain a higher level of productivity from their work forces than can civil service systems, they can use part-time labor where appropriate, and they can use less labor-intensive methods of service delivery. Partnering with the private sector allows local governments to take advantage of economies of scale. By contracting with several suppliers, governments can assure continuity of service. By contracting competitively for services, they can determine the true costs of production and thereby eliminate waste.

Cooperating with the private sector also allows governments to adjust program size incrementally as demand or needs change. Partnerships that partially or completely displace inefficient SOEs can help reduce government subsidies or losses and relieve fiscal pressures on the national treasury. PPPs can usually respond more flexibly to market signals, more easily procure modern technology, and develop stronger capacity to maintain infrastructure than can public agencies. Public-private sector cooperation can also generate jobs and income while meeting demand for public goods and services.

At a time when private transfers far outpace the flow of official development assistance, partnerships are often the most effective way for governments in developing countries to mobilize private and foreign investment capital for infrastructure expansion or improvement. And to the extent that PPPs achieve their objectives, they can contribute to increasing national productivity and economic output, assuring a more efficient allocation of scarce capital resources, accelerating the transition to a market economy, and developing the private sector.

HOW DO GOVERNMENTS AND THE PRIVATE SECTOR COOPERATE?

The ways in which governments and the private sector most frequently cooperate include contracting for services and facilities management, co-ownership or co-financing of projects, build-operate-transfer arrangements, informal and voluntary cooperation between government and the private sector, and passive government financing of the private provision of services.[11]

Contracting with Private Companies

Governments in countries with both advanced and developing economies are increasingly outsourcing the provision of services and infrastructure to private sector firms. Contracting is the method most frequently used by governments to elicit stronger private sector participation in providing public services and infrastructure. Contracting for infrastructure and services allows governments to arrange with private companies to provide services or facilities that meet government specifications. Generally, governments contract with private organizations to provide a service through three mechanisms: service, management, and leasing arrangements.

Service contracts. Under this arrangement a government agency contracts with a private firm to provide a specific service for a specified time. The United Kingdom's Private Finance Initiative extends services and provides infrastructure by purchasing services with defined outputs on a long-term basis from the private sector. The government uses PPPs to modernize government housing projects; obtain defense equipment; and expand schools, prisons, and hospitals.

In the United States, federal, state, and local governments contract with private organizations to help provide infrastructure and services that public agencies cannot offer efficiently or effectively on their own. US municipalities contract out more than 25 percent of their services to the private sector.[12] Services that local governments most frequently contract to private companies include street light maintenance, solid waste collection, street repairs, hospital management, mental health facilities, day-care programs, ambulance services, bus operations, and drug and alcohol treatment programs. Canada and most European countries also use private companies as public service providers, and an increasing number of developing countries are turning to private sector service contracts as well.

Contracting has become one of the most important methods of privatizing water and wastewater treatment services in many countries. In South America, the governments of Chile and Guatemala offered territorial concessions in large cities to companies that procure, purify, distribute, meter, and charge for water. In both countries, tariffs were approved by the national government, which also monitored water quality. In Peru, the government contracted to private companies many of the activities involved in water supply, such as meter reading, computer services, and billing and collection.[13]

Management contracts. Governments also use management contracts to provide services more efficiently while maintaining ownership control. Governments have contracted with international firms to privatize state-owned hotels in Africa and Asia; agro-industries in Senegal, Côte d'Ivoire, and Cameroon; and mining operations in Latin America and Africa. But management contracts have been used more extensively in Europe, North America, and many developing countries to provide a variety of services and infrastructure. In this form of PPP, a contractor takes over responsibility for operation and maintenance of a service facility for a specified time, with the freedom to make routine management decisions.

In Bahia, Brazil, the state government has contracted with private firms to manage new public hospitals that the government constructed and financed.[14] The state government sought management contracts with the private sector in order to transfer operational risk, improve the quality of medical care, and increase service efficiency. Through annual funding contracts that can be extended for five-year periods, the private companies recruit staff, manage facilities, and provide medical services for all public patients coming to the hospitals. The government pays for medical services based on a target volume of patients, and the operators receive reimbursement by achieving at least 80 percent of the target. In the United States and Canada, private companies also enter contracts to manage municipal or public hospitals; several states and local governments have given private contracts to operate correctional facilities; and some local governments contract with private companies to manage public utilities.

The Persian Gulf state of Abu Dhabi sought to bring commercial discipline and efficient management of its utilities by contracting with the private sector to manage electricity generation. It competitively tendered long-term management contracts with a private firm while maintaining its majority stake in the partnership.[15] In the 1980s several francophone African countries began using the "affermage system" through which the municipality constructs a facility and contracts with a private firm to operate and maintain it. In Côte d'Ivoire, the government joined with Societe de distribution d'eau de la Côte d'Ivoire, a private corporation, to supply piped water to households and to public fountains with coin-operated pumps. The government established rules for pricesetting, and surcharges on water fees were paid to the municipality to amortize the construction costs of the water system.[16]

In Poland, the government used management contracts to privatize state-owned enterprises during the 1990s.[17] Under the contract arrangement, groups of Polish or foreign managers could obtain the right to restructure and develop a state enterprise by submitting a business reorganization plan and making a down payment equivalent to about 5 percent of the value for which they estimate the enterprise can be sold after restructuring. The managers received shares in the SOE and could realize capital gains after the company was privatized. If the restructured SOE could not be privatized, the managers might lose all or part of their collateral. Managerial contracts have also been used to restructure SOEs that could not be immediately privatized and for which there was no prospect for capital gains. The managerial and business contracts shifted the responsibility and part of the cost of restructuring SOEs from the government to entrepreneurial managers and decentralized the privatization process to the enterprise level.

Lease contracts. Lease contracts are also used extensively for both public services and commercial operations. In Latin America and Africa, state-owned industries are leased to private companies for long-term operation. The government has leased electricity and water supply enterprises in Côte d'Ivoire; steel mills and refineries in Togo; and hotels and farm holdings in Jamaica. Companies leasing facilities assume responsibility for operation, maintenance, and replacement of nonfixed capital assets.

In the United States and some other countries, governments lease to private investors the development rights to land, water, or air space in order to provide services or infrastructure. The state of California, for example, leases air space above public highways and freeways to develop commercial buildings, hotels, and other infrastructure. The Washington, D.C. Metropolitan Transit Authority leases land and development rights to private investors to build stations with commercial and office space along the Metrorail System. The government can use the revenues from the leases to extend and maintain transportation infrastructure.[18]

Lease contracts are popular in other countries as well. In Sri Lanka, for example, local governments have for a long time rented municipal markets to private merchants. In Malaysia, the Municipal Council of Petaling Jaya turned to the private sector during the 1980s when it experienced declining revenues, mismanagement, and rising costs in the collection of parking fees. The council leased parking areas to private management firms and was thus able to retain control over parking services while relieving itself of management and financial responsibilities and still earning monthly rental income.[19] The State Railway Authority of Thailand (SRT) successfully experimented during the 1980s and 1990s with contracts with private firms to provide service on three intercity rail routes that were incurring substantial losses. The private companies leased passenger railcars and railway lines from the authority and paid it a fee every fifteen days. The private contractors covered the costs of railcar maintenance, cleaning, and optional concession services. The railway authority provided the use of railway stations and the personnel to manage them, as well as train drivers and guards.[20]

All three forms of contracting—service, management, and lease arrangements—allow the government to maintain ownership of public facilities and control over public services but also to benefit from private sector management and operation and derive an income from leases, management fees, or service concessions. Contracting with the private sector has increased efficiency, decreased vulnerability to employee actions and contractor failures, ensured protection against monopolistic behavior of contractors or government agencies, provided dual yardsticks for measuring and comparing performance, and provided more substantive knowledge and understanding of service delivery.[21]

Public-Private Joint Ventures

Privatization policies in many countries either require or allow the government to retain some share of the stock in profitable or politically strategic companies, making them, in effect, joint ventures. In Oman, the government developed a joint venture between Omani public and private companies and Maersk Sealand to expand and maintain its Salalah container shipping port.[22] In 2002, the municipality of Ajman in the United Arab Emirates formed a fifty-fifty joint venture—the Ajman Sewerage Company—with a consortium of Black & Veatch, Thames Water, and other companies to invest $100 million in a wastewater network that will deliver services to 300,000 people in the emirate. The government granted the joint venture a twenty-seven-year concession in which the company will recover its costs by levying tariffs for service to be paid by customers.

In other countries, national, regional, and local governments seek joint ventures with the private sector to overcome problems they cannot solve on their own. In Colombia, for example, the government of the Department of Caldas developed a joint venture with Aqua Pura S.A. to bring together five regional public sector groups and two regional private enterprises to manage coffee waste in several municipalities in the state. The joint venture partners helped coffee producers adopt new coffee washing technology to reduce water consumption and wastewater from coffee processing. The partnership also developed a comprehensive waste management plan for twenty-one towns in the region to reduce coffee processing waste pollution of rivers and streams.[23]

China has used joint ventures between foreign investors and state enterprises to obtain foreign technology and capital, learn foreign management and marketing techniques, increase foreign exchange-generating capacity, and promote joint research and development projects.[24] The

Chinese government also used joint ventures between SOEs and private foreign companies to make new investments in infrastructure and manufacturing facilities. The expansion of telecommunications equipment facilities in the Shanghai area, for example, was financed through joint ventures. Shanghai Bell Telephone Equipment and Manufacturing Company was taken over by a joint venture among China's Ministry of Posts and Telecommunications, Alcatel Bell, and the Belgian government to produces switches for telephone companies in China.[25]

To upgrade and expand container-shipping terminals at the port of Shanghai, the state-run Shanghai Port Authority formed a new joint venture company, Shanghai Container Terminals Ltd., with the multinational company Hutchinson Wampoa. The joint venture company, in which each side held a 50 percent share, was formed to upgrade and operate the container terminals under a contract providing for five years of tax-free operation, an additional five years with a 50 percent tax reduction, and special tax privilege.

Build-Operate-Transfer Agreements

Governments around the world use turnkey projects with consortia of private companies to build telecommunications, transport, shipping, airport, utility, and water and sewerage infrastructure. Governments in countries with both advanced and developing economies use build-operate-transfer agreements in which they buy or lease completed facilities constructed by private investors after the companies have recouped their investment and a reasonable return by operating the facilities for an agreed-upon time. In 2001, the Netherlands developed such an agreement with a consortium led by Siemens Corporation to design, build, finance, and maintain the superstructure of a high-speed rail system that will run from Amsterdam into Belgium. Financing for the project comes from the sponsors and from a twenty-eight-year loan from the European Investment Bank. The government is also using a build-operate-transfer agreement to finance and extend highways that will become toll roads that generate revenues to repay the capital and operating costs of the private consortia that will build and operate them.[26]

In the United States private companies sometimes provide the financing, design, construction, operation, and maintenance of water treatment or wastewater treatment facilities with a contract from one or more local governments. The companies provide services until they recover their investment and a fair profit, and then turn ownership over to the government. Cities extend their water supply systems through build-operate-transfer contracts with private corporations that make the capital investments in developing or expanding water supplies. Typically the private company obtains private financing to expand the system, with the city government contracting to purchase water from the company for an agreed-upon number of years for a per-gallon fee. At the end of the contract, the city can take ownership for an agreed-upon transfer fee or extend the contract for water supply.[27]

The government of South Korea is using a build-operate-transfer arrangement to develop and operate the Seoul Beltway and Daegu-Pusan highway as toll roads. It has given the Pusan NewPort Company sponsored by the Samsung corporation, CSX World Terminals, and local Korean contracting companies a fifty-year secured concession to develop a $900 million Pusan port expansion project using the PPP approach.[28] The Private Infrastructure Investment of Korea organization seeks financing and participation from private firms around the world in constructing, financing, and operating infrastructure in Korea.

Build-generate-transfer or build-operate-own arrangements have also been used extensively in Malaysia and Turkey to build telecommunications systems, highways, utilities, and water supply systems, and operate them under a concession from the government. Debt financing is usually highly leveraged and the private consortium takes a small equity position. It also seeks loans from international financing agencies and commercial banks using future revenues from the projects to repay them. These arrangements have been used in Malaysia to privatize the Labuan Water Supply System, the Ipoh Water System and the Larut-Matang Water Supply System, as well as the Kuala Lumpur Interchange and the North-South Highway.[29]

In Australia, the federal and state governments have used build-generate-own arrangements to expand public hospitals. Private firms build, own, and operate a public hospital under government supervision for about fifteen year periods. The operators provide fully accredited clinical services to all patients without charge and are reimbursed by the government based on a forecasted mix of patients. They also receive block grants for teaching.[30]

Another approach—build-operate-own-transfer—has been used to construct and operate independent power plants in China (Shajiao project) and Pakistan (Hab River project) as well as in the Dominican Republic and Costa Rica. These projects usually involve limited recourse financing in which capital is raised on the basis of cash flows and not on the collateral of project owners.

Passive Public Investment

Governments use passive public investment when they make grants, equity investments, loans, or guarantees to induce private sector organizations to participate in offering goods and services or construct infrastructures that are deemed to be in the public interest. Government agencies may offer guarantees or fiscal incentives to induce private organizations to provide infrastructure and services that contribute to economic development, or provide loans or subsidies to individuals or groups to purchase services, equipment, or housing from the private sector.

The government of Barbados, for example, created a Housing Credit Fund in the Ministry of Housing and Lands during the 1980s, through a loan from the U.S. Agency for International Development, to provide capital at below-market interest rates to private banks, trust companies, the Barbados Mortgage Finance Company, and other financial institutions to make loans—using regular commercial procedures—for low-cost housing in urban areas. This revolving fund substantially expanded the role of private commercial lenders in extending credit for housing to low-income households. Moreover, it worked with private builders and local officials who were responsible for building and land-use regulations to plan and obtain approval for the construction of housing units that low-income families could afford.[31]

In India, various federal and state government agencies have long encouraged private companies to become more heavily involved in land development and low-cost housing construction. In Ahmedabad, for example, a private construction and housing finance company played an active role in providing low-cost housing with support from local regulatory authorities. This private corporation assembled land for housing projects, obtained approvals from the Ahmedebad Urban Development Authority, helped organize cooperative societies that held title to land and performed maintenance functions after the project was completed, and obtained mortgage financing for beneficiaries from the Housing and Urban Development Corporation, a public agency. With government assistance and encouragement, the company was able to construct thousands of low-cost housing units in and around the city of Ahmedabad.[32]

State guarantees and incentives reduce private companies' costs or increase the potential for profits in activities that would, in their absence, seem too risky or unprofitable. These incentives may ultimately be less costly for government than providing services directly. Guarantees and incentives can mobilize private sector financial resources that would otherwise not be available to the government and assure that services are provided more flexibly and efficiently than by government agencies. However, both government officials and the private sector can abuse the guarantees and incentives unless they are carefully monitored and supervised.

Delegating Responsibility for Services or Infrastructure to the Private Sector

Governments in some countries are increasing private sector participation by delegating responsibility for some services and infrastructure to NGOs or simply leaving them to private enterprise. This is done through publicly mandated or regulatory requirements; by using merchant facilities; and by requiring developers to provide or financially support the services and infrastructure associated with residential, commercial, or industrial construction projects.

In the United States federal and state governments have often used regulations to shift responsibility to the private sector for providing services and infrastructure if their operations lead to public health, safety, or security hazards. Private sector organizations are required to invest in infrastructure and equipment that reduce or eliminate air and water pollution and to dispose of potentially toxic or hazardous wastes. More stringent environmental laws have spawned a strong private industry to supply environmental protection technology, equipment, and services to both the public and the private sectors. The Clean Air Act, the Resource Conservation and Recovery Act, the Comprehensive Environmental Response Compensation and Liability Act, and state and local environmental regulations have all stimulated more investments in environmental infrastructure in the United States. Clearly, investments by private companies in environmental protection technology and equipment relieve the public sector of cleanup costs and of increased public investment in the infrastructure required to cope with higher levels of air and water pollution.

Increasingly local governments in the United States and in other countries are requiring private developers of residential areas, commercial facilities, or industrial sites to provide the infrastructure and services required to treat wastewater and dispose of solid and hazardous wastes, and to provide access roads, utilities, and other types of facilities. The requirements for developers to finance infrastructure improvements directly may be a part of a local government's subdivision or building permit requirements or may be imposed through development fees, impact fees, purchase of sewer access rights, capacity credits, or other forms of exaction. Most state governments that have experienced rapid population growth and large-scale residential, commercial, and industrial development have given municipal governments the authority to impose development and impact fees to cover the costs of infrastructure construction or extension.[33]

Voluntary or Informal Public-Private Cooperation

Globalization and the widespread expansion of the operations of transnational corporations has led to increasing voluntary cooperation among private corporations, corporate foundations, international organizations, and national and local governments in addressing important social issues and in providing public services. For example in 2002, the Conrad N. Hilton Foundation pledged nearly $41 million to a PPP with the U.S. Agency for International Development and the governments of Ghana, Mali, and Niger to provide potable water and sanitation to rural villages in those countries. Participants in the PPP include UNICEF, World Vision, WaterAid, the Lions Clubs International Foundation, the Desert Research Institute, Winrock International, the World Chlorine Council, and Cornell University's International Institute for Food, Agriculture and Development.[34] The PPP will be responsible for drilling new water boreholes, developing alternative water sources, and providing safe hygiene and sanitation facilities and practices to more than 500,000 people in the three countries.

Through its partnership with Rotary International, Coca-Cola helps the government of India immunize its population against polio. Coca-Cola uses its extensive distribution network in India to provide resources and expertise in marketing and community mobilization, and makes employee volunteers available to support Rotary International's immunization drive. The Finnish telecommunications corporation Nokia launched a three-year, $11 million campaign with the International Youth Foundation and its own employee volunteers to help children with learning difficulties in public schools in South Africa, China, Mexico, Brazil, the United Kingdom, and Germany.[35]

The Bill and Melinda Gates Foundation contributed $50 million and the Merck Corporation matched the contribution with antiretroviral medicines, and by developing and managing a program to assist the government of Botswana in addressing HIV and other health problems. The project focuses on improving existing health-care capabilities for people with HIV infection; developing awareness, education, and voluntary testing and counseling programs; and expanding health-care infrastructure for treatment of tuberculosis, HIV-related infections, and HIV infection. The partners work with global health and development agencies, private sector supporters, private foundations, and other potential sponsors to prevent and treat HIV infection. Gates Foundation and Merck participation also helped persuade Boehringer-Ingelheim and Unilever to provide additional financial resources.

Several other pharmaceutical companies have also volunteered to assist governments in overcoming tropical diseases, especially in Africa. The World Health Organization (WHO) and national governments in Africa work together through a partnership with Merck, the African Programme for Onchocerciasis Control, and the Task Force for Child Survival and Development at the Carter Center on elimination of onchocerciasis. Pfizer works with WHO, the Edna McConnell Clark Foundation, and African governments on elimination of blinding trachoma, GlaxoSmithKline, WHO, and government health agencies have partnered to eliminate lymphatic filariasis and control drug-resistant malaria.[36]

The Open Society Institute Network, funded by international financier George Soros, developed a partnership with WHO to establish a worldwide information database to link scientists in developing and developed countries with leading scientific journals and databases, discussion groups, and funding sources.[37] The Open Society Institute in Hungary funded an extensive local government and public service reform project because it could provide information and assistance faster than governments or international aid agencies when the opportunities for reform appeared.

By working together international organizations, national governments, public interest groups, private foundations, and TNCs are also experimenting with new methods of corporate self-regulation. As part of the UN "Global Compact" TNCs and business organizations such as the Conference Board, International Chamber of Commerce, International Federation of Consulting Engineers, the International Petroleum Industry Environmental Conservation Agency, Enterprises pour l'Environnement, World Business Council on Sustainable Development, and European Business Network for Social Cohesion agreed to develop and support appropriate policies and practices on human rights, labor, and the environment. The participating corporations adhere to nine major principles, including the commitment to support and respect the protection of international human rights within their sphere of influence and make sure their own organizations are not complicit in human rights abuses. They develop standards and pledge to uphold freedom of association and the effective recognition of the right to collective bargaining; the elimination of employment discrimination and all forms of forced and compulsory labor; and the effective abolition of child labor. They also support pollution prevention measures; undertake initiatives to promote environmental protection; and encourage the development and diffusion of environmentally friendly technologies.

In many developing countries, governments leave some services entirely to NGOs or allow them to provide services of a higher quality or more comprehensive coverage than those provided by the public sector. For decades, cooperative organizations, trade unions, women's and youth clubs, and religious groups in Asia have all been involved in some aspect of public service provision.[38] NGOs and religious organizations provide health, education, and training programs that supplement those offered by governments.[39]

In the Philippines, for example, religious organizations have played an important role in supplementing the public education system by operating elementary and secondary schools, as well as colleges and universities. They run hospitals and health clinics and provide other social services that are either not available from the government or that are considered inadequate. In Vietnam, individual physicians or groups of medical personnel have been allowed to open private health clinics, especially in crowded urban neighborhoods, to improve access to health services and relieve pressures on state hospitals that lack sufficient beds, equipment, and medicines to provide adequate health care.[40] In India, the government registers and assists housing cooperative societies that buy land and obtain financing to build low-cost housing for their members. Housing cooperatives account for a substantial portion of all private formal housing production in urban areas in India.

WHAT CONDITIONS ARE NECESSARY FOR EFFECTIVE PUBLIC-PRIVATE COOPERATION?

PPPs offer governments in developing countries important means of expanding services and infrastructure and the private sector commercial opportunities to expand their businesses. However these complex arrangements can create problems for both the public and the private sectors if they are not properly designed and administered. They often displace public workers, thereby generating political opposition among public officials, labor unions, and public employee associations. If PPPs are not well designed and supervised, their services can become more expensive than those provided by government. Poorly designed and inadequately analyzed projects have failed in both rich and poor countries. Corruption can undermine public trust in PPPs if the contracting process is not transparent and carefully supervised. Lack of sufficient competition can turn PPPs into private monopolies that operate no more efficiently than SOEs. Overly restricting concessions or creating too many can deprive PPPs of economies of scale. Too-stringent government regulation can lead to deficiencies in service provision. Too lax and it may not hold private service providers sufficiently accountable.[41]

The cost of contract management can be substantial. In all cases, governments must compare carefully the costs of contracting out with the costs of providing services directly. The involvement of the private sector in providing services that were formerly free or that were subsidized by the government can increase their price and place poor segments of the population at a significant disadvantage. Governments of jurisdictions with large numbers of poor people must make adequate provision to serve those who may not be able to afford them under PPPs.

Experience suggests that if PPPs are to succeed, governments must:

- enact adequate legal reforms to allow the private sector to operate efficiently and effectively,
- develop and enforce regulations that are clear and transparent to private investors,
- remove unnecessary restrictions on the ability of private enterprises to compete in the market,
- allow for liquidation or bankruptcy of existing state enterprises that cannot be commercialized or privatized,
- expand opportunities for local private enterprises to develop management capabilities,
- create incentives and assurances to protect current state employees after PPPs take over service provision, and
- redefine the role of government from directly producing and delivering services to facilitating and regulating private sector service provision.[42]

The experience in the United Kingdom led the government to conclude that for PPPs to work effectively, the government must retain responsibility and accountability for deciding among competing objectives; define chosen objectives for services provision; set standards, criteria, and output targets; and safeguard the broader public interest.[43] National or local government agencies must have the capacity to decide on the level of services needed and the financial resources available to pay for them; set and monitor safety, quality, and performance standards; and enforce those standards and the output targets. As a director of the government organization Partnerships UK points out, "for the public sector, reforms would typically include a move from input-based to output-based contracting, which may require significant investment in developing skills and guidance based on best practices; enactment of enabling legislation—for example, to overcome issues of public sector *vires* (legal authority) and taxation of PPP contracts; and institutional reform to assist in prioritizing, providing resources for, and approving transactions."[44]

From its extensive experience with PPPs, the UNDP concludes that in order to succeed, national and local government officials must be receptive to finding alternative mechanisms to traditional public service provision and be willing to accept private-sector participation. They must choose appropriate projects that are conducive to private sector management and properly package the projects in order to avoid disproportionate transaction costs. Because PPPs often take a long time, strong public sector leadership and political commitment are essential to their success. PPPs work best when both the public and private sector partners have project "champions" as catalysts and sustainers. Such projects are sustainable if they are mutually beneficial to both government and private sector partners and if each can overcome adversarial posturing to build mutual trust.[45]

The UNDP points out that the tendering, procurement, and contracting procedures must be financially and operationally sound, open, transparent, and fair. "Any departure from the sealed-bid tender and contracting method will open the government to accusations of partiality or corruption."[46] In addition, the procurement process should

- state the desired end goal or output targets of the agreement and minimize overly specific requirements, so that the private sector can innovate and manage flexibly,
- ensure that the potential private-sector partners can be adequately compensated for or retain their intellectual property,
- include monitoring provisions of performance measures by a third party or autonomous government agency, and
- provide for renegotiating the terms of the agreement over time.

Ultimately, the success of PPPs depends not only on developing mutual trust between government officials and private sector executives, but on building and maintaining public confidence in the integrity of the partnerships. Trust and confidence can be undermined when the goals of the partners are ambiguous or when their objectives are unrealistic or in conflict. Incompatible organizational systems and management practices can also weaken PPPs, as can reluctance on the part of governments or the public to allow private companies to obtain a fair return on investment.[47]

CONCLUSION

As the foregoing descriptions clearly illustrate, governments around the world have experimented with many approaches to public-private sector cooperation. In most countries the size and impact of the private sector is growing. Private businesses, private voluntary organizations, and even informal sector enterprises are providing more of those goods and services for which user charges can be levied and from which private companies can derive a reasonable profit. Experience suggests, however, that no single approach to public-private sector cooperation is suitable for all countries or for all types of services and infrastructure. PPPs are not panaceas for all of the ills confronting governments in providing services and infrastructure.

Despite potential problems and complexities, PPPs that are carefully planned and implemented can help governments improve quality, reduce price, and extend coverage of services, and they can accelerate the construction of infrastructure and facilities that are crucial for economic development and social progress. PPPs and other forms of public-private cooperation can be valuable instruments for leveraging the resources of both the public and private sectors and of enhancing the capabilities of national and local governments to achieve their development goals.

NOTES

1. See Dennis A. Rondinelli, "Public-Private Partnerships," in *Handbook on Development Policy and Management,* eds. Colin Kirkpatrick, Ronald Clarke and Charles Polidano (Cheltenham, England: Edward Elgar, 2002): 381–388.

2. Dennis A. Rondinelli and Max Iacono, *Policies and Institutions for Managing Privatization: International Experience* (Geneva: International Labour Office, 1996).

3. J. Rivera, E. Brenes, and G. Quijandria, "The Tourism Industry in Costa Rica," in *Private Capital Flows and the Environment: Lessons from Latin America,* ed. B. S. Gentry (Cheltenham, England: Edward Elgar, 1998): 223–240.

4. E. S. Savas, *Privatization and Public-Private Partnerships* (New York: Chatham House, 2000).

5. United Nations Development Programme, *Joint Venture Public-Private Partnerships for Urban Environmental Services*, PPUE Working Paper Series, Vol. II (New York: UNDP, 2000): 8.

6. Mohammad A. Mustapha, "Telecommunications in Jordan: Performance, Policy Environment and Reforms Ahead," in *Towards Competitive and Caring Societies in the Middle East and North Africa,* eds. I. Diwan and K. Sirker (Washington, D.C.: World Bank, 1997).

7. Vuthiphong Priebjrivat and Dennis A. Rondinelli, "Privatizing Thailand's Telecommunications Industry: A Case Study of Politics and International Business," *Business and the Contemporary World* 6, no. 1 (1994): 70–83.

8. Gabriel Roth, *The Private Provision of Public Services in Developing Countries* (New York: Oxford University Press, 1987).

9. Dennis A. Rondinelli and Gyula Vastag, "Urban Economic Growth in the 21st Century," in *Migration, Urbanization and Development,* ed. R. Bilsborrow (Norwell, Mass.: Kluwer, 1998): 469–514.

10. United Kingdom, "Public Private Partnerships: The Government's Approach" (London: Her Majesty's Stationery Office, 2000).

11. B. S. Gentry and L. O. Fernandez, "Evolving Public-Private Partnerships: General Themes and Urban Water Examples," paper prepared for OECD Workshop on Globalization and the Environment (Paris: OECD, 1997).

12. E.S. Savas, "Global Perspectives on Local Issues," in *International Privatization: Global Trends, Policies, Processes, Experiences,* ed. O. Yul Kwon (Saskatoon, Saskatchewan: Institute for Saskatchewan Enterprise, 1990): 231–238.

13. Maureen Lewis and T. R. Miller, "Public-Private Partnerships in African Urban Development" (Washington, D.C.: USAID, 1986).

14. Rob Tailor and Simon Blair, "Public Hospitals," Public Policy for the Private Sector, Note No. 241 (Washington, D.C.: World Bank, 2002).

15. Taimur Ahmad, "Eastern Promises," *Project Finance* 229 (May 2002): 38–40.

16. Sandra J. Cointreau, "Environmental Management of Urban Solid Wastes in Developing Countries: A Project Guide" (Washington, D.C.: World Bank, 1982).

17. Ben Slay, "Poland: The Role of Managers in Privatization," *RFE/RL Research Report* 2, no. 12 (1993): 52–56.

18. U.S. Department of Transportation, *Private Sector Involvement in Urban Transportation* (Washington, D.C.: Federal Highway Administration, 1986).

19. Chee Hock Tan, "Use of Performance Analysis to Determine Privatization of Street Parking," paper prepared for seminar on Urban Finance and Management in East Asia (Kuala Lumpur, Malaysia: World Bank Economic Development Institute, 1987): mimeograph.

20. H. Levy and A. Menendez, "Privatization in Transport: Contracting Out the Provision of Passenger Railway Services in Thailand," World Bank-EDI Working Paper (Washington, D.C.: World Bank, 1990).

21. E. S. Savas, "Inter-city Competition Between Public and Private Service Delivery," *Public Administration Review* 41, no. 1 (1981): 46–52.

22. Taimur Ahmad, "Eastern Promises."

23. UNDP, *Joint Venture Public-Private Partnerships for Urban Environmental Services.*

24. P. D. Grub and J. H. Lin, *Foreign Direct Investment in China* (Westport, Conn.: Quorum Books, 1991).

25. Michael Selwyn, "Shanghai Bell: After the Pain, It's All Gain," *Asian Business* (March 1993): 9.

26. Michael Murray, "Does Anyone Give a PPP?" *Project Finance* 219 (July 2001): 21–22.

27. U.S. Environmental Protection Agency, *Public-Private Partnership Case Studies* (Washington, D.C.: USEPA): 99–102.

28. Natasha Calvert, "PICKO Promotes," *Project Finance* 231 (July 2002): 38–39.

29. Matthew L. Hensley and Edward P. White, "The Privatization Experience in Malaysia," *The Columbia Journal of World Business* 28, no. 1 (1993): 70–83.

30. Rob Taylor and Simon Blair, "Public Hospitals."

31. Royce LaNier, Albert Massoni, and Carol Oman, "Public and Private Sector Partnerships in Housing: A Background Paper" (Washington, D.C.: Technical Support Services Inc., 1986).

32. PADCO Inc., "India: Public-Private Partnerships in Land Development" (New Delhi, India: USAID, 1991).

33. U.S. Environmental Protection Agency, *Public-Private Partnership Case Studies,* 68–70.

34. U.S. Agency for International Development, "$41 Million Public-Private Partnership to Provide Clean Water in West Africa," Press Release 2002-097 (Washington, D.C.: USAID, 2002).

35. J. Burns, "Business Learns the Value of Good Works," *Financial Times,* December 18, 2000: 10.

36. Adetokunbo Lucas, "Public-Private Partnerships: Illustrative Examples," Background Paper No. 1 (Geneva: World Health Organization, Special Programme for Research & Training in Tropical Diseases, 2000).

37. World Health Organization, "Life Saving Scientific Information Boost Via Internet to Health Researchers in Africa, Central Asia and Eastern Europe," WHO News Release, 15/5/2000.

38. L. Ralston, J. Anderson, and E. Colson, "Voluntary Efforts in Decentralized Management," Working Paper (Berkeley: University of California, Institute of International Studies, 1981).

39. See Dennis A. Rondinelli, John Middleton, and Adriaan Verspoor, *Planning Education Reforms in Developing Countries* (Durham, N.C.: Duke University Press, 1990).

40. Jennie I. Litvack and Dennis A. Rondinelli (eds.), *Market Reform in Vietnam: Building Institutions for Development* (Westport Conn.: Quorum Books, 1999).

41. Ruth H. DeHoog, *Contracting Out for Human Services* (Albany, N.Y.: State University of New York Press, 1984); Harry P. Hatry, *A Review of Private Approaches for Delivery of Public Services* (Washington, D.C.: Urban Institute

Press, 1983); E. S. Savas, *Privatizing the Public Sector* (New York: Chatham House, 1982).

42. Dennis A. Rondinelli, "Privatization, Governance, and Public Management: The Challenges Ahead," *Business & the Contemporary World* 10, no. 2 (1998): 149–170.

43. United Kingdom, "Public Private Partnerships: The Government's Approach," 10–12.

44. Michael B. Gerrard, " Public-Private Partnerships," *Finance & Development* (September 2001): 48–51.

45. United Nations Development Programme, *Joint Venture Public-Private Partnerships for Urban Environmental Services;* see especially 32–35.

46. United Nations Development Programme, *Joint Venture Public-Private Partnerships for Urban Environmental Services:* 30.

47. Dennis A. Rondinelli and Sylvia Sloan Black, "Multinational Strategic Alliances and Acquisitions in Central and Eastern Europe: Partnerships in Privatization," *Academy of Management Executive* 14, no. 4 (2000): 85–98.

Part IV

Conclusion

13

The Competent State: Governance and Administration in an Era of Globalization

Dennis A. Rondinelli and G. Shabbir Cheema

IN A COMPLEX AND CHANGING GLOBAL SOCIETY there are few certainties on which governments can base their policies and still fewer universally applicable solutions to the problems that will inevitably arise in an uncertain world. Yet one scenario is highly probable. The twenty-first century will be an era of increasing global economic, social, and political interaction, in which states will have to play new and different roles than they had in the past. Debates over whether or not the nation-state will survive in a global society have largely been resolved. Even the most vehement critics of allegedly oversized, inefficient, and intrusive governments now recognize that the state will continue to be an important political institution that can, for good or ill, determine the welfare of billions of people. The challenge for political and administrative leaders in all countries is to redefine the role of the state and to build the institutional capacity of governments to play beneficial roles in helping citizens cope with the uncertainties and benefit from the opportunities of globalization.

All of the contributors to this book conclude that what is needed is not large and all-powerful governments that plan for and control all aspects of economies and societies but competent states that guide and facilitate economic growth, enhance human capacity, mobilize financial and human resources for development, promote and encourage private enterprise, protect economically and socially vulnerable groups, combat poverty, and protect the natural environment and physical resources through democratic, participative, honest, efficient, effective, and accountable political and administrative systems.

THE COMPETENT STATE

What is a competent state? Dictionaries define "competent" in at least three ways[1]:

1. "answering all requirements; suitable; fit; convenient, hence, sufficient; fit for the purpose";
2. "having ability or capacity; duly qualified"; and
3. "permissible or properly belonging to. . . ."

All three of these meanings help define a competent state. Clearly the state must meet the requirements of global interaction and increasing international interdependence. The competent state must fit people's needs as the citizens of a country define them. It must also fit global expectations as defined in such international agreements as the UN Millennium Development Goals (MDGs) and the Universal Declaration on Human Rights. And the competent state must have sufficient ability or capacity, with duly qualified leaders and officials, to achieve the purposes for which it exists. Finally, the competent state must be seen as permissible—legitimate in both a legal and a political sense—and properly belonging to the citizens of the country over which it exercises sovereignty.

The concept of the competent state has often been defined in times of adversity by the shortcomings and weaknesses of governments in achieving sustainable economic and social development and protecting human rights and freedoms. In the late 1970s and early 1980s—when many developing countries were undergoing political turmoil, economic recession or stagnation, and social disintegration—the state was severely criticized by international financial organizations and by internal political and social dissidents. The harshest criticisms were of states with authoritarian governments that sought to plan excessively and control exclusively the nation's economy, leading to stagnant or declining rates of economic growth, widespread poverty, and political repression. Governments that practiced central economic planning and management came under the harshest criticism. Political economist Charles Lindblom summarized succinctly the weaknesses of centrally planned systems, noting that they were characterized by:

- a strong concentration of political power and authority in the hands of a single ruler or a small group of party leaders,
- political leaders committed to achieving collective goals determined largely by ideological criteria,

- state ownership of all or most of the productive assets in society,
- centralized organization and direction of the economy by the ruling party or government,
- use of a wide range of controls (including coercion) to assure conformance to planned goals and targets,
- suppression of individual political freedoms and social pluralism,
- use of a privileged mobilizing organization—such as a political party—to guide society toward collective goals, and
- the substitution of formal organization (large, complex, and hierarchical party or government bureaucracies) for other forms of social coordination.[2]

In such states, the inability of central planning authorities to comprehend and calculate the myriad complex interactions in the economy and to raise standards of living quickly undermined their capacity to control or guide development in any meaningful way. Scarce resources were allocated neither by efficient market signals nor by competent technical analysis and planning. Hungarian economist Janos Kornai pointed out that in place of market signals, resources were allocated through a set of nonprice signals emanating primarily from the national economic plan, but also from frequent bureaucratic directives, the exchange of information horizontally among authorities on the same hierarchical level, breakdowns and catastrophes, and grumbles or protests from subordinate bureaucratic units as requirements became unrealistic or intolerable.[3]

Although the immediate task of reform governments that succeeded those authoritarian regimes was to abolish the central planning apparatus and reduce the state's control over production and prices, the failures of command and control and the complex challenges of implementing economic, political, and administrative reforms helped redefine state roles. Although many "failed" or "incompetent" states were in developing countries, governments in countries with advanced economies that were suffering from economic stagnation and social inequities were also forced to redefine their functions. Even democratic western industrial countries—where governments owned or managed significant sectors of the economy, incurred large and continuing budget deficits, overregulated the private sector, failed to deliver public services efficiently and effectively, and discouraged entrepreneurial effort—came under increasing criticism.

During the 1980s and 1990s, government was often characterized as large, bloated, highly politicized, inefficient, excessively regulatory or controlling, sometimes corrupt, and often parasitic.[4] In their book *Reinventing Government,* which influenced reform in the United States and

in other economically advanced and developing countries, David
Osborne and Ted Gaebler offered another view of the competent state.[5]
They described ten characteristics of what effective governments should
be:

1. catalytic—they should "steer rather than row" and see that services are provided rather than always delivering them directly,
2. community-empowering in ways that encourage local groups to
   solve their own problems rather than dictating bureaucratic
   solutions,
3. competitive rather than monopolistic by deregulating and privatizing those activities that could be carried out by the private sector or NGOs more efficiently or effectively than public agencies,
4. mission-driven rather than rule-bound, setting goals and allowing employees to find the best ways of meeting objectives,
5. results-oriented—they should fund effective outcomes rather
   than inputs,
6. customer-driven in meeting the needs of citizens rather than
   those of the bureaucracy,
7. enterprising in earning revenues rather than just spending tax
   resources,
8. anticipatory—investing in the prevention of problems rather
   than spending to solve problems after they occur,
9. decentralized—working through participation and teamwork
   among government agencies at different levels and with groups
   outside of government, and
10. market-oriented in solving problems through market forces
    rather than larger government programs.

These ten characteristics, or ones similar to them, became the principles for government reinvention for many federal agencies and state
and local governments in the United States, the United Kingdom, Canada,
Australia, New Zealand, and other countries during the 1990s.

The concept of a competent state was also shaped by the economic
and social problems of developing countries during the 1980s and
1990s and by the demands placed on their governments by globalization
during the early years of the twenty-first century. It became clear in the
large number of developing countries experiencing slow economic
growth, especially in Eastern Europe, South Asia, Sub-Saharan Africa,
and South and Central America, that governments would have to
restructure their economies to produce higher value-added products and

services and become more outward-oriented in a globalizing system of trade and investment. Governments in developing countries faced substantial challenges in diversifying their exports from primary commodities and raw materials, achieving economic stability, adjusting exchange rates, commercializing agriculture, and building manufacturing and services industries. Most governments in developing countries had little choice but to strengthen market systems and accelerate growth to alleviate poverty and raise living standards through job creation.

New concepts of the competent state evolved from all of these sources and others. Even international financial institutions and development assistance organizations that were most critical of incompetent states during the 1980s now recognize the important roles that governments play in implementing effective and affordable social assistance, basic education, health, and small business development programs in order to maintain political stability, attract FDI in both labor- and technology-intensive industries, and improve the labor and managerial skills needed to participate in international trade and investment.

As this book discusses, many states in the developing world continue to face challenges in coping with globalization. Some developing countries have shortages of educated and trained human capital and managerial talent to accelerate economic growth and reduce poverty. Others must find new ways of increasing capital inflows to make the investments needed in basic infrastructure and services to facilitate both domestic enterprise and foreign trade and investment. It became clear by the end of the twentieth century that competent states, especially in the poorest developing countries, must build their institutional capacities to overcome political and social instability, weak private sectors, and high levels of corruption in government that undermine the confidence of foreign and domestic investors and that increase political risk. Since the early 1990s, governments in countries with both advanced and emerging market economies have seen economic reform and public sector institution-building become permanent requirements for initiating and sustaining economic and social progress.

THE ROLES OF COMPETENT STATES

This book makes a strong case for redefining the state's role in creating and sustaining viable economies, reducing poverty, and raising standards of living. It describes a set of fundamental roles or functions that competent states must perform effectively in a globalizing society.

These roles and functions all contribute to achieving equitable, sustainable, and participative economic and social development reflected in the UN MDGs and in other international declarations of human aspirations. The fundamental role of the state is to achieve sustainable economic and social progress that leads to higher standards of living for all people. The UN Millennium Declaration called for states and international organizations to promote freedom, equality, solidarity, tolerance, respect for nature, and shared responsibility.

Although the contributors to this volume see a crucial role for the state in achieving sustainable human development and reducing poverty, none argue that government can achieve these goals alone. The concept of a competent state that emerges here is one of collaborative governance in which national governments work in partnership with the private sector, organizations of civil society, other states, and international organizations through democratic and participative processes. The major roles and functions of competent states identified in this book are depicted in Figure 13.1.

In the twenty-first century, three important roles of a competent state will contribute to achieving sustainable human development. As Rondinelli and Cheema point out (chapter 1), Bertucci and Alberti confirm (chapter 2), and Agosín and Bloom describe (chapter 4), one of these roles is creating an enabling environment for participating effectively in a globalizing economy so that all segments of the population have the opportunity to benefit from international trade and investment. In an increasingly global society, the inability of some countries or population groups to benefit from international economic interaction virtually assures their inability to achieve socially equitable national economic growth. Second, to achieve socially equitable economic growth, especially in the poorest developing countries, as Agosín and Bloom contend and Pasha argues (chapter 5), the state must focus on pro-poor policies that combat poverty and enhance the capacities of people normally bypassed in the distribution of the benefits of economic growth to participate more effectively in productive activities on which their livelihoods depend. Third, the state has a crucial role in strengthening the capacity of public institutions to promote socially equitable economic growth, enable participation in the global economy, and combat poverty.

Creating an Enabling Environment
for Participation in the Global Economy

Achieving sustainable human development in the twenty-first century, as outlined in the MDGs, requires the competent state to create an

Figure 13.1 Roles of the Competent State

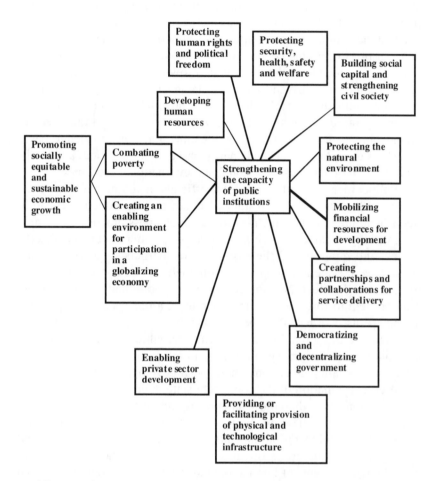

enabling environment in which individuals and enterprises can participate in and benefit from global economic interaction. The heads of state
that ratified the UN Millennium Declaration believed "that the central
challenge we face today is to ensure that globalization becomes a positive force for all the world's people."[6]

The competent state must respond to the opportunities and risks that
globalization brings to all areas of modern life—the economy, society,
communications, transportation, trade, and investment. Bertucci and
Alberti, Rondinelli, and Agosín and Bloom all describe the trends that
are driving the most recent cycle of globalization to which the state
must respond in order to create an enabling environment for participation in and sharing of the benefits of international trade and investment.

Bertucci and Alberti point out (chapter 2) that national economic and social development is being driven increasingly by the multinational regionalization and internationalization of trade and investment and that the competent state participates effectively in shaping the international rules of global economic interaction. In Chapter 1, Rondinelli and Cheema document the worldwide growth in exports, imports, and FDI that, in turn, is driven by and accelerates the mobility of all factors of production (capital, technology, know-how, labor and property ownership) by rapid technological development especially in the telecommunications and transportation, by the emergence of knowledge-based industries to replace labor- and energy-based manufacturing, and by the rapid growth of services in national and international economies.

Political leaders and government officials in competent states must recognize that these trends result in similarities in production capabilities around the world; in the need for agile business practice by companies seeking to meet growing international demand for speed, efficiency, and quality; and the expansion of markets required to attain economies of scale and scope.[7] As Rondinelli points out (chapter 3), all of these trends affect the competitiveness of individual firms and often require them to forge international strategic alliances and cooperative arrangements in order to compete. In a global society the state must create a climate of national competitiveness in which enterprises, localities, and regions can engage profitably in international transactions and contribute to national economic and social development.[8]

A crucial function of the competent state, therefore, is to create the enabling conditions that allow its citizens and enterprises to participate effectively in globalization. Expanding the participation of countries more fully in globalization depends on their governments' ability and willingness to structure political, economic, and social institutions to meet the requirements of international markets. Creating an institutional structure for market economies and economic growth is a complex, long-term process. Market economies developed in Western industrial countries over more than 200 years. Few developing countries or those in transition from centrally-planned to market systems can pursue all of the changes simultaneously. In some of these countries, a new institutional structure may take generations to put into place. Since the late 1980s, however, states have been under increasing pressure, from within and without, to accelerate the process of institution-building to create or strengthen their economies so they can participate more effectively in globalization.

Combating Poverty

At the core of the MDGs is a challenge to UN Member States both to pursue socially equitable economic development and reduce poverty. When countries integrate more tightly into the global economy, as Agosín and Bloom note (chapter 4), they also become more vulnerable to international economic cycles and external financial forces that can adversely affect poor countries and poor groups within all countries. The competent state must go beyond conventional macroeconomic adjustment, trade and investment liberalization, and exchange rate reform needed to create an enabling environment for economic growth—and even beyond policies aimed at capital accumulation, labor force expansion, total factor productivity, and infrastructure expansion that accelerate economic growth—to achieve sustainable human development. Agosín and Bloom also point out that the competent state must enact and implement policies and programs in health, education, small and medium-size enterprise development, gender equity, democracy, social capital formation, and environmental protection that are focused specifically on enhancing human capacity to combat poverty. States that seek to achieve sustainable human development must help expand human capacities and strengthen social capital so that the poor can participate effectively in economic development.

Pasha (chapter 5) goes further. He argues that the competent state, especially in developing countries, must place poverty reduction at the core of the development process to ensure that people living in poverty participate in and benefit from globalization and economic growth. The competent state combats poverty and increases participation in economic growth through policies and programs that direct resources to the sectors in which the poor earn their livelihoods (agriculture and food production), to the areas in which the poor live (rural and underdeveloped regions), to the factors of production they possess (largely unskilled labor), and to the outputs they consume (food and basic necessities).

Strengthening the Capacity of Public Institutions

Institutional capacity building is the process through which individuals and organizations in any country strengthen their abilities to mobilize the resources needed to overcome economic and social problems and to achieve a better standard of living as generally defined in that society. Institutions include both sustainable organizations and widely accepted rules of behavior in both the public and private sectors.

This book identifies at least ten major roles for the state in strengthening the capacity of public institutions to promote socially equitable economic growth, combat poverty, and create an enabling environment for participation in globalization. The competent state strengthens the capacity of public institutions to:

- develop human resources,
- protect human rights and political freedoms,
- protect security, health, safety, and welfare,
- build social capital by strengthening civil society,
- protect the natural environment,
- mobilize financial resources for development,
- create partnerships and collaborations with the private sector and NGOs for service delivery,
- democratize and decentralize government,
- provide or facilitate the provision of physical and technological infrastructure, and
- enable private sector development.

Although each of these elements of institution building is important in its own right, increasingly they are interrelated and together affect the ability of the competent state to achieve social and economic development goals. The state's capacity to contribute to socially equitable economic development depends on the ability of the leaders of national and local governments, NGOs, institutions of civil society, and businesses and industries to adjust rapidly to complex international social, political, and economic changes.

The challenge facing all states in the twenty-first century is to create a system of governance that promotes and supports efficient economic interaction and that, at the same time, advances the health, safety, welfare, and security of its citizens. All states face continuing challenges in renewing political institutions, finding new modalities of governance, and expanding political capacities to guide national economic activities without undue intervention and control. They must create a political system that can elicit at least a minimum level of public consensus on social and political goals; encourage political, business, and civic leaders to articulate social and economic priorities; and guide the actions of public and private organizations toward economic objectives that benefit society.

Among the means available to strengthen the capacity of public institutions are constitutional, electoral, governance, and administrative and civil service reforms. Constitutional reforms restructure and revise the basic principles and institutions of governance; establish the structure of government as a federal, federation, or unitary system; identify the purpose and powers of the state; delineate the powers and limitations of and relationships among legislative, executive, and judicial branches of government; and clarify the responsibilities and obligations of government and citizens. As Cheema points out (chapter 6), electoral reforms create new types of and bases for representation, establish or revise the qualifications for registration and voting, modify election rules and voting procedures, determine the process of candidate selection, prevent corrupt or unfair voting practices, guarantee voting rights, and determine how the public can hold elected officials accountable. Kauzya points out (chapter 10) and Work confirms (chapter 11) that governance reforms delineate the units of government at national, regional, and local levels; their roles and responsibilities; the relationships among them that can strengthen mechanisms for decision-making, interaction, coordination and cooperation; and create procedures for dispute resolution and settlement. Administrative reforms, as Cheema observes, improve the quality of government by specifying the procedures of bureaucratic accountability, of decision-making by rule of law, and of the role of the judiciary in maintaining them; they also strengthen the efficacy and transparency of financing, procurement, contracting, accounting, and other management functions. Civil Service reforms establish or adjust the duties, responsibilities, and obligations of public employees; pay levels; recruitment procedures; incentives; training and career development rules; and ethical standards.

The competent state often plays a crucial role, as Cheema contends, in creating or strengthening institutions that establish ethical norms of behavior and transparency in government and the private sector, And as Bertucci and Alberti, Rondinelli, and Agosín and Bloom argue (chapters 2, 3 and 4), the state's role is crucial in setting and enforcing legal rules, developing and sustaining appropriate macroeconomic policies, liberalizing trade and finance, protecting property rights, and privatizing the ownership of state enterprises and land. In many countries, governments play a catalytic role in the growth of small and medium-size enterprises and in accommodating the needs of transnational corporations.

The competent state strengthens the capacity of public institutions to collaborate effectively with the private sector and organizations of civil society. Rondinelli notes (chapters 3 and 12) that businesses and industries are the primary generators of jobs, income, and wealth in all countries. Increasingly they must operate across national borders and, in

some sectors, collaborate closely with governments in providing services. The competent state, Rondinelli argues, builds private sector
capacity to deliver social services as well as to produce commercial
products through deregulation, privatization, management contracts
with private organizations, joint ventures, outsourcing, and other forms
of PPP. Malik and Waglé (chapter 8), emphasize the importance of
political, civic, and business leaders being able to adjust quickly and
continuously to changes in the terms and conditions of global trade and
investment, in order to maintain a nationally viable economy and to
include the poor in productive economic activities.

With the growing recognition that the state plays a pivotal role in
economic development has come the realization that the functions of
government must change drastically to position countries effectively in
a global system of trade and investment. The competent state sometimes
plays a catalytic role in providing or arranging for the provision of public services and infrastructure needed for economic production. The
state can help break the bottlenecks to economic expansion by investing
directly in productive activities during the early stages of economic
growth and creating favorable conditions for private enterprise development in later stages.

As Sisk observes (chapter 9), globalization requires the state not only
to arrange for the provision of conventional physical infrastructure such as
roads and utility systems, but increasingly it must also take a key role in
strengthening the infrastructure required to promote technological innovation, apply knowledge, and expand information systems. Expanding
knowledge-oriented infrastructure requires governments to collaborate
with the private sector and with universities and research institutes in creating Knowledge, Innovation and Technology Systems (KITS). The competent state is increasingly an electronic state—e-government provides
broader access to information about public institutions, allows public
agencies at different levels of administration to cooperative more effectively, and makes it easier for citizens to obtain public services. Sisk also
points out that the competent state must find new ways of supporting
research and development if it is to remain competitive in the global marketplace and to achieve the UN MDGs. To do so the state must strengthen
the capacity of public institutions to build partnerships with knowledge-
based industries, broker knowledge and information, promote diversity
and pluralism in knowledge and information generation, and disseminate
and apply knowledge in both the public and private sectors.

The competent state, as Rondinelli points out (chapter 3) and Malik
and Waglé note (chapter 8), provides a social safety net for the most

vulnerable groups in society until they can develop their capacities to participate productively in the economy. In every society, the state has a responsibility to create and maintain social assistance programs for the disabled, disadvantaged, or the poor who are adversely affected by economic reforms.

A recurring lesson of economic and social development experience over the past half century is that central government alone cannot achieve economic and social equity. Kauzya and Work contend that states must often deconcentrate or devolve authority, resources, and responsibilities to local governments and NGOs to elicit greater participation in political and administrative decision-making and to deliver social services essential to creating a strong economy. Pasha (chapter 5), and Malik and Waglé both expect a competent state to create social safety nets for the poor and economically disadvantaged, not only through national public agencies, but also through local governments and community organizations.

Strengthening the capacities of public institutions to empower organizations of civil society to participate in economic, social, and political activities will be required of all states in an era of globalization. Civil society organizations not only supplement services provided by the private sector and maintain a check on government power, they also help distribute the benefits of economic growth more equitably within society, and offer opportunities for individuals to improve their standards of living. Civil institutions channel people's participation in economic and social activities and organize them into more potent forces for influencing public policies. Institutions of civil society have an important role in mitigating the potentially adverse impacts of economic instability, creating efficient mechanisms for allocating social benefits, and providing a voice for poorer groups in political and governmental decision-making.

Competent states, as Kauzya points out (chapter 10) must strengthen not only the capacities of national bureaucracies, but build local capacity as well. Strengthening governance capacity can be done through vertical decentralization of authority, responsibility, and resources to subnational administrative units, local governments, and other organizations working at the local level; and through horizontal decentralization that empowers local communities. Strengthening local governance capacity, as both Kauzya and Work note, involves a variety of stakeholders, including central government agencies, local governments, civic society organizations, community groups, the private sector, and international donor organizations. Indeed, they observe that the capacity of all organizations operating at the local level needs strengthening in order to achieve socially equitable economic development. The state can play an important role in empowering these organizations to participate in what Kauzya argues are five essential functions: priority-setting, planning, producing, paying or financing, and consumption. All of these functions are critical in engaging local groups, and in encouraging them to take ownership of development projects and programs.[9]

Shende emphasizes (chapter 7) that the competent state strengthens government's fiscal architecture to mobilize the financial resources needed for development. Although managing domestic resources has always been an important role for the state, national governments must now develop greater competence in managing foreign financial resources as well. States face increasing challenges in widening the tax base, enforcing tax compliance, and managing tax competition. As tax systems become more complex, Shende argues, the state must take a stronger role in ensuring that the incidence of taxes falls equitably on all groups in society. It must also develop new sources of revenue for financing essential economic and social programs and tap into revenues generated by international business opportunities that globalization creates. The state must support a fiscal architecture that not only strengthens central government revenues but also the central governments' capacity to expand local government finances. The success of democratization depends on decentralizing participation in public policy-making and the implementation of government programs. The success of decentralization depends, in turn, on local administrative and political units having adequate revenue and spending powers. Central governments can strengthen the fiscal capacity of local governments by, among other things, expanding taxing and revenue-raising authority for local governments, allowing them to raise taxes from a wider variety of local sources, and using a greater number of tax instruments. In some countries the central government has created special funds that can be replenished from national revenue sources such as customs, excise or import taxes, or regular budgetary assignments that are set aside from line agency budgets to be used to finance costly capital investments. In other countries the state provides statutory payments to local governments from fixed percentages of recurrent revenues of central, state, or provincial government budgets as unrestricted grants, thus giving local administrations more flexibility to meet local needs and demands.[10]

The competent state also protects natural resources and the quality of the physical environment, which can be impacted both positively and negatively by economic growth. Unsustainable industrialization, commercialization of agriculture, urbanization, and use of technology contribute to global climate change, the degradation of water resources, air pollution, the loss of biological diversity, ozone depletion, forest destruction, desertification, degradation of land, and overconsumption of energy, water, and land resources. But an increasing number of studies conclude that economic growth, in and of itself, is not the problem; rather it is the way in which growth is pursued. Governments that pursue sustainable economic growth can, in fact, maintain ecological systems and protect the environment. Economic growth is associated with lower fertility and slower population expansion—which reduce population pressures on natural resources—and with income increases that can be used in part for pollution control and prevention and energy conservation. Energy efficiency generally improves with economic growth. People with adequate sources of income are not as likely as the poor to destroy forests for firewood or engage in slash and burn agriculture.

Governments can use market principles to overcome environmental degradation by internalizing the costs of environmental pollution for individuals and businesses through taxation and fees, eliminating pollution subsidies, and enacting other measures to ensure that polluters pay.[11] Moreover, open markets that attract FDI can also be beneficial; most transnational corporations transfer environmental practices to their foreign affiliates that are far superior for preventing and controlling pollution than those used by domestic firms in developing countries.[12] Of course, economic growth alone is not sufficient to reverse or prevent environmental degradation; governments and the private sector must take specific actions to prevent or overcome market failures and use sound regulation and market-based instruments to protect common resources.

CONCLUSION

The twenty-first century began a new era of globalization, not only for economic trade and investment, but for technological, social, and political interaction as well. Because of the necessity in an era of globalization for all nations to participate through open markets in international trade and investment, states can no longer centrally plan and manage national economies or merely provide traditional public services. Global competitiveness will require states in nations at all stages of economic development to strengthen the institutional capacity of government to generate and allocate resources efficiently to create the enabling conditions for achieving equitable economic and social development. The state's roles will change drastically from controlling, directing, and intervening in the economy to supporting and facilitating productive economic activities; providing adequate infrastructure and social overhead capital; creating and maintaining a competitive business climate; assuring fair market access; protecting the interests of workers and consumers; and providing for the health, safety, and security of its citizens.

States that redefine their roles and functions can play a positive role in helping citizens and enterprises participate more effectively and share in the benefits of globalization in all of its dimensions. The competent state must continually reinvent government through innovation and quality improvements and strengthen its relationships with citizens, the private sector, and organizations of civil society. The competent state must take a strong role in shaping the rules of global interaction so that all countries can benefit equitably from the opportunities and minimize the burdens of globalization. During the twenty-first century the competent state must be efficient, effective, participative, honest, transparent, professional, responsive, and collaborative if it is to achieve the goals of socially equitable economic growth and sustainable human development.

REFERENCES

1. *Webster's New Universal Abridged Dictionary*, 2nd ed. (New York: Simon & Schuster, 1983).

2. See Charles E. Lindblom, *Politics and Markets: The World's Political-Economic Systems* (New York: Basic Books, 1977): chapter 18.

3. Janos Kornai, *The Socialist System: The Political Economy of Communism* (Princeton, N.J.: Princeton University Press, 1992): 157–159.

4. For a detailed assessment of the problems of European, North American and Asian-Pacific countries see Organization for Economic Cooperation and Development, *Assessing Structural Reforms: Lessons for the Future* (Paris: OECD, 1994).

5. David Osborne and Ted Gaebler, *Reinventing Government* (Boston, Mass.: Addison-Wesley Publishing, 1992).

6. United Nations, "United Nations Millennium Declaration," Resolution A/55/L.2 (New York: United Nations, 2000): Section I.5.

7. John D. Kasarda and Dennis A. Rondinelli, "Innovative Infrastructure for Agile Manufacturers," *Sloan Management Review* 39, no. 2 (1998): 73–82.

8. See Jack N. Berhman and Dennis A. Rondinelli, "Urban Development Policies in a Globalizing Economy: Creating Competitive Advantage in the Post–Cold War Era," in *Post Cold War Policy, Vol. I: The Social and Domestic Context,* ed. William Crotty (Chicago: Nelson-Hall, 1995): 209–230.

9. See Dennis A. Rondinelli, *Development Projects as Policy Experiments: An Adaptive Approach to Development Administration,* 2nd ed. (London and New York: Routledge, 1993).

10. Dennis A. Rondinelli, "Financing the Decentralization of Urban Services in Developing Countries: Administrative Requirements for Fiscal Improvements," *Studies in Comparative International Development* 25, no. 2 (1990): 43–59.

11. See Dennis A. Rondinelli, "A New Generation of Environmental Policy: Government Business Collaboration in Environmental Management, *Environmental Law Reporter* 41, no. 8 (2001): 10891–10905; and Dennis A. Rondinelli, *Rethinking U.S. Environmental Protection Policy: Management Challenges for a New Administration* (Arlington, Va.: IBM Endowment for the Business of Government, 2000).

12. Dennis A. Rondinelli and Gyula Vastag, "Multinational Corporations' Environmental Performance in Developing Countries: The Aluminum Company of America," in *Growing Pains: Environmental Management in Developing Countries,* eds. Walter Wehrmeyer and Yacoob Mulugetta (Sheffield, England: Greenleaf Publishing Ltd., 1999): 68–83.

About the Contributors

Manuel R. Agosín is Chief Economist for the operations department that deals with Central America, Mexico, Haiti and the Dominican Republic in the Inter-American Development Bank. He is also Professor of Economics at the University of Chile. He obtained his Ph.D. in Economics from Columbia University. At the United Nations, he was an economist and manager of various units in charge of economic research and technical assistance in areas related to development and international trade, finance, and foreign direct investment. He has published numerous articles in international journals and edited books published in Chile and abroad.

Adriana Alberti is Chief Technical Advisor, Division for Public Administration and Development Management, Department of Economic and Social Affairs, United Nations. She holds a Ph.D. in Political and Social Sciences from the European University Institute in Florence, and has worked since 1992 on governance issues including at the University of Bologna and Princeton University. She has published a number of articles and is editor and co-author of the first issue of the United Nations *World Public Sector Report on Globalization and the State* (2001).

Guido Bertucci is Director of the Division for Public Administration and Development Management, Department of Economic and Social Affairs, United Nations. He has served the United Nations in a number of capacities for over twenty-five years in the area of human resources, financial management and administration. He graduated with a degree in Political Science from the Catholic University of Milan, Italy and holds a post-graduate degree in Administrative Sciences from the same university. From 1971 to 1974, he was Associate Professor of Comparative Constitutionalism at the Catholic University of Milan. From 1992 to 1993, he was an Associate Professor of Public Administration at New York University, Robert F. Wagner School of Public Service.

261

David E. Bloom is Clarence James Gamble Professor of Economics and Demography, and Chairman of the Department of Population and International Health, at the Harvard School of Public Health.

G. Shabbir Cheema is Principal Adviser and Program Director, Division for Public Administration and Development Management, United Nations. As a senior United Nations official for more than fifteen years, he has provided leadership in crafting democratic governance programs at the country level, and designing global research and training programs in electoral and parliamentary systems, human rights, transparency and accountability of government, urban management and decentralization. He received his Ph.D. in political science in 1973 from the University of Hawaii. He has taught at Universiti Sains Malaysia, University of Hawaii, and New York University. He has authored or edited eight books and numerous book chapters and journal articles on governance and public administration.

John-Mary Kauzya is Chief of Governance and Public Administration Branch in the Division for Public Administration and Development Management of the United Nations where he has also served as Inter-regional Adviser on Governance Institutions and Systems. He has been a lecturer in public administration and management at Makerere University in Uganda and the Deputy Director of the Uganda Management Institute before joining the United Nations. He holds a Ph.D. from the Université Paris 1, Panthéon-Sorbonne, specializing in public administration and management.

Khalid Malik is a development practitioner with over twenty-five years experience. He is Director of the Evaluation Office at the United Nations Development Programme, and was formerly United Nations Representative in Uzbekistan. Educated as an economist at the universities of Oxford, Cambridge, Essex and Punjab, he has held a variety of key managerial, technical and policy positions in the United Nations Development Programme in the field and at headquarters. He has edited books and authored articles on a range of topics, including capacity development, poverty and inequality, post-conflict, evaluation and results-based management.

Hafiz A. Pasha is a United Nations Assistant Secretary-General and United Nations Development Programme Assistant Administrator and Director of the Regional Bureau for Asia and the Pacific. He has an

M.A. from the University of Cambridge and a Ph.D. from Stanford University, and over twenty-seven years of experience of research, teaching and public service. He has served as the Federal Minister for Finance and Economic Affairs, Deputy Chairman of the Planning Commission, Education Minister and Commerce Minister in three governments in Pakistan. Earlier, he was the Vice Chancellor/President of the University of Karachi, Dean and Director of the Institute of Business Administration, Karachi, and Research Professor and Director of the Applied Economics Research Centre, University of Karachi.

Dennis A. Rondinelli is Glaxo Distinguished International Professor of Management at the Kenan-Flagler Business School at the University of North Carolina-Chapel Hill. Rondinelli has done research on international development policy, planning and management in Asia, Central Europe, Latin America, and Africa. He has authored or edited sixteen books and published more than two hundred book chapters and articles in scholarly and professional journals. In 2002, he was appointed to the Expert Committee on Public Administration of the United Nations Economic and Social Council.

Suresh Narayan Shende was educated in India, France and USA. He worked in the Indian Revenue Service from 1961 to 1997, and as Inter-regional Adviser in Resource Mobilization at the United Nations Department of Economic and Social Affairs from 1997 to 2003. He has undertaken numerous UN technical assistance missions to developing countries.

Jennifer Sisk is an ICT and e-Government Policy Advisor with the United Nations Department for Economic and Social Affairs. Ms. Sisk has worked within the United Nations system for over six years on science and technology policy issues, focusing on ICT for development. Ms. Sisk has a B.A. from the University of California Berkeley and an M.A.L.D. from the Fletcher School of Law and Diplomacy, Tufts University.

Swarnim Waglé is an economist working on trade, World Trade Organization, and human development issues at the regional United Nations Development Programme Asia Trade Initiative, Hanoi. Trained at the London School of Economics and Harvard University, his academic interests span issues of growth, trade, poverty and social relations. He has also worked at the BBC in London and the World Bank in Washington, DC.

Robertson Work is Director of the global Decentralised Governance Programme and Principal Policy Advisor on Decentralisation at the United Nations Development Programme in New York. Before his thirteen years with the United Nations Development Programme he worked twenty-one years with a non-governmental organization, the Institute of Cultural Affairs, as Executive Director in Malaysia, the Republic of Korea, Jamaica and Venezuela.

Index

Abu Dhabi, 224
Accountability. *See* Transparency and accountability
Adler, P., 144–45
Administrative accountability, 100
Administrative decentralization, 50, 196
Administrative reforms, 252, 253
Affermage system, 224
Africa: AIDS epidemic in Sub-Saharan, 72; corruption in, 108, 114; infant mortality rates in Sub-Saharan, 5; managerial and lease contracts, 224, 225; regional recessions in 1980s and 1990s, 3
Agrawal, A., 152
Agriculture: dumping of agricultural surpluses, 125; pro-poor agricultural growth, 88
Aid, foreign, 125–26, 150
AIDS, 72, 77
Air fuels tax, 140
Algerian Front de Libération Nationale, 107
Annan, Kofi, 25
Arab Common Market, 40
Asia: anticorruption policies in, 113–14, 115; civic engagement networks, 144; corruption and its impact in, 106–7, 108; East Asian financial crisis of 1990s, 65, 78, 89; exports performance and exchange rates, 64–65; infant mortality rates, 5; institutional development in, 37; pro-poor growth process and East Asian economies, 84; pro-poor policies in China, 85; regional recessions in late 1990s, 3; saving rates in East Asia, 66
Asian Development Bank, 8, 46, 53, 108, 124
Association of Southeast Asian Nations (ASEAN), 40
Australia, 228

Baby-boom generation, 69
Banco Sol, 76
Bangladesh, 76, 89–90, 92, 104
Banking sector. *See* Financial institutions
Bank Rakyat Indonesia Unit Desa, 76
Barbados, 229
Bill and Melinda Gates Foundation, 231–32
Biotechnology, 165–66
Bolivia, 76
Borderless virtual world, 21
Botswana, 114
Brazil, 224

Bribery, corruption and, 104, 106, 108, 110, 111, 112
Brinkerhoff, D., 151, 153
Build-operate-transfer agreements, 227–28
Bureaucratic corruption, 101–2
Business development, 42; developing, attracting, and retaining TNCs, 45–46; privatizing state enterprises, 42–43; promoting small enterprise development, 43–45
Business organizations, 232

Campaign finance, 101, 103, 106
Capital flows, 64, 65
Carbon tax proposals, 139, 140
Caribbean region, 5, 229
Chang, Ha-Joon, 37
Chhibber, Pradeep, 107
China, 85, 226–27, 228
Civic engagement, 143, 158–59; benefits, costs, and constraints, 150–52; defining, 145–46; going beyond, 148–52; leap from micro level to macro level, 152–55; link between social capital and, 143–45; macro-level policymaking, 155–57; at the micro level, 149–50; policy implications, 147–48; PRSPs, macro-level civic engagement, 157–58
Civic Traditions in Modern Italy (Putnam), 144
Civil service, 48–49; civil service reforms, 252, 253; corruption and its impact in the, 104, 108, 111, 117
Civil society, 25; pro-poor policies and, 94; strengthening and supporting civil society institutions, 55–56
Clean Air Act, 230
Coca-Cola, 231
Coleman, James, 144
Colombia, 226
Commission of the European Communities, 51
Communications infrastructure, 52
Communication technologies. *See* Information and communication technologies (ICTs)
Competent state, 243–47, 257–58; combating poverty, 250–51; creating an enabling environment, 249–50; roles of competent states, 247–57; strengthening the capacity of public institutions, 251–57
Competitiveness in a globalizing economy, 33–36, 56–57; business development

policies, 42–46; creating an institutional structure for market competition, 37–38; improving government efficiency, accountability, and responsiveness, 46–51; initiating and sustaining macroeconomic reform, 38–41; protecting the economically vulnerable, 52–54; providing physical and technological infrastructure, 51–52; roles of government in fostering, 36–56; strengthening legal institutions for economic transactions, 41–42; strengthening and supporting civil society institutions, 55–56

Comprehensive Environmental Response Compensation and Liability Act, 230

Conrad N. Hilton Foundation, 231

Constitutional reforms, 252–53

Construction sector, pro-poor growth and, 88

Contracting, with private companies, 222–26

Corporate tax rates, 129

Corruption: causes of, 109–13; combating, 113–15; components of reforms, 115–17; controlling corruption and establishing ethical norms, 46–48; forms of, 100–102; impact on economic development and poverty eradication, 106–8; magnitude of, 108–9; and the quality of democratic process, 102–6

Corruption Perceptions Index 2002, 47

Corrupt Practices Investigations Bureau (Singapore), 114

Costa Rica, 228

Cross-border corruption, 112–13

Cross-border shopping, 136

Customs unions, 40

Daubon, Ramon, 148

Debt: debt financing, 228; debt relief, 125; public debt, 132–34

Decentralization. *See also* Governance, decentralizing: administrative, 50; debureaucratization and, 27; decentralizing governance, 195–218; decentralizing government, 49–51; pro-poor policies and, 94; vertical and horizontal, 183

Deconcentration, decentralization and, 50, 199

Delegation, decentralization and, 50

Demand-side policies, 44

Democratic governments, and social capital, 69–70

Democratic Peoples Republic of Korea, 85

Democratic process, corruption and quality of, 102–6

Democratic state, hallmarks of a, 23–24

Demographic change, 68

Demographic transitions, 68–69

Developing countries: economically vulnerable in, 53, 54; economic growth of, 3–4, 7–8; economic restructuring policies in, 90; globalization and expansion of, 19–20; institutional reform in, 26; KIT practices in, 166–67, 168–69; liberalization in, 61; openness to the international economy in,

63–64; political corruption in, 47, 103, 104–5, 106; Poverty Reduction Strategy Papers prepared by, 83–84; property rights in, 40–41; small business development in, 43, 44; taxation in, 128, 129, 130–31, 138

Devolution, decentralization and, 51, 94, 199

Digital communications technologies, 52

Directorate on Corruption and Economic Crime (Botswana), 114

Divestment decentralization, 197

Domestic corruption, 111–12

Domestic resource mobilization, 122–24

Domestic saving, 66

Dominican Republic, 228

Dreze, J., 145

East Asian financial crisis, 1990s, 65, 78, 89

Economically vulnerable, protecting the, 52–54

Economic development: applying ICTs in, 164–65; impact of corruption on, 106–8

Economic growth. *See also* Competitiveness in a globalizing economy: financial resources for, 122–23; globalization and, 3–4, 7–8, 18–19; liberalization and promotion of fast, 65–67; virtue of trust in, 144

Economic and Social Commission for Asia and the Pacific (ESCAP), 55

Economic unions, 40

Economist, The, 61

Edgerton, J., 146

Edna McConnell Clark Foundation, 232

Education: enhanced higher education, 77; improving quality of, 68; smaller families and access to, 68–69

Edwards, M., 148

Elections, politically corrupt, 104–5, 111

Electoral reforms, 252, 253

Elite hegemony syndrome, 103

El Salvador, 76

Entrepreneurship, globalization and, 18

Environmental issues: global environmental tax, 139, 140; ICTs for environmentally sound technologies, 165; U.S. environmental regulations and infrastructure, 230

Esman, M., 148

Ethical norms in government, establishing, 46–48

European Union (EU), 40, 113, 140

Exchange rates, stabilizing, 64–65

Excise duty, 129, 135

Executive branch: corruption in the, 105; reforming the, 27

Factor accumulation, 66

Families, shift from larger to smaller, 68–69

Financial accountability, 99

Financial institutions. *See also* International Monetary Fund; World Bank: allocation of bank credit, 92; oversight of the banking system, 67; support for small business, 76

Financial management, public sector capacity building in, 28

Financial resources, 121–22, 140–42; alternative financial instruments, 139–40; domestic resource mobilization, 122–24; factors affecting financial resources mobilization, 134–39; foreign, 124–26; mobilization of government funds, 126–34
Fiscal decentralization, 197
Fiscal deficits, 86, 87
Foreign aid, 125–26, 150
Foreign direct investment (FDI): economic globalization and, 3, 4, 19; freeing of non-FDI capital flows, 64; liberalization of, 61, 64, 65; pro-poor policies and, 90; small business development and effects on, 43; TNCs and increases in, 45
Foreign financial resources, 124–26
Fragmented patronage and extended factionalism syndrome, 103
Free trade agreements, 64
Free trade areas, 39–40
Free trade, globalization and, 19
Front Islamique du Salut, 107
Fukuyama, F. F., 70, 144
Functional perspective of corruption, 100
Fundación Calpiá, 76

Gaebler, Ted, 245–46
General Agreement on Trade and Tariffs (GATT), 18
Ghai, D., 155
Global economy, integration into the, 63–65
Globalization, 1–2, 17–19; benefits of, 4–6; corruption and, 112; and development of civil society institutions, 55; and economic growth, 3–4; emergence of a globalizing society, 2–8; and financial resources, 125, 138–39; global interdependence and global social networks, 18; good governance and, 29–30; and its impact on the private sector, 220; and its impact on the state, 20–22; opportunities and challenges of, 19–20; problems of, 6–8; and redefining the role of the state, 22–25
Globalization and liberalization, 61–62, 77–78; action points, 74–77; interactions, 71–74; Sphere 1: integration into the global economy, 63–65; Sphere 2: promotion of fast economic growth, 65–67; Sphere 3: development of human and social capital, 67–71; three spheres of development policy, 62–63
Goldsmith, A., 151, 153
Governance: corruption and poor, 109; e-governance, 164; governance reforms, 252, 253; ICTs for good, 164; rethinking governance and the role of the state, 8–9
Governance, decentralizing, 195, 216–18; commitment and participation, 205; decentralized governance, 196–209; enabling environment for, 199, 202–3; initiative and leadership, 207–8; lessons

learned, 209–16; making reforms operational, 208–9; participation, 204–5; partnerships, 205–7; service delivery and institutional structures, 203–4
Governance, local, 181, 182–83, 191–92; capacity assessment, 188–91; capacity building, 183–84; capacity building for participation, 4 Ps + C concept, 184–88; elements of good, 181–83; holistic capacity building, 186–88; vertical and horizontal decentralization, 183
Government: applying ICTs in, 164; controlling corruption in, 46–47; decentralizing, 49–51; democratic governments and social capital, 69–70; e-government policies, 174–75; KITS and role of, 171–75; making public administration more responsive, 48–49; mobilization of government funds, 126–34; strengthening judicial institutions, 49
Government bonds, 133
Grameen Bank of Bangladesh, 76, 92
Grand corruption, 108, 110
Green Revolution, 88
Gross domestic product (GDP): and the economically vulnerable, 53; economic globalization and, 3, 4, 5
Group of Seven (G-7) initiative, 157

Hanifan, Lyda J., 144
Health care: access to quality, 68, 77; applying ICTs to healthcare sector, 165
Heavily Indebted Poor Countries (HIPC) Initiative, 125, 133, 157
Hirschman, A. O., 146
HIV/AIDS, 72, 77
Hong Kong, 113–14
Housing cooperatives, 233
Human resource development, public sector capacity building in, 27–28
Human and social capital, development of, 67–71
Huntington, S., 152

Income tax rates, 129
Independent Commission Against Corruption (ICAC), 113–14
India: corporate partnerships, 231; housing cooperative societies in, 233; passive public investment in, 229; political corruption in, 102; pro-poor growth process in, 85–86; pro-rich services in, 91; trade liberalization in, 89–90
Indonesia, 102
Infant mortality rates, 5, 68, 69
Information and communication technologies (ICTs), 163; economic development and poverty alleviation, 164–65; KIT and development, 166–67; sector applications, 165–66; transforming government and governance, 164
Information technology (IT), 27; innovation and information technology capacity

building, 28–29; technological infrastructure and, 52

Infrastructures: delegating responsibility for services and, 230–31; KIT, 167–68; physical and technological, 51–52

Institute of Management Development, 35

Institutional reform, public sector capacity building in, 26–27

Integrity Pact (South Korea), 115

Intelligent democratic state, hallmarks of an, 23–24

InterAmerican Development Bank, 33, 35

Interest group bidding syndrome, 102–3

International Finance Corporation, 43–44, 221

International Monetary Fund (IMF): corruption in government, 47, 113; impact of structural adjustment policies, 53; Poverty Reduction Strategy Papers for financing by, 83–84, 157; public debt, 133

International Red Cross, 19

International trade: economic globalization and, 3–4, 19; legal standards for, 41–42; liberalizing trade and investment policies, 39–40

International Youth Foundation, 231

Investment liberalization, 18

Investments, public and private, 67, 87, 221

Japan, 11, 84

Johnston, Michael, 102–3

Joint ventures, public-private, 226–27

Jordan, 220

Judicial systems: corruption in the judiciary, 105–6; reforming, 26–27; strengthening judicial institutions, 49

Kakuei, Tanaka, 111

Kenya, 154

Knowledge, innovation, and technology (KIT) systems, 163, 167–68, 175; current landscape in developing countries, 168–69; and development, 166–67; e-government policies, 174–75; knowledge brokering, 173–74; partnerships, 173; research and development, 172–73; role of the public sector, 169–75; in sector applications, 165–66; strategic framework and policy, 171–72; value-added activities, 172–75

Korea, 84

Kornai, Janos, 245

Korten, David C., 146

Kpundeh, Sahr J., 111

Kwon, S., 144–45

Labor laws, 41

Land reform, 84, 92

Land taxes, 130

Latin America: corruption in, 108, 112; infant mortality rates, 5; lease contracts, 225; regional recessions in early 1980s, 3; saving rates in, 66

Lease contracts, 225, 226

Legal framework: pro-poor policies and rule of law, 93; strengthening legal institutions for economic transactions, 41–42

Liberalization. See Globalization and liberalization

Life expectancy, 68

Lindblom, Charles, 244–45

Macroeconomic adjustment, 64

Macroeconomic policies: civic engagement and, 155–57; of pro-poor growth, 86–87

Macroeconomic reform, 38; creating or strengthening property rights, 40–41; implementing structural adjustment policies, 38–39; liberalizing trade and investment policies, 39–40

Malaysia, 84, 93, 225, 228

Management contracts, 223–25, 226

Market-centered perspective of corruption, 101

Market decentralization, 197

Markets: competitive market economy, 34–35; creating an institutional structure for market competition, 37–38; dependence on legal institutions, 41; globalization and market failures, 6–7; and integration into the global economy, 63–65; market fundamentalism, 20

Massachusetts Institute of Technology (MIT), 197

Mathur, H. M., 155

Merck Corporation, 231, 232

Microeconomic or microsector policies, of pro-poor growth, 87–88

Microenterprises, 76

Microfinance, 149

Mill, John Stuart, 152

Moralist-normative perspective of corruption, 100

Mortality decline, 5, 68, 69

Multinational firms: cross-border corruption and, 112–13; tax competition among, 136

Narayan, D., 148

Nepal, 93

Netherlands, 227

Nokia, 231

Nongovernmental organizations (NGOs): globalization and, 19; pro-poor policies and, 94; and public service sector, 233

North American Free Trade Agreement (NAFTA), 40

Oakley, P., 152

Openness, to the international economy, 63–64

Open Society Institute Network, 232

Organization for Economic Growth and Development (OECD), 4, 5–6, 113

Osborne, David, 245–46

Pakistan: build-operate-transfer agreements, 228; financial sector liberalization in, 89; land reform in, 92; political corruption in,

104, 105; pro-poor growth process in, 87;
pro-rich services in, 91; rise of rural poverty
in, 88
Parliaments, politically corrupt, 104, 105
Partnerships. *See also* Public-private
partnerships (PPPs): decentralized
governance, 205–7; KITS and public-
private, 173
Passive public investment, 229–30
Patronage machine syndrome, 103
Payroll taxes, 128–29
People's Action Party (Singapore), 114
Petty corruption, 107–8
Pfizer, 232
Pharmaceutical companies, 231, 232
Philippines, 92, 102, 105, 233
Physical and technological infrastructures,
51–52
Pluralism, knowledge diversity and, 174
Poland, 224–25
Policy failures, globalization and, 7
Political accountability, 99–100
Political corruption, 101–6, 109–11, 112
Political decentralization, 196
Political parties, corruption of, 105, 111
Poverty, 75. *See also* Pro-poor policies:
applying ICTs in poverty alleviation,
164–65; combating, 250–51; globalization
and, 7; impact of corruption on poverty
eradication, 106–8; national competitiveness
and, 35; Participatory Poverty Assessments,
157; taxes and poverty reduction, 132
Poverty Reduction Strategy Papers (PRSPs),
83–84, 157–58
Private Finance Initiative (UK), 223
Privatization: and impact on poverty, 89; of
SOEs, 42–43, 110, 219, 221
Pro-market reform, 70
Property rights, macroeconomic reform and
creating/strengthening, 40–41
Property taxes, 130
Pro-poor growth, 76, 84, 85–86;
macroeconomic policies of, 86–87
Pro-poor policies, 83–84; framework for
poverty reduction, 94–95; macroeconomic
policies, 86–87; microeconomic or
microsector policies, 87–88; nature of,
85–92; political economy of, 92–94;
redistributive policies, 91–92; restructuring
policies, 88–91
Protectionist policies, economic globalization
and, 3–4, 20
Public administration, responsiveness of, 48–49
Public debt, 132–34
Public institutions, strengthening the capacity
of, 251–57
Public interest-institutionist perspective of
corruption, 101
Public office-legalistic perspective of
corruption, 100–101
Public-private partnerships (PPPs), 219, 236;
advantages of, 221–22; build-operate-transfer

agreements, 227–28; contracting with
private companies, 222–26; delegating
responsibility for services and infrastructure,
230–31; interest in, 220–21; passive public
investment, 229–30; public-private ventures,
226–27; voluntary or informal public-private
cooperation, 231–33; what conditions are
necessary for effective, 233–36
Public sector: decentralization, 50, 196–97;
KITS and role of the, 169–75
Public sector capacity building, 26; human
resource development, 27–28; innovation
and information technology, 28–29;
institutional reform, 26–27; resource
mobilization and financial management, 28
Putnam, Robert, 69, 143, 144

Ramirez, A., 75
Ranis, G., 75
Recessions, worldwide, 3
Reinventing Government (Osborne and
Gaebler), 245–46
Religious organizations, 233
Republic of Korea, 64
Research and development, KITS and
government-sponsored, 172–73
Resource Conservation and Recovery Act,
230
Resource mobilization and financial
management, public sector capacity building
in, 28
Robb, C., 157
Rodrik, D., 153
Roh Tae Woo, 110
Roodt, M. J., 152
Rose-Ackerman, Susan, 106, 107
Rotary International, 231
Rwanda, 181, 188–90

Sales tax, 129, 135
Save the Children, 19
Saving rates, 66
Scientific research, ICTs for basic, 165–66
Sen, A. K., 145, 154
Service contracts, 223, 226
Singapore, 114
Smadja, Claude, 61
Small business: promoting small enterprise
development, 43–45; support for, 76–77
S.M.A.R.T. objectives, 189
Social capital, 55; and civic engagement,
143–59; development of human and, 67–71
Social safety nets: for the economically
vulnerable, 54; to tackle poverty, 83–84
Soros, George, 20, 232
Southern Africa Customs Union, 40
South Korea, 115, 228
Sovereignty, state, 21
Soviet Union, former, 70, 77
Sri Lanka, 75–76, 225
State-owned enterprises (SOEs), privatization
of, 42–43, 110, 219, 221

State, role of the: globalization and, 17–22,
    29–30; public sector capacity building,
    26–29; redefining, 22–25; rethinking
    governance and, 8–9
Stewart, F., 75
Structural adjustment policies, implementing
    macroeconomic, 38–39
Supply-side policies, 44

Taiwan, 64
Tanzi, V., 127
Tariffs, 90, 125, 138
Taxation: enforcing tax compliance, 135, 137;
    global taxes and fees, 139–40; managing tax
    competition, 135–37, 138; resource mobili-
    zation through, 127–32; tax administration,
    123–24, 130; tax expenditures, 91; tax
    havens, 137; tax and nontax revenues, 122,
    127; tax policy, 130; widening the tax base,
    134–35
Technological innovation, globalization and, 18
Thailand, 84, 102, 220, 225
Tobin tax, 139, 140
Tocqueville, Alexis de, 144
Trade: coordinating trade liberalization and
    resource mobilization, 137–39; economic
    globalization and, 3–4, 18, 19; liberalizing
    trade and investment policies, 39–40; trade
    liberalization, 64, 89–91
Transnational corporations (TNCs): developing,
    attracting, and retaining, 45–46; economic
    growth and expansion of, 4
Transparency and accountability: applying
    ICTs in government for increased, 164;
    combating corruption through, 99–100;
    pro-poor policies and, 93–94
Transparency International, 47
Transportation infrastructure, 52
Trickle-down effect, 83
Turkey, 228
Twain, Mark, 1

United Arab Emirates, 226
United Kingdom, 223, 234–35
United Nations Conference on Financing
    Development, 19
United Nations Conference on Trade and
    Development (UNCTAD), 35, 39, 45
United Nations Development Programme
    (UNDP), 62, 76; and decentralized
    governance, 195, 197; *Human Development
    Reports*, 5, 7, 67, 145, 158, 166;
    Management Development and Governance
    Division of the Bureau for Development
    Policy (MDGD/BDP), 197; poverty
    alleviation, 54; and PPPs, 220, 235

United Nations Food and Agriculture
    Organization (FAO), 5
United Nations Millennium Declaration, 8–9,
    26, 83, 94, 121, 163, 164, 165, 166, 170,
    248, 249; Millennium Development Goals
    (MDGs), 9, 26, 83, 95, 168, 244, 248, 249,
    250; Road Map, 163, 164, 165, 166
United Nations (UN): Global Compact, 25,
    232; increasing numbers of NGOs, 19; study
    on causes of corruption, 109–11; *World
    Public Sector Report 2001*, 22
United States: build-operate-transfer
    agreements, 227–28; contracting with
    private companies, 223, 225; shifting
    responsibility to the private sector, 230
Universal Declaration on Human Rights, 244
Uphoff, N., 148
U.S. Agency for International Development,
    229, 231

Value-added tax (VAT), 128, 129, 138
Vietnam, 85, 233
Virtuous spirals, 74, 75
Voluntary organizations, and public-private
    cooperation, 231–33

Women, changing roles of, 68–69
Woolcock, M., 143, 147, 148
World Bank, 124; civic engagement projects,
    150, 154; Comprehensive Development
    Framework, 62–63; corruption in govern-
    ment, 47, 113; globalization and poverty, 7;
    impact of structural adjustment policies, 53;
    institutional development and market
    efficiency, 38; national competitiveness and
    poverty, 35; Poverty Reduction Strategy
    Papers for financing by, 83–84, 157; private
    investment, 221; public debt, 133; small
    business development and policy changes,
    44–45; strengthening judicial institutions, 49
World Competitiveness Yearbook, 35
World Development Report 2000/2001, 147
World Economic Forum, 35, 61
World Institute for Development Economics, 91
World Intellectual Property Organization
    (WIPO), 168
World Summit on Sustainable Development, 19
World Trade Organization (WTO), 18, 27;
    globalization and liberalization concerns, 61,
    64; international trade agreements standards,
    40; in KIT infrastructure, 168; negotiations
    in Seattle, 77–78; pharmaceutical
    partnerships, 232

Zee, H., 127
Zero-rate band, 128

Also from Kumarian Press...

International Development

Better Governance and Public Policy
Capacity Building for Democratic Renewal in Africa
Edited by Dele Olowu and Soumana Sako

Confronting Globalization
Economic Integration and Popular Resistance in Mexico
Edited by Timothy A. Wise, Hilda Salazar and Laura Carlsen

Going Global: Transforming Relief and Development NGOs
Marc Lindenberg and Coralie Bryant

Governance, Administration & Development: Making the State Work
Mark Turner and David Hulme

Sustainable Livelihoods: Building on the Wealth of the Poor
Kristin Helmore and Naresh Singh

Worlds Apart: Civil Society and the Battle for Ethical Globalization
John D. Clark

*Conflict Resolution, Environment, Gender Studies, Global Issues,
Globalization, Microfinance, Political Economy*

Pathways out of Poverty
Innovations in Microfinance for the Poorest Families
Edited by Sam Daley-Harris

Promises Not Kept: Poverty and the Betrayal of Third World Development
Sixth Edition
John Isbister

Running out of Control: Dilemmas of Globalization
R. Alan Hedley

Rural Progress, Rural Decay
Neoliberal Adjustment Policies and Local Initiatives
Edited by Liisa L. North and John D. Cameron

The Spaces of Neoliberalism: Land, Place and Family in Latin America
Edited by Jacquelyn Chase

Where Corruption Lives
Edited by Gerald E. Caiden, O.P. Dwivedi and Joseph Jabbra

Visit Kumarian Press at **www.kpbooks.com** or
call **toll-free 800.289.2664** for a complete catalog.

Kumarian Press, located in Bloomfield, Connecticut, is a forward-looking, scholarly press that promotes active international engagement and an awareness of global connectedness.